THE COPYRIGHT THING
DOESN'T WORK HERE

T0338113

THE COPYRIGHT THING DOESN'T WORK HERE

Adinkra and Kente Cloth and Intellectual Property in Ghana

Boatema Boateng

FIRST PEOPLES
New Directions in Indigenous Studies

University of Minnesota Press

Minneapolis

London

Publication of this book was made possible, in part, with a grant from the Andrew W. Mellon Foundation.

An earlier version of the Introduction was published as "Square Pegs in Round Holes? Cultural Production, Intellectual Property Frameworks, and Discourses of Power," in *CODE: Collaborative Ownership and the Digital Economy*, ed. Rishab Ayer Ghosh (Cambridge, Mass.: MIT Press, 2005); copyright 2005 by MIT Press. An earlier version of chapter 2 was published as "Walking the Tradition–Modernity Tightrope: Gender Contradictions in Textile Production and Ghanaian Intellectual Property Law," *American University Journal of Gender, Social Policy, and the Law* 15, no. 2 (2007); copyright 2007 by American University. An earlier version of chapter 4 was published as "African Textiles and the Politics of Diasporic Identity-Making," in *Fashioning Africa: Power and the Politics of Dress*, ed. Jean Allman (Bloomington: Indiana University Press, 2004); copyright 2004 by Indiana University Press. An earlier version of chapter 5 was published as "Local and Global Sites of Power in the Circulation of Ghanaian Adinkra," in *Global Communications: Toward a Transcultural Political Economy*, ed. P. Chakravartty and Y. Zhao (Lanham, Md.: Rowman and Littlefield, 2008); copyright 2008 by Rowman and Littlefield.

Published by the University of Minnesota Press
111 Third Avenue South, Suite 290
Minneapolis, MN 55401-2520
http://www.upress.umn.edu

Library of Congress Cataloging-in-Publication Data

Boateng, Boatema.
    The copyright thing doesn't work here : Adinkra and Kente cloth and intellectual property in Ghana / Boatema Boateng.
        p. cm. — (First peoples: new directions in indigenous studies)
    Includes bibliographical references and index.
    ISBN 978-0-8166-7002-4 (hc : alk. paper) —ISBN 978-0-8166-7003-1 (pb : alk. paper)
    1. Adinkra cloth—Law and legislation—Ghana. 2. Kente cloth—Law and legislation—Ghana. 3. Textile fabrics—Law and legislation—Ghana. 4. Textile design—Law and legislation—Ghana. 5. Copyright—Textile fabrics—Ghana. 6. Intellectual property—Ghana. I. Title.
KRX1115.B63 2011
346.66704'82—dc22

                                                                        2010047170

Printed in the United States of America on acid-free paper

The University of Minnesota is an equal-opportunity educator and employer.

18 17 16 15 14 13 12 11   10 9 8 7 6 5 4 3 2 1

Contents

Introduction Indexes of Culture and Power

ADINKRA AND KENTE FABRICS are made by ethnic groups in Ghana, and until 1996, I saw them as expressions of cultural identity and kente, in particular, as a highly desirable—and elusive—status symbol. Like many Ghanaians, I valued adinkra cloth not only for its association with mourning but also as the source of a pool of symbolic designs that I considered mine by right of citizenship. I regarded kente as a kind of coming-of-age symbol because women often acquired it through marriage or by attaining enough economic independence to purchase it for themselves. When my grandmother died and left her kente to those granddaughters who had been named after her, I realized its additional significance as a means of transferring wealth. While waiting to find out whether inheritance, marriage, or disposable income would land me with my first serious three-piece women's set of kente, I bought a few token samples and one piece of adinkra cloth—all made for the tourist market. I took them along with me when I traveled abroad to study and occasionally deployed them as visual reinforcements of my Ghanaian identity and as antidotes to homesickness.

Then, in November 1996, I read an article in *Public Agenda,* a Ghanaian newspaper, which radically transformed my perception of adinkra and kente cloth. The article reported that imitation Ghanaian kente cloth was being mass-produced by East Asian countries without any compensation to the originators of the designs. Noting the payment of royalties by U.S. musician Paul Simon for the right to use a popular Ghanaian highlife tune, and also referring to the benefits to the local music industry that had resulted from an intensive national copyright protection program, the article stated, "Yet the issue of copyright protection for folklore remains largely a hidden issue, not only inside Ghana, but on the international front as well." Quoting the director of the country's Copyright Board, the article spoke of efforts by African countries to lobby for a treaty for the international protection of

1

folklore and the need for royalties paid for such folklore to accrue to the state "on behalf of the unknown creators of the ancient kente designs or drum rhythms, traditional tunes, etc."[1]

These comments were all the more interesting because they were made eleven years after Ghana revised its copyright law to include so-called folklore among protected creative works. Even earlier, in 1973, Ghana had tried to protect indigenous designs like those of adinkra and kente cloth in a textile designs registration decree passed under the country's industrial property laws. More recently, Ghana has introduced a law on geographical indications that seeks to protect kente, among other products, through the following clause in the definition of protected goods: "any product of handicraft or industry and include[ing] Kente."[2] Despite these measures, adinkra and kente have been imitated throughout most of the history of modern Ghana, and ironically, such imitations have proliferated in the country and abroad since the passage of the 1985 copyright law.

The *Public Agenda* story marked the beginning of my interest in the treatment of "folklore" and related forms of cultural production as intellectual property. It transformed kente and adinkra from personal markers of identity, prestige, and adulthood into indexes off which one could read and explore a wide but interrelated range of legal, political, economic, cultural, and social issues. These included the uneasy fit between folklore and intellectual property law, the implications for different legal subjects of the state's claim to represent "unknown creators" of Ghanaian folklore, the different practices of appropriation around cultural production, and the ability of a country like Ghana to mediate in the international regulatory arena in order to protect its interests.

This book examines these issues in relation to three sets of questions. First, what are the differing principles of authorship and alienability in the production of adinkra and kente and in intellectual property law, and what happens when these two systems meet? Second, what kinds of legal subjects are brought into being in the encounter? Third, what kinds of appropriation practices are found around adinkra and kente, on what kinds of claims are they based, and what implications do they have for Ghana's copyright protection of folklore?

While copyright law is the primary legal means of folklore protection in Ghana, my discussion extends to other areas of intellectual property law because the complex nature of cultural products like adinkra and kente makes it clear that they cannot be fully accommodated by just one kind of intellectual property protection. The Ghanaian copyright law protects the *designs* of adinkra and kente cloth. This makes all appropriations in all media equally problematic. Yet when one places these textiles into their context of use, it is clear that those designs have greatest significance when bound up with the material object of cloth. Simply protecting the designs, therefore, fails to get at the conditions under which those designs gain an important part of their value. The use of industrial property laws shows an awareness of this on the part of Ghanaian lawmakers. Yet the textiles registration decree that best reflected this awareness has been repealed, and its substitute, the Industrial Designs Act of 2003, makes no similar provision. Apart from the differing philosophical premises of folklore and intellectual property law, the individual categories of intellectual property law limit what can be protected and prove inadequate in the case of complex cultural products like adinkra and kente.

Even though kente cloth is also produced by the Ewe people of southeastern Ghana, I focus on Asante kente and adinkra because of the peculiar position of the Asante state in modern Ghana. Asante formerly controlled most of the territory that is now known as Ghana, and adinkra, kente, and other forms of material culture were systematically incorporated into Asante culture. Although much diminished in size and power, Asante continues to occupy an important place within Ghana, and focusing on these products makes it possible to examine issues that come up because of the political significance of adinkra and kente for both Asante and Ghana. One such issue is the politics of constructing state or national cultures, as evident in the cycles of appropriation by which these textiles first became Asante and have now also become Ghanaian.

Another feature of these fabrics that makes them important for this study is that, originally, all adinkra cloth and certain kente designs were reserved for the exclusive use of the Asante ruler, or *Asantehene*, in a system that some commentators have likened to copyright.[3] While adinkra and kente are no longer reserved for the Asantehene, there are still restrictions around the production of his cloth. Certain cloth producers are designated as makers of the king's adinkra and kente, and the importance that cloth producers attach to this designation can be seen in their view that the Asante state is prior to Ghana in any ownership claims to the cloth. This makes it possible to consider the issues that arise from other systems for regulating cultural appropriation that run parallel to copyright protection. It also raises the issue of the relationship between the modern state and indigenous states existing within its boundaries.

In order to explore these issues, I conducted life histories and interviews in 1999, 2000, and 2004 with twenty-two Ghanaian cloth producers and artists who produce adinkra and kente or draw on the cloth designs in their work. Life histories belong to a set of methods that include personal narratives and testimonials and entail recording respondents' accounts of the phenomenon under study as it has evolved in the course of their lives.[4] A key concern in this method is to give voice to marginalized groups, and I chose life histories because, with the exception of a few exemplary figures, the voices of folklore producers have been virtually absent from the debates on copyright protection in Ghana.

The life histories method also provides respondents with more scope for discussing their work in their own terms rather than in predetermined analytical categories. While seeking to give voice to cloth producers, I am also mindful that some of their views may make them vulnerable to retaliation or attack. Therefore, in cases in which the opinions expressed by adinkra and kente producers and other respondents have the potential to draw such sanctions (especially from the state) or inflame existing tensions among different groups with an interest in copyright law, I do not reveal the speakers' identities unless the views concerned are already a matter of public record.

The democratic potential of the life histories method must be balanced with the recognition that the narratives recorded through this method are not necessarily direct representations of reality but constructed by both narrators and researchers. In an inversion of this construction, one prospective respondent disparaged the method and refused to participate in the study because he perceived the focus on individual lives as secondary to the more important subject of the history of the craft. Clearly, for this individual, there was a preferred narrative that he saw as incompatible with the method. For a few other respondents, the method was an opportunity to emphasize their singularity as practitioners of the craft. While the life histories method is open to manipulation for respondents' own agendas, this very openness gives the method its value because it also enables respondents to provide unanticipated insights on the subject.

In addition to life histories, I conducted interviews with several Ghanaian policymakers and policy advisors and with two musicians who are active in the music lobby for copyright reform in Ghana. In 2004, I also observed a meeting organized by a committee of the Ghanaian parliament to collect views on a draft copyright bill before it was passed into law. I further conducted a content analysis of *Essence* and *Ebony* magazines in 2003 as a basis for discussing African American use of adinkra, kente, and other African textiles. Finally, I drew on secondary data, including legislation and policy documents. In the course of undertaking this research, it became clear why, to borrow a phrase from an adinkra maker, "the copyright thing doesn't work here"—that is, why, although intellectual property law has worked well for its originally intended purposes throughout Ghana's history, the encounter between the law and folklore is an uneasy one.

The Asante and Ghanaian Historical Contexts

The West African nation of Ghana has its immediate political origins in the British colony of the Gold Coast. Prior to British colonial control, however, most of the territory was subject to the authority of the Asante kingdom that emerged in the early eighteenth century and reached the height of its political power by the mid-nineteenth century. In addition to territory, Asante controlled the major trade routes extending north to the bend of the Niger River and south to the Atlantic Ocean.[5] A number of communities of wood-carvers, metalworkers, and cloth weavers sprang up around the Asante capital, Kumasi, and became the basis for a distinctive culture harnessed to the Asante state through deliberate policies of co-optation and royal patronage. Apart from establishing itself as a military, political, and economic power, Asante also became an important center of cultural production. Workers in the communities around Kumasi linked the aesthetic features of their products with Asante values and historical events and persons, making them expressive of a distinctly Asante identity.

In the mid-nineteenth century, Britain began to establish a foothold in the territory that is now Ghana—first in coastal areas that were not subject to direct Asante control. After half a century of struggle, Asante fell to the British and became part of the colony of the Gold Coast. British colonization was met almost from the outset with nationalist thought and struggle that grew as British control expanded.[6] Nationalist leaders identified culture as an important element and began the work of building a national culture in the early twentieth century. With the Akan (who include the Asante) forming the dominant ethnic group in the territory, Akan culture became an important resource for cultural nationalism.[7] Nationalist leaders also claimed a link between the Akan people and the ancient kingdom of Ghana.[8] Along with Mali and Songhai, this was one of three important West African kingdoms that flourished between the fifth and sixteenth centuries.[9] Travelers to ancient Ghana documented its wealth and power—features that were particularly evident in Asante. Thus, even though ancient Ghana had been located much farther to the west and north, its name became a focal point of nationalist struggle, and the British colony of the Gold Coast gained independence as the nation of Ghana in 1957.

Even as they claimed a distinctive indigenous or "traditional" culture for the nation, the early leaders of Ghana were keen to build a *modern* nation—that is, a nation that followed the forms of governance established in Europe during the Enlightenment period and exported around the world through colonization. Ghana thus retained colonial legal, administrative, and educational systems, and while it gradually adapted these systems to national priorities and conditions, their main philosophical underpinnings and structural features remained intact. The new nation also maintained parallel systems of indigenous (or "customary") and Western-style national laws and, in some cases, such as marriage, recognized a third system: Islamic law.

This recognition of indigenous laws and institutions had a precursor in the European colonial policy of "indirect rule" (as opposed to rule through settler communities that exercised direct dominance over local populations). In this version of colonization, Britain and other European powers exercised authority through small groups of colonial administrators and also through indigenous rulers who were willing to cooperate. Recalcitrant political rulers were replaced or subdued, and where there were no such rulers, the colonial authorities imposed them: "The tribal leadership was either selectively reconstituted as the hierarchy of the local state or freshly imposed where none had existed, as in 'stateless societies.'"[10] In the Gold Coast, societies like the Ga and Dangbe, which were organized under the authority of priests and priestesses, were made to adopt the Akan institution of kings or "chiefs."[11]

Ghana's postindependence retention of indigenous political systems was not solely a means of rule by proxy but a necessary accommodation for two main reasons. First, nationalist leaders supplanted indigenous rulers and needed to overcome resistance from the latter. Second, the degree of recognition accorded those rulers by ordinary Ghanaians meant that they could not be removed without undermining citizens' support for the nationalist project itself. After a process of struggle, Ghanaian leaders were obliged to provide a place for indigenous rule within the new nation.[12] The country's current constitution provides for a National House of Chiefs composed of the "paramount" rulers of the country's ethnopolitical groupings, and in 2006, Ghana also established a Ministry of Chieftaincy and Culture. Through these measures, the country recognizes "the institution of Chieftaincy [as] the kingpin of Ghanaian traditional culture."[13]

Apart from state recognition, indigenous rule continues to derive much of its significance from ordinary Ghanaians who recognize the political authority of both national and indigenous states. For many people, the authority of the indigenous state may be a more immediate reality than that of the national state. This helps to explain the strength of allegiance expressed by some adinkra and kente producers toward the Asantehene, who is an important source of adinkra's and kente's prestige as cultural products. This cultural distinctiveness, which is claimed not only for Asante but also for Ghana, is an important factor in the latter's efforts to protect adinkra and kente designs using intellectual property law.

Intellectual Property Law

Intellectual property law encompasses a range of laws governing rights over cultural production. The oldest and most well known of these are copyright, patent, and trademark laws. These respectively protect artistic works, scientific and industrial innovations, and symbols or words that distinguish a business or product from its competitors. Other intellectual property laws are geographical indications and rights of publicity.[14] Geographical indications laws safeguard products associated with specific locations by preventing the use of the location name for competing products made in other places. Rights of publicity protect well-known individuals from the unauthorized use of their images and other distinctive features.[15]

Intellectual property laws and the rights they grant have been defined in a range of ways, such as "property that is the product of creativity and does not exist in tangible form,"[16] "legal rights [that] can attach to information emanating from the mind of a person if it can be applied to making a product that is made distinctive and useful by that information,"[17] and "rule-governed privileges that regulate the ownership and exploitation of abstract objects in many fields of human activity."[18]

Although the variations in these definitions indicate the complexity of intellectual property law, a number of important common features exist. First, these laws create property rights in *intangible* cultural goods, making them amenable to commercial exchange. As the last two definitions show, intellectual property laws also govern cultural production that is "useful," and they are concerned with "ownership" and "exploitation." Usefulness here is typically understood in economic terms, and in most cases "profitable" can be substituted for "useful" in Posey and Dutfield's definition. However, it is important to note that Posey and Dutfield's work is mainly concerned with the creative work of indigenous peoples that also derives its usefulness from noneconomic applications such as sustaining religious life, reinforcing community identity, and fostering physical healing.[19] "Exploitation," in

Drahos's definition, can also be understood as *economic* exploitation. Intellectual property law is therefore bound up with the commodification of culture.

The terms *ownership* and *property* point to alienability as a central premise of intellectual property—that is, the view that cultural products or knowledge can be separated (or alienated) from other such products or knowledge and privately owned and transferred from one owner to another.[20] This seems quite normal until one considers the wide range of cultural goods that circulate under other principles, such as custodianship or sharing. In certain female spheres of cultural production, like knitting and quilting, individual women constantly create new designs, and for several generations they did not claim ownership rights over these but freely shared them with other women.[21] In indigenous societies, cultural production often circulates under principles of custodianship or protection but is considered inalienable—that is, it "can belong to no human being."[22]

Intellectual property laws also manage a tension between two competing views: one, that cultural production can and should be privately owned, and the other, that public access to such production is necessary for continued creativity and innovation.[23] The rights granted by intellectual property laws are therefore temporary, and after a specified period of time, the rights granted to the author or inventor expire, and the invention or creation concerned passes into the "public domain" where it may be freely accessed and used by anyone. In the last few decades, corporations in industrialized nations have successfully pressed for the extended duration of intellectual property rights—especially in the area of copyright law—and this trend is reflected in the laws of other countries, including Ghana.[24] The range of works protected under the law has also expanded, leading to expressions of concern over the "enclosure of the commons" and its implications for future creativity and the access to information considered to be essential in democratic societies.[25]

Another feature of intellectual property law that is important to this discussion is the distinction between the creators of a work and the owners of that work. In the case of the first intellectual property rights—copyright—these were initially granted to publishers and only later to authors as the idea of the creative individual took hold.[26] Under current conditions, the costs of creative work and its economic exploitation are beyond the means of many individuals, making artists and scientists dependent on entities that possess the resources to support their work and exploit it economically. These may be commercial or noncommercial entities, with universities in the latter category. As noted by Posey and Dutfield, "In the twentieth century, modern societies are increasingly dominated economically by corporations that employ researchers and inventors. As a result, the IPR [intellectual property rights] often go not to individuals but to the corporations, government agencies, or universities that employ them or fund their research."[27]

This means that even though intellectual property rights are premised on an individual author or inventor, increasingly those rights are held by businesses that have the status of personhood before the law rather than by actual persons.[28] Although the "moral rights" principle in copyright law allows the creators of a work to be recognized as its authors (right of paternity) and also to have a say in how it is modified (right of integrity) even after the economic rights have been transferred, this principle is a rather marginalized one in intellectual property law. In international intellectual property agreements, for example, moral rights are upheld in the Berne Convention but not in the more recent and legally binding Agreement on Trade-Related Aspects of Intellectual Property Rights (TRIPS Agreement) of 1994.

Intellectual property laws fall into two subcategories: copyright laws and industrial property laws. This is essentially a division between the arts, on the one hand, and science and industry, on the other, and follows the organization of the law in the first two international intellectual property conventions established in the nineteenth century: the 1883 Paris Convention for the Protection of Industrial Property, which deals with patents and trademarks, and the Berne Convention of 1886 governing copyright. The distinction is a blurred one, especially with the late twentieth-century emergence of technologies like computer software that cross the boundary between copyright and patent law.[29] However, it operates institutionally, and in the United States, one government office regulates copyright law and another regulates patents and trademarks.

Intellectual Property Law in Ghana

Ghana has had laws governing the three main areas of intellectual property law throughout most of its existence. In the institutional separation noted previously, industrial property laws have always been administered by the Ministry of Justice that oversees legal affairs. The oversight of copyright law, on the other hand, has moved from the Ministry of Information to a National Commission on Culture and, more recently, to the Ministry of Justice. Even with this latest move, copyright law is administered by one department within the ministry and industrial property laws by another, thus retaining traces of the old separation of copyright from industrial property laws. This division poses additional challenges in using intellectual property law to protect cultural products like adinkra and kente.

Ghana inherited its intellectual property laws from Britain through colonization but gradually reformed them to reflect national priorities. In the case of copyright law, for example, the earliest law in the territory was Britain's Imperial Copyright Act of 1911, followed by the 1961 Copyright Act enacted four years after the country's independence from Britain.[30] Subsequent reforms of Ghanaian copyright law took place in 1985 and 2005. In some instances, special laws were passed to protect specific interests. For example, as noted earlier, a textile designs registration decree was passed in 1973 as an industrial property law. This was aimed at protecting the local textile industry in response to pressure from industry groups.[31]

The 1985 reform of the country's copyright law was also partly in response to intense lobbying from musicians in the recording industry and also due to technological changes that facilitated the widespread copying of music. This legal reform occurred at a time of increased momentum in the global movement to protect indigenous knowledge from exploitation by groups and individuals from outside the communities of origin. The World Intellectual Property Organization (WIPO), which administers the major international intellectual property agreements (such as the Berne Convention), provided a hospitable forum for this movement. Another important organization in this area was the United Nations Educational, Scientific and Cultural Organization (UNESCO). In 1982, after several attempts by various governments to include folklore protection in international intellectual property agreements, WIPO and UNESCO convened a Committee of Governmental Experts on the Intellectual Property Aspects of the Protection of Expressions of Folklore. The Committee adopted the *Model Provisions for National Laws on Protection of Expressions of Folklore against Illicit Exploitation and Other Prejudicial Actions.*[32]

In protecting folklore under copyright law, Ghana drew on the model provisions. However, although produced by two major international organizations, these provisions are not supported in other instruments administered by WIPO, such as the Berne, Paris, and Rome conventions that govern the international protection of literary and artistic works, industrial property, and performers' and producers' rights. They are also not supported by the TRIPS Agreement, which has become the most important instrument for regulating intellectual property internationally. Nonetheless, as a member of WIPO interested in preventing the exploitation of "national" culture,

Ghana used the opportunity of the 1985 copyright law reform to include folklore among works protected under the law.

A fundamental challenge in this protection of folklore under copyright law arises from the standard premise, within intellectual property law, that such cultural production belongs in the public domain. This stems from the perception of folklore as communally produced in contrast to the law's conceptualization of the author or inventor as an individual. Intellectual property law has its origins in Western Enlightenment thinking, which focused on the individual as the bearer of rights. This was reinforced by eighteenth-century Romantic thinkers who held that authorship is the result of individual genius and inspiration.

As will become evident in this book, folklore production is, in fact, both individual *and* communal. However, rather than completely abandoning standard intellectual property principles, Ghana upholds the legal premise of an individual author in using copyright law to protect folklore. The standard options within the law are for the rights over a work to be vested in actual or corporate legal persons. The initial choice, in the 1985 law, was to consider the creators of folklore as ethnic communities and unidentified individuals and vest the rights in the state and in perpetuity. This was a contested solution, since a number of Ghanaian commentators assert that in many instances the "unidentified" creators of folklore are in fact well known.[33]

Further, in a variation on the author–owner division, and even though the language of the law described this arrangement as custodianship rather than ownership, this solution made the state the effective owner of local cultural production that fit the legal definition of folklore. As a result, while Ghana successfully reinterpreted the standard legal norms of ownership to suit its specific conditions, it did so in ways that followed the trend of strengthening the rights of the institutional owners of cultural products over the rights of the individual creators of those products. In this, Ghana's legal protection lost its emancipatory promise as it effectively wrote the individuals and communities that produce folklore out of the law.

The 2005 law goes some way toward addressing this issue with regard to adinkra and kente designs. While retaining the work of unidentified authors as part of Ghanaian folklore over which the state (represented by the president) has custody, the 2005 law includes adinkra and kente designs only within the definition of folklore "where the author of the designs [is] not known."[34] Therefore, in principle, individual creators of folklore may now claim formal, legal authorship over these designs. However, to do so is to pit themselves against principles of authorship that are contrary to those under which they produce. It also requires them to adopt unfamiliar forms of legal subjectivity.

Further, the nod toward the fact of individual creativity in folklore production does not change the widely held view that folklore is communally produced and therefore belongs in the public domain. As a result, Ghana's copyright protection of folklore is at variance with the norm in most international intellectual property law agreements. As noted earlier, the country has also used certain industrial property laws to protect the designs of adinkra and kente cloth. These include the textile designs registration decree mentioned earlier and the more recent geographical indications law. The latter holds considerable promise as an option because in such laws, the question of whether creativity is individual or communal does not factor into protection. Rather, geographical indications are premised on traditions of cultural production that are specific to particular locations.

Terms of the Debate

The marginal status of "folklore" in intellectual property law is an important index of the status of different kinds of knowledge and cultural production. The term has an especially troubled history in its application to the cultural production of non-Western societies. The second-class status of folklore within intellectual property law is therefore not only legal but also discursive. Folklore is the term used in the Ghanaian copyright law, following the UNESCO/WIPO model provisions. However, the association of the word with the Eurocentric and essentializing practices of colonial anthropology makes it less than ideal.[35] The persistence of that association makes the term especially problematic when it is used to denote a form of intellectual property, since it immediately places the cultural production it designates in an inferior status to cultural forms that are produced according to the "scientific" and "artistic" conventions of the West and routinely accorded intellectual property protection.

Similar problems occur with the term *indigenous knowledge*, which often refers to cultural production that has medicinal and agricultural applications. Since this term is used almost exclusively to refer to the cultural production of non-Western peoples, it has the result of naturalizing Western cultural production. Knowledge is thus an unmarked category when it is produced within the conventions of Western science. Outside those conventions, it is marked as common, folk, or indigenous. The result is a ranking that accords the status of "science" to indigenous knowledge only when it is brought within the sphere of the former. The mechanism through which this transfer occurs is often appropriation enabled by intellectual property law.

Paulin Hountodji links the problem of terminology with the structural location of knowledge production in the Third World—especially Africa. He argues that most African knowledge production is exogenous, that is, produced in accordance with the dictates of the North. He calls for an approach to knowledge production that is "endogenous" or "experienced by society as an integral part of its heritage." He further argues that the term *endogenous* is preferable to *indigenous* as a marker of knowledge because

> the indigenous is what appears to the foreign observer—explorer or missionary—as a purely local curiosity that has no effectiveness outside its particular context. The term always has a derogatory connotation. It refers to a specific, historical experience, precisely one of integration of autochthonous cultures into a world-wide "market" in which these perforce are pushed down to inferior positions.[36]

While this is a compelling argument, endogenous knowledge does not resolve the unmarked and therefore default status of Western knowledge. While it is conceptually useful for distinguishing different systems in order to challenge exogenous practices of knowledge production, endogenous knowledge can only undermine the hierarchy of different knowledge production systems when it is applied to all such systems.

Traditional knowledge has gained wide currency as a more respectful alternative and is reflected in the shift in WIPO from terms like folklore and indigenous knowledge. This is the most common of a range of terms that include the word *tradition*—for example, "traditional resource rights."[37] However, these suffer from the same marking described previously and do little to undermine the inferior status ascribed to tradition in relation to modernity. Ultimately, these newer terms leave intact the hierarchical relationship between the knowledge of Western science and that of indigenous peoples, local communities, and Third World nations. Given this hierarchy, terms like *folklore, indigenous knowledge,* and *traditional knowledge* can only be provisional rather than definitive, and this is how I use them in this book.

I also use these terms interchangeably with *cultural production* and *knowledge* to signal my rejection of the hierarchy. Drawing on the insights of feminist theorists like Sandra Harding and Patricia Hill Collins on the gender and racial politics of knowledge production, I argue that the cultural production of indigenous peoples and local communities is delegitimized as knowledge through the hegemony of Western systems of knowledge production.[38]

Through the terminology just discussed, they are also discursively marked as "subjugated knowledges." Viewed in this way, it becomes clear that the relative value and legitimacy of different kinds of knowledge is not inherent but a function of their social, cultural, and epistemological contexts. Their ranking relative to each other from a Western scientific and legal perspective is revealed as political and ideological rather than natural, and intellectual property law's privileging of "scientific" and "artistic" creations becomes a means whereby this ranking is reinforced.

Some commentators have argued that, given problems like those outlined previously, to use intellectual property law to protect indigenous and local cultural production is to cede the ground to the epistemologies of the dominant framework.[39] They call for a radical rethinking of authorship and alienability, taking into account non-Western principles that privilege community above the individual and custodianship over ownership. This challenge has been taken up by both activists and scholars and to some extent by this project, but to focus exclusively on such a rethinking can obscure the need to examine the conditions that lead to both indigenous peoples and Third World nations seeking to protect their cultural production within the admittedly imperfect framework of intellectual property law. This book argues that countries like Ghana are already implicated in the larger framework of modernity of which intellectual property law forms a part. Therefore, the task of unthinking the law's dominant concepts of authorship and alienability of culture cannot be undertaken in isolation from that of unthinking European and North American colonization and imperialism in all their guises and present-day manifestations.

Sites of Struggle

At its most fundamental level, intellectual property law regulates the circulation of culture. Since it does not treat all modes of cultural production equally, the law is also a site for the exercise and contestation of power. Therefore, this book is, in essence, an exploration of the different ways that power is exercised over and through culture. The place of adinkra and kente in the Asante and Ghanaian contexts points to their status as culture in the anthropological and aesthetic senses of the word—that is, products that are specific to a social group and reflect its beliefs and values and exemplify aesthetic distinctiveness. These fabrics' importance as the basis for different claims by a range of actors from individual Ghanaians and diasporic Africans to the Ghanaian state also reflects the view that "in our period . . . of accelerated globalization" culture is a resource.[40]

My primary interest in discussing adinkra and kente in relation to intellectual property law is in the ways that they are sites of struggle over meaning. In this respect, they are elements of culture in the constitutive sense proposed by neo-Marxist cultural scholars like Néstor García Canclini. From this perspective, culture can be defined as "all practices and institutions involved in the administration, renewal, and restructuring of meaning."[41] As will become evident in the following chapters, different kinds of claims over adinkra and kente reveal their multiple and contested meanings in relation to gendered, ethnic, national, and racial identities. They also undermine standard meanings of legal subjectivity and the figure of the author in cultural production.

Power, as I explore it here, is equally multidimensional and arises from a number of different sources, including the dominant legal understanding of cultural production and producers as well as the imposition of intellectual property law as a universal framework for regulating cultural flows. While that imposition initially occurred through the extension of Western norms to the rest of the world through colonial and imperial projects, it continues to operate through modernization programs and international regulatory regimes like TRIPS. In addition to the hegemony of intellectual property law and its conceptualization of cultural production and producers, the Ghanaian state exercises power in its use of the formal mechanism of the law to reinforce one set of meanings of adinkra and kente, namely, that they are national rather than ethnic culture. In the contests over meaning, it is clear that the state has superior power in its ability to institutionalize certain definitions. At the same time, that power is not absolute, since the state has modified those definitions in response to challenges from Ghanaians.

Popular contestation of the meanings imposed by the state occurs not only directly through traditional political action like lobbying but also through appropriation and consumption practices that subvert those meanings. As different players invest adinkra and kente with different kinds of significance through intellectual property regulation, through narratives of tradition and heritage, and through the production and consumption of imitations, the locus of power shifts depending on which meanings become dominant either explicitly or implicitly. These shifts are also gendered, as male dominance in handmade cloth production gives way to female dominance in appropriation of that cloth. It is evident from these contests that power, in relation to adinkra and kente and their protection, is located in both institutions and practices. Further, it is bound up with social identities and also has important geopolitical dimensions. Therefore, in examining different players' ability to assert certain meanings over others, I am interested in their differing sources and practices of power.

In exploring this multifaceted interaction between culture and power, I draw on a number of theoretical sources. My analysis of power is first of all a materialist one that anchors the struggles examined here in histories and structures of dominance. Those histories are essential for understanding the normalization of intellectual property law as a universal form and the structure of the current international regulatory regime. However, an exclusive focus on such structures can obscure the ways in which they are challenged and subverted through group and individual *practices* of production, appropriation, and consumption.

From a classical Marxist perspective, culture is purely superstructural—that is, it is dependent on the "base" of economic relations—and is further an ideological tool for buttressing unjust power relations. This approach is reflected in Immanuel Wallerstein's discussion of the uses of culture in the world system, especially in relation to race and gender.[42] While this perspective is useful for understanding both the role of culture in maintaining the world system and the gendered nature of much cultural appropriation, it leaves very little scope for resistance. Classical Marxist perspectives are also inadequate in accounting for power relations in contexts like Ghana and Asante that do not map neatly onto frameworks of modernity. Social relations in these contexts cannot be fully explained in terms of class struggle organized around the relations of production. An especially useful set of insights comes from Lisa Lowe and David Lloyd's distinction between "Western Marxism" and "Third World Marxism." They note that "the challenge to the privileging of class antagonism as the exclusive site of contradiction requires a critique of Western Marxism's assumption of the universality of capitalist development."[43]

Even as they point out the need to displace class struggle as the focus of Marxist analysis, Lowe and Lloyd also emphasize the importance of feminist, antiracist, and other oppositional struggles as "in themselves occupy-[ing] significant sites of contradiction that are generated precisely by the differentiating process of advanced globalizing capitalism."[44] This allows for the possibility of resistance in forms other than class struggle. Further, in acknowledging race, gender, and other oppositional locations as sites of both oppression and resistance to structures of power, Lowe and Lloyd's analysis makes it possible to combine third-world Marxism with alternative analytical frameworks such as the "African feminism" of scholars like Amina

Mama and Oyèrónkẹ́ Oyêwùmí.[45] These frameworks also challenge dominant understandings of gender oppression and resistance.

Drawing on the work of Michel Foucault, I also conceive of power as discursive in its operation, and throughout this book, I link structures of power with discourses of power.[46] Discourses are not simply ideological statements used to justify one course of action over another; rather, they set the conditions for action. For example, the discourse of modernization as a desirable goal for all nations shapes Ghana's retention and use of Western legal systems even when they are incompatible with its goals. Discourses also shape the kinds of action that individuals can undertake and therefore, to some extent, the kinds of people they can be. In this way, they produce subjects, and this is evident in the case of intellectual property: the discourses of the law produce exemplary subjects—those whose modes of cultural production conform to the law—and anomalous ones who, like adinkra and kente makers, produce culture in alternative ways. The discussion of terms in the previous section indicates yet another discursive level at which power operates in relation to cultural production.

While discourses are powerful, they do not close off all alternatives because they are multiple rather than unitary. Further, they exist in a state of flux and competition with each other. When viewed in terms of Antonio Gramsci's concept of hegemony, it becomes possible to conceive of discourses as shifting over time.[47] One can therefore conceive of practices that challenge dominant discourses as counterhegemonic, with the potential for displacing hegemonic discourses. These can in turn cause shifts in more structural forms of power. The idea of hegemony is therefore a valuable one for conceptualizing culture as a site of both domination and resistance and for conceiving of the possibility of changes in power relations around culture.

It is through this set of theoretical sources that I examine the questions of authorship/alienability, legal subjects, and cultural appropriation that arise from Ghana's intellectual property regulation of adinkra and kente. In examining these issues, this book also intervenes in the debates on culture as a site and means of political struggle in relation to modernity, the nation, globalization, and the construction of social identities. That struggle occurs not only between the different groups that have a stake in adinkra and kente but also in the conflict over what it means to be modern and a nation as well as what it means to be a subject nationally and globally.

In the case at hand, these struggles are mediated by intellectual property law, which is theorized here as a productive force that shapes what it regulates in specific ways, with a number of outcomes for different players.

Nationhood and Western-style national laws are among the primary means by which countries like Ghana fulfill the imperative to be "modern," and such laws are, in effect, technologies of modernity. Modernity here is understood as "an overarching periodizing term to denote a historical era" as well as the state of being modern.[48] That state is achieved through modernization, which refers to a prescriptive set of principles for achieving Western-style development.[49]

A discussion of Ghana's legal protection of *anything* is therefore also a discussion of the imperative to be modern and of the technologies of modernity as well as one set of responses and the power implications of those responses. While meeting the demand to be modern through nationhood, Ghana's formal political space includes state-sanctioned "traditional" systems of indigenous authority, as noted earlier. Therefore, for many adinkra and kente producers, the ruler of the Asante state is not only an important authority figure but also a potential mediator between them and the national state. Within the space of the modern nation, therefore, one finds institutions and practices that both contradict and resist dominant understandings of modernity and nationhood.

Global and Local Dimensions

The claims of the African diaspora over African culture and the mass production of imitation adinkra and kente cloth by entrepreneurs based in countries other than Ghana add a global dimension to Ghana's intellectual property protection of these textiles. In order to make its copyright protection of folklore completely effective, Ghana must intervene in global markets and in the international regulatory sphere, raising questions of the place of the nation under present conditions of globalization. I understand globalization to be not so much a new phenomenon as an old one that has gone through different phases, with the current phase marked by increased and intensified interconnections between different parts of the world.[50] This analysis reflects the view that different parts of the world have been incorporated into a capitalist world system in which the economic division of labor and attendant structural inequalities take on a global dimension.[51] From this perspective, the manner in which Ghana emerged as a modern nation-state is a part of this process of globalization.

The last thirty years of this process have seen the expansion of neoliberalism as a governing principle of global relations. Market principles have therefore gained ascendancy for governing a range of social and economic relations. In the international regulatory sphere, these principles have led to intellectual property being governed predominantly as a trade issue. The strongest institutional manifestation of this is the TRIPS Agreement of 1994, which was drawn up in the General Agreement on Tariffs and Trade (GATT). The latter was replaced in 1995 by the World Trade Organization. In the TRIPS/WTO regime, decision making is closely linked to economic power, placing countries like Ghana at a distinct disadvantage.

At the same time, it is important to note that the appropriation Ghana seeks to challenge occurs not only in the Western industrialized nations that dominate the international regulatory sphere. Some Ghanaians point to China as a major threat to both the mechanized and artisanal textile industries.[52] Appropriated versions of kente are also made in Korea, India, la Côte d'Ivoire, and most recently, in Ghana itself.[53] Due to these sources of appropriation, it is mistaken to characterize the issue solely in North–South terms as one of an appropriating North and an exploited South.[54] Largely unhampered by mid-twentieth-century ideological barriers, global economic integration now links East, West, South, and North in complex networks that undermine any simple notions of Western economic hegemony. While the North–South distinction is useful and points to continuing structural differences between different world regions, it does not exhaust all the dimensions of global cultural flows. The book therefore draws attention to multidirectional flows of commodification and appropriation that are local, regional, and global.

Apart from indexing the global dimensions of adinkra and kente production, appropriation, and consumption, diasporic claims point to the use of these fabrics in constructing social identities. Such identity construction is also evident in Ghanaians' use of adinkra and kente and these textiles' association with the Asante ethnic group, and this construction often occurs through nationalist projects. As such, adinkra and kente highlight different axes of subjugation and resistance in local, national, and global contexts. The local here is understood as a site within the nation-state but distinct from it—a distinction that is important because the nation cannot always be assumed to fully represent the interests of local communities in the international sphere. At the same time, I do not conceive of the local as a pristine space uncontaminated by globalization. Rather, it is articulated to global processes in different ways—through national policies that facilitate cloth producers' contact with tourist markets, for example. It is at the local level that the practices of individuals and groups are most discernible. It is also often at this level that the relationship between different social identities and the cultural products under discussion here becomes most visible.

I further distinguish between different instances of the local in relation to the debates on intellectual property law and traditional knowledge. For example, the local in Ghana is not the same as the local in Native American "nations" in the United States, and yet the two are related. In analyzing the link between them, it is helpful to follow the example of scholars like Chandra Mohanty who conceptualize the Third World not solely in terms of geographic location but also histories of subjugation.[55] While the terms *One-Third World* and *Two-Thirds World* have been suggested as preferable alternatives to the earlier, hierarchical binaries of *First World, Third World,* and *North* and *South,* I consider that the new set of terms does not completely resolve the problem.[56] Further, it does not address the invisibility of indigenous peoples in the term *Third World,* noted by Shohat and Stam.[57] I therefore prefer to retain *Third World* in the sense suggested in Mohanty's earlier work and interpret it as an indicator of relations of subjugation rather than a ranking of world regions.[58]

A focus on such histories makes it possible to link the struggles of people in different locations while recognizing that the diverse ways in which they are articulated to economic and political institutions and histories lead to differences in the nature of their struggles. Thus, one can link the struggles of continental and diasporic Africans and those of indigenous peoples and Third World nations without homogenizing those struggles. It is necessary to highlight those links because, although they are not the focus of this book, indigenous peoples have been central to the debates and international policy initiatives regarding forms of culture that typically fall outside the scope of intellectual property law. The struggles of indigenous peoples over their cultural production therefore constitute an important precedent to the project undertaken here, and it is important to establish how both kinds of projects are related.

Following the United Nations' Working Group on Indigenous Peoples, indigenous peoples are those who have endured settler colonialism and resisted integration into the dominant economic, political, and cultural systems.[59] Shohat and Stam go further and note the presence of a "Fourth World" of indigenous people "within all of the other worlds."[60] While both indigenous peoples and most Third World nations are shaped by having experienced European colonization, the latter have achieved a degree of political independence and nationhood. For indigenous peoples, therefore, the struggle over indigenous knowledge is bound up with continuing struggles for political liberation, and this is a legitimate basis for distinguishing between their struggles and those of Third World nations like Ghana. However, since "flag independence" for such nations has seldom translated into economic liberation, and they therefore persist in conditions more accurately described as neocolonial than fully independent, their struggle for liberation can hardly be described as complete. In their common experience of colonization and their ongoing efforts for full emancipation, therefore, one can identify an affinity between the interests of both groups.

It can further be argued that, as a Third World nation, Ghana's relationship with industrialized nations around the appropriation of local culture is similar to that between those nations and indigenous people. In the current phase of globalization, both have witnessed the accelerated appropriation of their cultural production—from plant knowledge to ritual and utilitarian objects—for global markets. However, even as it argues for the protection of "national" cultural production, the Ghanaian state must navigate the claims and interests of the country's different ethnic groups whose cultures make up the composite that is regarded as national culture. Otherwise, it risks standing in relation to ethnic groups within the country in ways that may be all too similar to the relationship between "settler democracies" and indigenous peoples.

To complicate matters further, the Ghanaian case shows that the country's ethnic groups cannot uniformly be conceived of as embattled or oppressed minorities. As the example of adinkra and kente shows, the ethnic group in question is sometimes a dominant one. Yet cloth producers who exercise considerable power in the context of the ethnic group and the Asante state may consider themselves marginalized in the larger civic space of the nation-state. Additionally, gender can trump ethnicity when women move cultural production from a sphere of male privilege into one of female economic power.

It is this complex network of power relations around cultural production that this book discusses. To a discussion on authorship and ownership that tends to focus on cases of dispossessed indigenous peoples against the state—often a Western industrialized state—this book offers the case of an African nation where the state itself may be marginalized internationally even as it exerts power nationally and locally.[61] The power and legitimacy of the Ghanaian state vary depending on whether it is making ownership claims over culture as a Third World nation in the international sphere or as a government in relation to its citizens. Its relatively marginal status in the global economy may lend it a certain moral authority in making claims internationally that it cannot assume in exercising power over its citizens at home. The book further provides a case in which attention to the exercise and negotiation of power at local and national levels and to factors such as gender and ethnicity, lineage and citizenship, challenge accounts of unrelieved victimhood.

Adinkra and Kente Fabrics

Adinkra and kente are among those arts that became an important part of Asante culture in the eighteenth and nineteenth centuries. There are varying accounts of the origins of these textiles, and in the case of adinkra, one popular version is that it was introduced into Asante in 1818 when the Asante defeated and killed Adinkra, the rebellious leader of Gyaman, near the current border between Ghana and the Ivory Coast. The life of the king's son, Apau, was spared on condition that he teach the Asantehene's cloth makers how to make the cloth that the Gyaman king had been wearing when he was killed.[62] Those cloth makers were located at Asokwa, and the town became, and continues to be, the official source of the Asantehene's adinkra cloth. Some accounts date Asante cloth production to the Bron and Denkyira states that preceded Asante. By these accounts, cloth making at Asokwa was initiated by cloth makers from Denkyira who defected to Asante when the Asante defeated their kingdom in 1701—more than a century before the 1818 war with Gyaman.[63]

Adinkra is made by stenciling patterns onto cloth using *badie*, a black dye made from tree bark. The background cloth is sometimes made of smaller pieces sewn together with brightly colored *nhwemu* stitching to form a larger piece (see Plate 1). The patterns are composed of distinctive symbols, each of which has a specific meaning. Symbols are named for important figures and events and also for proverbs reflecting Asante values. The adinkra symbolic system has been characterized as a form of writing that refutes standard accounts of African societies as preliterate prior to contact with Europeans.[64] The most well-known adinkra symbol is the *(minnsuro obiaa) gye Nyame,* or "(I fear none) except God," symbol whose name is often given simply as Gye Nyame, or "Except God." Although it denotes courage in its original meaning, the Gye Nyame symbol has come to stand for the power of God and has therefore been adopted by many Ghanaian Christians as a symbol of their faith. Apart from the individual names of symbols, adinkra is also named for the secondary designs formed by the arrangement of the symbols on the cloth.

Adinkra is strongly associated with mourning, and this is reinforced by some of the explanations of the word. Apart from being the name of the king of Gyaman, "adinkra" includes the Akan word for message, *nkra.*[65] It is also a contraction of the Akan words for taking leave of someone, *di nkra*. The connection with death is further made on the basis of the Akan word for the soul, *kra*, the argument being that a "dinkra is the parting or send-off message or intelligence that the soul carries to and from God."[66] When the symbols are stenciled onto a white background, however, adinkra cloth can also be used for celebration.

Kente is a form of strip weaving and as such is one example of a form of textile production that is widespread in many parts of West Africa. In Ghana, there are three main kinds of strip weaving. One form is practiced by the Gonja and other ethnic groups in the northern part of the country, and the Gonja town of Salaga has long been a center of textile production.[67] Strip weaving in northern Ghana has a relatively simple color palette of cream, indigo, black, and white and is often woven in solid color or stripes. Another form of strip weaving is found among the Ewe people in the southeastern part of the country. This form, *adanudo*, is also known as kente and has double-woven bands that contrast with the single-weave background.

Asante kente cloth is made from strips in a single weave with alternating double-woven panels such that when the strips are sewn together, the effect is similar to a checkerboard. It is noted for its vivid colors and the abstract motifs woven into the strips, unlike Ewe kente in which the colors are more subdued and the motifs more lifelike. Like adinkra, the motifs used in Asante kente cloth weaving have specific names; however, the cloth is usually named for the colors and design of the background, which is often striped. As with adinkra, kente is named for historic figures and events and also for Asante values. The design *kyeretwie*, or leopard catcher, for example, symbolizes courage, while *aberewa ben*, or "wise old woman," indicates the respect accorded older women in Asante society (see Plate 2). Another design, *Oyokoman*, is named for the Oyoko clan. One especially rich and prestigious version of these and other designs is called *adweneasa* or *adwenasa*, a name that refers to the weaver's skill. Literally, it means that the weaver has exhausted both his creativity and the motif pool in producing it. In reality, it simply means the cloth is composed entirely of double-woven panels.[68] While the motifs in kente cloth are usually abstract, weavers have expanded their aesthetic frameworks by weaving elements like words, numbers, and adinkra symbols into cloth. These are usually strips intended for use as stoles or as decoration (see Plate 3).

As noted earlier, some accounts trace Asante textile production to earlier Akan kingdoms, and one account also suggests Gyaman as a possible source of kente weaving.[69] However, popular myths around Asante kente cloth trace its origins to two brothers in the town of Bonwire. The two are said to have observed a spider weaving its web and created the cloth by imitating the spider. The Ewe people have a similar story of the origins of their cloth, and weavers in each of these two ethnic groups claim to have taught the craft of weaving to the other group, leading to rival claims over the true origins of kente. Yet another origin story claims that one Otaa Kraban learned the craft at Salaga, suggesting that weaving was introduced to Asante from cultures further to the north.[70] Asante control of trade routes and cloth-producing states to the north, like Gonja, suggest the possibility of northern influence, if not northern origins. Indeed, one participant in this study reported that in earlier times the Asantehene would sometimes send his kente weavers to the Gonja weaving center of Salaga to produce his cloth.[71]

The main centers of Asante cloth production are the towns of Bonwire and Ntonso for kente and adinkra respectively.[72] Both towns appear on national tourist maps, while Bonwire has added recognition from the Asante royal house as the official source of the Asantehene's kente. The head of the Asantehene's weavers is therefore appointed from Bonwire in a line that is said to go all the way back to the two brothers in the popular myth of origin.[73] Bonwire's standing as a center of kente production is further supported in both official and unofficial national narratives. Thus, for example, a popular song about kente weaving by distinguished Ghanaian composer Ephraim Amu specifically refers to kente weaving at Bonwire.

A third town, Adanwomase, near Bonwire, is also important as the official source of the Asantehene's *white* kente. While Asante kente is famous for its vivid colors, it was initially woven in cream and blue—the colors of natural cotton and indigo dye. White and blue cloth that approximates this original palette is important for celebration, and weavers continue to produce cloth in these colors. While national and royal patronage have combined to make Ntonso, Bonwire, and Adanwomase the most prominent centers of production, they are part of a cluster of cloth-producing communities. Cloth production has also spread beyond those communities, as cloth makers often combine cloth production with farming and other occupations and migrate temporarily to other parts of Ghana where opportunities for those occupations are better. Despite such migration, Asante cloth production is most heavily concentrated in Ntonso, Bonwire, and surrounding towns (see Map 1).

Asokwa, the earliest center of adinkra production in Asante, has almost disappeared from public consciousness and is absent from tourist maps.

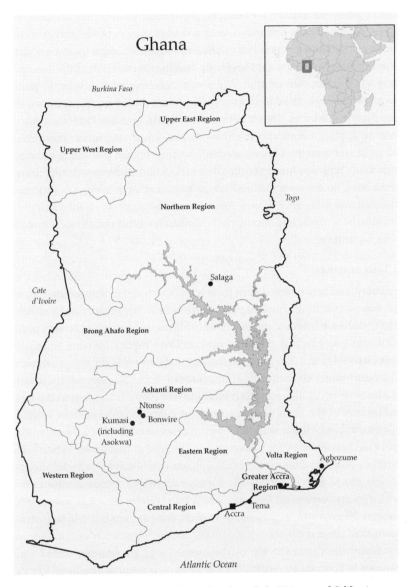

Map 1. Ghana. Data obtained July 2009 from gdata through the University of California, Berkeley, at http://biogeo.berkeley.edu/bgm/gdata.php. Attribution given in accordance with CC Attribution, Nonprofit, Share-Alike license terms.

The name now refers to a huge suburb of the Asante capital, Kumasi, while the original community is hidden behind lumber mills on the edge of the suburb. That community is now officially known as Asokwa Old Town. In this book, I follow the practice of adinkra producers and refer to the community simply as Asokwa. Despite its current obscurity, Asokwa remains important as the official source of the Asantehene's adinkra cloth. Most cloth producers quoted in this book came from these four centers of cloth production—Asokwa, Ntonso, Bonwire, and Adanwomase. One was located at Tewobaabi, a community adjoining Ntonso, while a few others came from Kumasi and from the national capital, Accra. As noted previously, adinkra and kente makers often combine cloth production with other occupations. They may do so simultaneously or go back and forth between cloth production and other professions. Apart from farming, some of the cloth producers in this study had also worked as teachers, construction workers, and factory workers.

Cloth Matters

Adinkra and kente cloth derive their importance not only from their association with both Asante and Ghanaian cultural nationalism but also from the social and economic significance of cloth as a commodity in many parts of Ghana. In much of southern and central Ghana, cloth is a bearer of identity and status and also specifies one's state—whether one is grieving or celebrating. This is indicated by the kind of cloth, its color, and the accessories with which it is worn. Thus, white and blue cloth, when worn with white accessories, signifies celebration—for example, the birth of a child. The same cloth, worn with black accessories, signifies death—either of a very old person or a very young one. In the case of the former, white celebrates a long life, while in the case of children, white is worn in defiance of death. Black cloth unequivocally signifies death and, in combination with red, denotes deep mourning or crisis.[74] Cloth is also a means of storing and transferring wealth, especially for women, who are less likely than men to own fixed property.

Kente cloth is at the top of the hierarchy of celebration, status, and wealth in this system. Adinkra cloth is near the top of the hierarchy of mourning depending on the stage of mourning and the wearer's relationship to the deceased.[75] It is superseded in significance by black and red cloth, which, apart from denoting deep mourning, also signal a close relation to the deceased. Over the past century, other textiles have been incorporated into this system of value and use. These include imported luxury fabrics like lace and brocade as well as "African" prints. The prints represent a particularly interesting example of indigenized foreign fabric: they began as Dutch imitations of Indonesian batik and were originally introduced into Africa by the Dutch East India Company in the late nineteenth century. West African soldiers also brought batik cloth home from their service in colonial armies in Southeast Asia during the Second World War.[76] The Dutch company Vlisco has been the producer of some of the most prestigious brands for the African market for several decades. Vlisco is now a multinational corporation that includes a number of African textile manufacturing companies in its production network.[77] Design elements from Indonesian batik continue to feature in contemporary designs from Ghanaian textile factories within and outside the Vlisco group in an interesting and continuing cycle of appropriation.

The prints are assigned varying levels of value depending on how and where they are produced. Wax block prints in which the batik technique is combined with roller printing are at the more prestigious and expensive end of the scale, while "fancy" prints are the cheapest and least prestigious. Apart from their history and design, these prints are also distinctive in their proportions, which approximate those of adinkra and kente cloth. They are usually about forty-eight inches wide and sold in multiples of two yards, up to a maximum of twelve yards. In local markets in Ghana, better quality cloth is sold only in lengths of six yards ("half-piece") or twelve yards ("full piece"). Women's clothing requires a half-piece, which is then divided into three smaller pieces similar to a three-piece set of adinkra or kente cloth. A full piece is divided into four- or five-yard lengths that, when joined together lengthwise, are about the size of a man's kente or adinkra cloth and worn in the same way.

Ghanaians distinguish between these prints and other kinds of fabric and signal this distinction not only in the way they use those fabrics but also in language. For many Ghanaians—especially among ethnic groups in the central and southern parts of the country—the word *cloth* has an evocative quality and substance that makes it more than a mere synonym for words such as *fabric* and *textile*. This distinction carries over into English, in which the word has been imbued with the same depth of meaning as the Akan *ntama* or *ntoma*. This practice linguistically aligns such cloth with kente, which is properly called *serekye nwentoma* (silk woven cloth) and adinkra or *ntiamu ntoma* (printed or stenciled cloth). Thus, some adinkra and kente makers distinguished between their cloth and cotton prints by referring to the latter as "textiles *ntoma*," that is, cloth made in a textile factory.

Where the Akan *ntoma* is used to refer to other kinds of fabric, the intended use is often specified—for example, for a dress or suit—and where the use is unspecified, the default meaning is usually the kind of cloth described earlier. The linguistic distinction between cloth and other kinds of fabric also occurs in the English language, with Ghanaians typically using *cloth* for the cotton prints described earlier and *material* for everything else, such as "curtain material" or "dress material." Finally, *cloth* also refers to a specific kind of clothing made from this kind of fabric (and also from adinkra, kente, lace, etc.): either a three-piece ensemble, in the case of women, or a large piece wrapped around the body and draped over one shoulder, in the case of men. It is regarded as traditional, in contrast to Western clothing, and *cloth* is therefore used as a synonym for the more formal "traditional attire."

Given the social importance of cloth in many parts of Ghana, it is not surprising that adinkra and kente producers regard the appropriation of their work in textile form more seriously than in other forms. The designs of adinkra cloth, in particular, easily lend themselves to appropriation in nontextile media such as jewelry, masonry, and stationery (see Figure 1). In Ghana, they appear in the insignia of churches and universities and in the openwork walls of patios and courtyards. Adinkra designs also appear in a number of different textile forms, particularly batik, which has become a major Ghanaian cottage industry in the last three decades. A less widespread form is screen-printing, while a third is factory-printed cloth.

Mechanized cloth production has become increasingly important as a site of adinkra and kente appropriation. In comparison with adinkra, kente designs are less widely imitated in nontextile media, but several attempts have been made to produce it in textile form. For example, Ghana's University of Science and Technology is reported to have produced a broadloom imitation.[78] In the broadloom technique, the distinctive designs are woven into the fabric, as with handwoven cloth. In the 1980s and 1990s, another broadloom version, Spintex kente, named for the factory that produced it, was very popular in Ghana. It was not an exact reproduction of kente, but it used many of kente's motifs and was accepted as an approximation and used as a substitute for some purposes. Spintex kente was also popular in the African American market, but competition from East Asian factories led to a decline in its production in Ghana, and by 2000, it was available only on commission.[79] In the meantime, imitation kente in *printed* form became increasingly popular beginning in the late 1980s. Although printed imitations of both adinkra and kente are ranked low on the cloth hierarchy by some Ghanaians, they are still very popular.

Figure 1. Gold jewelry with adinkra charms.

When it first appeared in Ghana, printed kente tended to be used for more mundane purposes than the handwoven version, while imitation adinkra quickly became accepted wear at funerals. Thus, the distinction made by Ghanaians between handmade and factory-printed cloth was initially stronger in the case of kente than in the case of adinkra. That distinction seems to be diminishing as imitations more closely reproduce handwoven kente designs and as Ghanaians increasingly use it for special wear and not just street clothing. This trend toward increased acceptance of imitations suggests a general shift in the value system guiding the use of cloth (see Plate 4 and Plate 5).

These printed versions are the most widespread forms of imitation kente and adinkra cloth and are more likely than imitations in other media to be regarded by adinkra and kente producers as appropriations. Most cloth producers were critical of the imitations and considered that they demeaned their craft and the prestige of the cloth. Some also perceived the imitations as a direct threat to their livelihood. One dissenter, an adinkra maker at Ntonso, considered imitations in all forms—textile and nontextile—to be fair in an open market. These mass-produced appropriations of adinkra and kente have been a key factor in making these textiles the subject of Ghanaian intellectual property law.

Authorship, Identity, Citizenship, and the Modern Nation-State

In discussing the wide range of issues around the ownership and intellectual property protection of adinkra and kente in this book, I return repeatedly to the three main questions posed at the beginning of this chapter. First, what are the differing principles of authorship and alienability in the production of these fabrics and in intellectual property law, and what happens when these two systems meet? Second, what kinds of legal subjects are brought into being in the encounter? Third, what kinds of appropriation practices are found around adinkra and kente, on what kinds of claims are they based, and what implications do they have for Ghana's copyright protection of folklore?

I take authorship and alienability (and the connection between alienability and ownership) as my starting point, and in chapter 1, "The Tongue Does Not Rot: Authorship, Ancestors, and Cloth," I examine and evaluate the concepts and categories of intellectual property law (particularly copyright law) against the authorship practices of Asante cloth producers. Rather than taking the law as my point of departure and questioning whether adinkra and kente producers measure up to its standards of authorship, I look at cloth makers' creative and authorizing practices and consider the norms of authorship and ownership embedded in these. I examine the ways in which those norms challenge the ones assumed in intellectual property law and complicate the view that traditional knowledge production only involves communal authorship. I also consider how cloth producers' creative practices translate into ownership claims over adinkra and kente. I further examine cloth makers' views on the interrelated nature of the aesthetic and physical features of adinkra and kente cloth—features that the law separates by protecting only the designs. I also consider adinkra and kente producers' knowledge transmission norms and what these suggest—first, about cloth production as a specialized commons and, second, about the concept of the commons as an alternative mode for understanding the production and management of culture.

In chapter 2, "The Women Don't Know Anything! Gender, Cloth Production, and Appropriation," I consider the gendered nature of adinkra and kente production and the extent to which it translates into male privilege in cloth-producing communities. I argue that any claims of exclusive male dominance and female subjugation must be tempered by the fact of gender interdependency in cloth production. I also discuss challenges from women—particularly women who control the local cloth trade. Gendered authorship translates into gendered ownership claims around cloth when men resist women's cloth production in local communities and when women register cloth designs as their intellectual property. I further show that gendering around cloth production occurs not only according to the identity of those who produce it but also according to the sphere in which cloth production occurs—and the perception of that sphere as traditional or modern. Added to this is the gendered nature of the law itself. I consider the ways in which these different kinds of gendering occur, the consequences of their interaction for authorship and ownership, and how they complicate our understanding of the gender of cultural production and appropriation.

In chapter 3, "Your Face Doesn't Go Anywhere: Cultural Production and Legal Subjectivity," I compare adinkra and kente producers with musicians as citizens who differ radically in their willingness and ability to insist on state attention to their interests. Since Ghana's independence in 1957, lobbying groups have been instrumental in shaping various aspects of the country's intellectual property law. The relationship between lobbying and legal change consistently demonstrates that ownership claims around different kinds of cultural production are dependent not only on authorship, gender, ethnicity, and citizenship but also on the capacity to relate to the state as a citizen and legal subject. I also show how the law brings certain kinds of subjects into being. Citizenship does not automatically translate into the status of legal subject. Rather, that status is produced by the discourses of the law that authorize not only certain kinds of cultural production but also certain kinds of subjects.

In chapter 4, "We Run a Single Country: The Politics of Appropriation," I examine ethnic, diasporic, and national identities as the basis for ownership claims around adinkra and kente. Adinkra and kente producers regard ownership of their cloth as properly belonging to their communities, ethnic group, or the Asantehene. When one moves from these producers to Ghanaian artists who use the cloth designs in their work, ethnicity gives way to citizenship as a basis for ownership claims, yet those claims do not translate into an endorsement of state ownership of those designs. Perceptions both within and outside cloth-producing communities often challenge state ownership. At the same time, to the extent that citizens claim these designs as Ghanaian rather than ethnic, they confirm the legitimacy and success of the state's ongoing project of cultural nationalism.

An additional dimension emerges from diasporic claims to African cultures and cultural products, particularly in the context of Black cultural nationalism in the United States since the 1960s as well as the pan-Africanist movement that peaked in the mid-twentieth century and linked continental and diasporic nationalist aspirations. In harnessing adinkra, kente, and other African cultural elements to Black cultural nationalist projects, the diaspora also becomes an important market and therefore an additional incentive for the production of imitations of adinkra—and especially kente. Along with a Ghanaian public that is increasingly accepting of imitations, Africans in the diaspora ensure that the rewards for producing imitations are at present greater than any sanctions against such production. They also shift the issue of appropriation into the global sphere and highlight the multidirectional circuits of commodification and appropriation that Ghana must deal with in protecting folklore.

In chapter 5, "This Work Cannot Be Rushed: Global Flows, Global Regulation," I consider some of the issues raised by the circulation of adinkra and kente in global markets. I first outline the context of globalization within which these and other forms of indigenous culture circulate and the impact on local sources of production. I argue that the challenge for Ghana, in this context, is to restore the link between Ghanaian production sources and global markets or at least to intervene in those markets in ways that reduce some of the losses caused by consumption practices that undermine the importance of people like adinkra and kente producers as sources of cultural goods for global markets. I then briefly survey the nature of the international regulatory framework for intellectual property, the significant changes that have occurred in that framework over the past few decades, Ghana's position in that framework, and the country's prospects for regulating the appropriation of its cultural production.

I also take into account the ascendancy of China in global textile markets. While China is not the only producer of imitation adinkra and kente, its influence makes it a useful example for considering the challenges that Ghana faces in global markets as well as the ways in which China's growing economic importance opens an additional axis to that of North–South relations of power around appropriation, namely, a South–South or South–East axis. Finally, I consider what the Ghanaian case suggests about the place of the nation under conditions of globalization.

In the Conclusion, I draw out the different meanings of intellectual property law in relation to Ghana's working out its identity as a modern nation as well as its place in the world under current conditions of globalization. I also propose alternatives to the current regulatory order. I first examine the different kinds of power relations around the production, consumption, appropriation, and protection of adinkra and kente, as discussed in the preceding chapters. In doing so, I discuss the ways in which the exercise of power by different actors at local, national, and global levels occurs both through institutions and structures, such as laws, as well as through discourses that reinforce certain kinds of structural power.

I also consider the ways in which power is often subverted because individuals act in multiple spheres. For example, the relatively marginalized status of cloth producers in the legal sphere does not necessarily mean that they are excluded from agency in all the spaces available to citizens in the postcolonial state, since they may be active in other spheres, such as the tourism industry, as well as other sites in the global economy. Finally, I explore the concept of the commons, along with metaphors drawn from environmentalism, to propose alternative regimes for managing the production and circulation of culture in ways that transcend the hierarchies of knowledge and culture enshrined in intellectual property law. Such alternatives can strengthen and expand the creative spaces in which adinkra and kente producers work.

In chapter 1, I turn to an examination of those spaces. Ultimately, my hope is that they can lead us to options for managing cultural production that undermine the hegemony and, indeed, the relevance of "the copyright thing."

Chapter 1   The Tongue Does Not Rot
Authorship, Ancestors, and Cloth

We Asantes, we believe that we should pray. It is not idol worship. . . . We pray to remember our ancestors who have died who brought this work.

—Kwabena, kente weaver, Bonwire

Earrings are not cloth.

—Nana Baffour Gyimah, adinkra producer, Tewobaabi

KOFI, AN ADINKRA MAKER, raised the subject of property rights in cultural production before I could even explain my mission in wanting to talk to him. Several researchers had come to the community asking him and others about their craft, he declared angrily. He and his fellow cloth producers had shared their knowledge but had gained nothing from it. Clearly, as he saw it, knowledge about adinkra making belonged to those who made the cloth in his community, Asokwa, and they deserved to benefit from it. This was only one of the ways in which I encountered adinkra and kente makers as producers of knowledge, and it suggested a relationship to their cultural production that was analogous to the relations protected under intellectual property law but with some important differences.

The underlying premises of intellectual property law typically exclude cultural producers like adinkra makers or kente weavers as holders of the kinds of legal rights routinely granted those who write books and produce music and films. The law conceives of rights-holding cultural producers as individuals and deems "traditional knowledge" to be communal in its production. As such, traditional knowledge belongs outside the sphere of intellectual property law. While Kofi's views do not entirely contradict this concept, they do not completely confirm it either. In the weeks and months following

35

this encounter, he and other adinkra and kente cloth makers revealed creative practices that supported the view, advocated by indigenous peoples and several nations, that traditional knowledge combines both individual and communal creativity.

In this chapter, I examine the ways that Ghanaian adinkra and kente makers conceive of themselves as creative persons with rights over their work, focusing on two key aspects. The first is the nature of the creative process in cloth production and the ways that communal and individual creativity combine in such production. An important aspect of that creativity is its temporal dimension, as living cloth makers link their creative work with that of deceased cloth makers. While this is partly a reflection of the wider society, the way that time factors into both adinkra and kente production restores to creative work features that are eliminated in the framework of intellectual property law. The second aspect of cloth making has to do with knowledge transmission norms that challenge intellectual property law's relegation of cultural products like adinkra and kente to the public domain, or "commons." Instead, cloth makers' norms of knowledge transmission delineate the boundaries of a *restricted* commons that cannot be equated with an open one.

Based on this examination, I consider what cloth makers' views and practices reveal about the differences between ways of organizing creative activity in the realms of traditional knowledge on the one hand and intellectual property law on the other. I argue that attention to actual practices of cultural production in the two areas reveals considerable similarities in underlying ideas about creative work and the rights of those who do such work. At the same time, there are variations that complicate any easy equation of cultural production in different spheres. Some of the strongest variations occur in the points of emphasis in the organization of creative work. Thus, while proprietary benefits are a concern in both of the systems I discuss here, they receive differing degrees of emphasis. Following from this, I also argue that adinkra and kente makers' views and practices around their work provide resources for rethinking key elements in the debates on intellectual property law, such as the idea and social functions of the author, and the nature of the commons.

Individuals in Spatial and Temporal Communities

The view that traditional knowledge is communally created holds, to some extent, in the case of adinkra and kente. This aspect of creativity in cloth production came up in a number of ways in cloth makers' life history narrations. At the most general level, it emerged in connection with the rivalry between four centers of cloth production: Bonwire and Adanwomase, which produce kente cloth, and Asokwa and Ntonso, which produce adinkra. With the exception of Ntonso, these centers are also the official sources of the Asantehene's (or Asante ruler's) cloth.

Cloth makers claimed their communities either as the origins or the most important centers of adinkra or kente production, and those at Asokwa and Adanwomase were most emphatic in making such claims. This is not surprising, since both communities have been overshadowed by Ntonso and Bonwire respectively. Although Asokwa remains the official source of the Asantehene's adinkra cloth, it has been superseded by Ntonso as a major center of production. While cloth makers at Ntonso acknowledged Asokwa as the origin of adinkra cloth in Asante, they dismissed the significance of that fact with comments like "It [adinkra making] first came to Asokwa, but they didn't hold onto it."[1]

Weavers at Adanwomase made no such concessions and claimed that *all* kente weaving originated from their town, even though they have official recognition as the source of only the Asantehene's *white* kente (woven in the original palette of white and blue). Bonwire, by contrast, is not only the official source of the Asantehene's cloth in the striking colors associated with Asante kente but is also widely regarded as the origin of all kente weaving in Asante and is famous for its cloth well beyond the area. Cloth makers also made communal claims over adinkra and kente when asked from whom permission should be sought in order to reproduce cloth designs. Most identified their communities, while some also identified the Asantehene.

Such claims over the origins of adinkra and kente encompass cloth production as a whole and can therefore be distinguished from claims over individual designs. They are demands for recognition as the sources of the most distinctive examples of a socially important commodity. It is therefore not surprising that cloth makers should make claims at the level of cloth making in its entirety. In some cases, however, they combined this with claims over the creation of specific designs at a communal level. An example of this is the following quote from Kofi at Asokwa about his community's status as a source of authentic adinkra designs, recognized at the Asantehene's palace.

And then what we came and met, the old ones [symbols] that the elders used, that is what has a name [prestige] at the palace, you see? So that is why at first Asokwa was the only place where the chief's cloth was made.[2]

Another example came from the Asokwa cloth makers' response to a locally produced book of adinkra symbols and their meanings.[3] They identified a number of symbols and their names as coming from their community, saying, in some cases, that those designs were "from the elders." In other cases, they challenged the names given the designs by the book's author. Other symbols they did not recognize at all. Most significantly, their reaction to symbols that they considered improperly named was one of indignation. They declared that only the person who created a symbol had the right to name it—a point that was repeated by cloth makers in other locations. However, in this case, they claimed that right for the community, and they saw the assignment of unfamiliar names to adinkra designs that they claimed to have originated with individuals at Asokwa as an infringement against the community.

Even as they made communal claims over designs, adinkra and kente producers also referred frequently to the creative work of individuals, citing both their own designs and, in the case of adinkra, designs created by stencil carvers in their communities. (Adinkra stencils are made from pieces of dried gourd and may be carved by a specialist or by the person who uses them). As noted earlier, cloth makers specifically linked the right to name designs to the act of creating a design. Naming thus emerged in cloth producers' narratives in different communities as an important element in the creative process and one that established the group or person assigning the name as the creator of the design.

One study participant at Ntonso specialized in designing and carving stencils not only for use by cloth makers but also for general sale. A cloth maker in the community described the carver's creative process as follows: "The knowledge that God gives to him, when he wakes up, whatever art has appeared to him, he carves it when he rises. *Then he names it himself*" (emphasis added). Other cloth makers also described the creative act in these terms—as an act of inspiration. In doing so, they revealed views very similar to eighteenth-century European Romantic ideas of creativity and authorship as the result of individual inspiration—in this case, accompanied by the right to name the result of that inspiration. At Bonwire, this naming right is formally recognized in a system in which individual weavers can gain official recognition from community leaders as the creators and namers of specific designs.[4]

The adinkra makers of Asokwa also gave several examples of naming as a right. In the most detailed of these, they described a symbol, *Nyame nti* (because of God), created and named by a specific individual in the early years of Ghana's independence. In their account, the cloth maker was treated badly by a client, a politician's wife, who refused to pay him the full amount he demanded for cloth that she commissioned from him. As Manu recounted it,

> She even insulted him, an elderly man. So when she went away, he carved this symbol to say that she was not the one who was going to provide him with his livelihood and she could take the work [without paying the price he asked]. So *because of God* . . . he carved it. . . . So if you go and sit there and call it, let's say, *Koforidua forest* so that it will sell, it means your imitation is wrong. So to get the name of the symbol, you have to get the person who carved it. So at all times when you ask, you ask, "Who carved it?"

This example is significant in providing a detailed account of an individual creative act and for underscoring naming both as an integral part of that act and as a right. The same cloth makers also showed me several designs carved by another deceased elder to whom they made specific reference, and one of them reinforced the importance of naming with the words, "because if I am the carver and I have carved my symbol, *I* am the one who names it. It is not you who are sitting by the side who if you should happen to see it, then you give it any old label." Thus, even as cloth makers at Asokwa claimed their community as the origin of several designs and assigned the naming rights over those designs to their community, they also gave several examples of the same right as an individual one.

Such individual creativity occurs without exclusive individual control over designs, however. To quote Manu again,

> It is like here, the copyright thing does not work here, so when he [the creator of a new design] carves it, it is at the beginning that he hides it so that he can use it to work with a little, but when he's done that for a while anyone can, someone can go and ask and say, "Give me this stamp of yours and let me use it."[5]

Explaining the principle behind this sharing, Manu continued, "In the old days they loved each other." That "love" might simply be the practical outcome of the difficulty of preventing others from copying a design in the relatively small communities where cloth producers live and work. The assertion of brotherly love is also undermined by the fact that there is a certain amount of rivalry between individual cloth producers as creators of new designs. One cloth maker went as far as to assert, "Weavers are thieves!" Doran Ross also details the experience of a weaver at Bonwire who complained of other weavers copying his designs.[6]

At the same time, at least one cloth maker expressed an aversion to being perceived as greedy, and that may be a factor in the ethic of sharing described by Manu. That sharing also shows the relation between individual and communal creativity, where the former represents the initial phase in the life of a design. Long after designs pass into the general pool, however, cloth producers continue to identify them by reference to the individuals who designed and named them.

Cloth makers' references to individual creative work are also significant in including the work of deceased cloth makers. While the *Nyame nti* example was the most detailed account of the work of a specific deceased person provided in adinkra and kente makers' narratives, it was not the only reference of this kind. Cloth producers frequently referred to the creative work of "the elders" or "the ancestors," and one such reference came from Yaw Boakye, an adinkra maker at Ntonso. Explaining the rationale behind charging fees whenever knowledge of the craft is passed on, he said,

> At first I would never have spoken to you unless you had brought a bottle of imported drink that I would use to pray to the ancestors before saying anything to you.[7] That's the customary way. . . . Because you are coming to remind me of my grief [for] the person who taught me and has died and my mother and others. . . . The ancestors say, after all, that when a person dies their tongue does not rot. The person's body has decayed, how will their tongue not rot? It is the words that they spoke and left behind that do not pass away that we express by saying that when a person dies their tongue does not rot.[8]

Cloth makers' references to the ancestors are partly a reflection of the wider society and bear some explanation. In Akan society, the realms of the dead and the living are closely interrelated, and death does not prevent the participation of the deceased in the present or, indeed, the expectation that they will do so—if only by bearing witness to the actions of the living.[9] Past members of the community therefore continue to feature in it, and they are invoked in the celebration of all major rites of passage, such as naming ceremonies at which new members are admitted into the community and funerals at which newly deceased members are seen off.

The practice of invoking ancestors in African societies is a touchy subject because it has often been misconstrued as worship—hence the disclaimer about idol worship in the quotation at the head of this chapter. The term *ancestor veneration* is sometimes substituted as a more accurate description of the practice, and some have gone even further in suggesting that the term *ancestor* itself is misleading. Those invoked, it is argued, are not ancestors but deceased elders, and their place in society is similar to that of living elders, although the nature of the recognition accorded them is different because of their deceased status.[10] This helps to explain adinkra and kente producers' use of the same terms, *nananom* and *mpanyinfo*, to refer to both living and deceased elders. The first varies in meaning according to context and can refer to elders, royalty, grandparents, or grandchildren, while the second literally means "elders."

One of the most important means by which deceased elders are summoned to participate in the world of the living is through the offering of libations. This carries over into the world of work where apprenticeship fees for the learning of a trade usually include drinks that are offered to the ancestors when the apprentice is admitted for training and when she or he is discharged. While a cash fee directly compensates the cloth maker for his work of knowledge production and transmission, it does not necessarily ensure due recognition of the ancestors. Including drinks in the fees institutionalizes such recognition by providing the medium through which the ancestors are ritually invoked.[11]

The Akan proverb "The tongue does not rot," in pointing to the endurance of words—and creative acts—underscores the view that a person's words and actions are not curtailed by their physical death. This locates cloth makers in communities that are not only spatial but also temporal. Deceased elders are both pioneers and coauthors with living cloth makers, and death does not lessen the importance of those roles. Thus, the living not only recognize individual acts of creativity but continue to do so even after the individuals concerned have died as, for example, in the case of the *Nyame nti* adinkra design.

Yet another way that cloth makers signaled the importance of the ancestors in their work was in their reactions to the research method. In the life histories method, respondents recount their lives in relation to the research topic. In this case, individual cloth makers were asked to focus their narrations on their practices as producers of adinkra and kente. The method enabled them to express themselves at great length and depth and to shape the study and its areas of emphasis by introducing topics that they considered important. As a participatory method, it seemed well suited to introducing cloth makers' voices into a national intellectual property protection debate that has largely excluded them.

In addition to introducing unanticipated issues into the study, cloth producers also shaped it through their disapproval of the method itself, indicating that they found the focus on their individual views and experiences misplaced. In an oblique rebuke, Nana Ntiamoah Mensah said, "Weaving, it is my heritage, my ancestors' heritage. If you had come and said you wanted to ask about the origins of weaving, I would have explained it to you, but that is not what you asked."[12] As his narration progressed, however, he anchored the account of his long life as a cloth maker in the history of cloth making and the practices of "the ancestors." This was a recurring pattern, and other cloth makers similarly linked their individual lives and practices with those who had gone before them.

The relationship between living and dead cloth producers signals a number of fundamental differences in the practices around authorship in adinkra and kente production and those prevailing in intellectual property law. For one thing, there are differences in the way that time factors into the concepts of the author and authorship. Within intellectual property law, the demarcation is clear between authors who have died and authors who are living. The authorship of the former is of consequence before the law only if their intellectual property rights have not yet expired.[13]

While few formal rights accrue to authors in the case of adinkra and kente, recognition of authorship does not end with death—or after a specified period following that death. As a result, the ancestors whose names are invoked by living practitioners as their coauthors may extend from Otaa Kraban, one of the "inventors" of kente weaving in the eighteenth century, to the deceased maternal uncles of a living craftsman. The temporal demarcation between past and present authors is thus of far less significance in the case of adinkra and kente than it is in intellectual property law.

In sum, adinkra and kente are produced in creative communities that are both spatial and temporal and that recognize individual creative work. Successful communal claims of origin and prominence attract rewards from both the Asante and national states. The national state literally puts key production centers "on the map" of tourist attractions, and it is as members of communities that cloth producers achieve a place in national tourist networks and metaphorically on the map of Asante royal culture. When recognition by either the national or Asante state is at stake, therefore, the communal aspects of adinkra and kente production (and design) become most important.

Since contested claims make it difficult to locate rights over creativity in specific communities, they seem to support some of the arguments against protecting traditional knowledge in intellectual property regimes. Those arguments point to the difficulty of identifying the exact creators and owners of such knowledge. At the same time, when cloth producers make claims over individual designs rather than over adinkra and kente as kinds of cloth, they undermine the view that traditional knowledge is only communal in its production.

The ample evidence of individual creativity in adinkra and kente design means that focusing solely on communal creative processes fails to account fully for the way that cloth designs come into being, especially since the practice of naming designs occurs not only at the community level but also individually. At this level, cloth makers' claims move decisively into the territory of proprietary claims over creative work analogous to those protected by intellectual property law.

At the same time, even though individual cloth makers constantly create new designs and assert rights over them, particularly the right to name designs, they do not assert those rights to the extent of completely separating their creative work from the creative work of others. The creative processes around cloth production are thus neither solely communal nor solely individual. Further, since they also transcend time as measured in individual lives, they cannot be adequately captured by an exclusive focus on living cloth producers. Adinkra and kente makers' references to the ancestors are important for understanding the different ways that time is organized in relation to cultural production and the implications for such production of different modes of temporal organization.

While the individual dimension of traditional knowledge production is widely recognized by indigenous peoples and nations pressing for the legal protection of such knowledge, the fiction of exclusively communal production continues to be deployed against such efforts, especially at the international level. Yet a strategy that reversed this and emphasized individual over communal creativity in order to gain protection would diminish traditional knowledge and leave unchallenged some of the basic premises of intellectual property protection.

To take the case of Ghana's copyright protection of adinkra and kente, for example, it would be a fairly simple step to strengthen the recognition of individual creativity, and, indeed, the current version of the law allows for such recognition. However, an exclusive focus on individual creativity in adinkra and kente production obscures the important functions of the communal dimension of traditional knowledge production. Communal claims show that adinkra and kente are valuable not only for the individual designs used in their production but even more as genres of cloth. A system of protection based on the individual designs is therefore inadequate—any protection must extend to the level of the genre. At that level, protection must engage with the communal dimensions of cloth production and with the physical medium of cloth itself.

As contested and unstable as communal claims may be—especially in the case of spatial communities—they also highlight aspects of *all* creative work that intellectual property law obscures. In addition, adinkra and kente makers' references to the ancestors, and thus to the temporal dimension of their creative communities, are important in highlighting different ways of organizing time and their implications for cultural production. The different ways that the temporal and spatial dimensions of communal creativity are organized in adinkra and kente production and in intellectual property protection open up our understanding of the nature of authorship and authorization in creative work. These operate in the two systems of cultural production to support different kinds of claims that reflect the different sets of values in which such production is embedded.

Authors and Time in Intellectual Property Law

Within intellectual property law an author (or inventor) is the individual who creates an "artistic" or "scientific" work. When such a work is created by several individuals, each one must be clearly specified. A work may also be created by a corporation (or its employees), in which case the corporation is granted the status of an individual author or inventor—that is, a "legal person." The law is able to operate across these variations in the ways that a work is actually produced because they all rest on the principle of authorship as the creative work of clearly identifiable individuals. Within this scheme, creativity resides in individuals, not in diffuse communities, especially when the latter are not formally constituted into legal entities such as corporations. Another important requirement of authorship, in this scheme, is that creative works are not only individually produced but also original and innovative. Traditional knowledge, on the other hand, is viewed as adapting what already exists and is therefore considered to be neither original nor innovative.

It is now widely acknowledged that communal creativity in traditional knowledge is composed of individual creative efforts that go beyond mere adaptation.[14] Critics have also argued that works routinely protected by intellectual property law, such as books and music compositions, are "intertextual" in nature—that is, they draw on previously created work.[15] If this is so, then such works are also the product of creative communities, although, in this case, those communities may be spatially dispersed. The fact of intertextuality further undermines the distinction between innovative books and music and noninnovative traditional knowledge. Why, then, is individual creativity ignored in one system of cultural production and underscored in the other such that one is viewed as exclusively communal and the other as exclusively individual? It is partly due to the history that has placed the two systems in a specific structural relation to each other. It is also a result of the points at which value resides in the two systems, leading to different points of emphasis, and I now consider these in turn.

The conceptualization of creative work enshrined in intellectual property law is not a natural phenomenon but a historical construct. It fixes a shift from a communal to an individual view of creativity that occurred in Europe when a number of factors combined to make individual claims over creative work socially and economically profitable. Those factors included the invention of the printing press that enabled the mass production, sale, and profitability of texts. Another was the Enlightenment emphasis on the individual as the seat of agency along with the idea, among Romantic poets, that creativity was the result of individual inspiration and genius.[16]

This period also saw the shift in the organization of time from a circular to a linear model, in one account.[17] In the circular model, events occurred in a recurring and predictable cycle centered around the sacred, such that there were no sharp distinctions between past and present, unlike the secular linear model in which such distinctions were a central feature. The shift of focus to the individual and to the secular concept of linear time became hallmarks of the historical era of modernity. Rather than remaining specific to a particular social and historical context, these ideas were universalized as much of the world came under European control. Intellectual property law gives concrete form to these shifts in the conceptualization of creativity and time and owes its naturalized status partly to the process by which "modernity" was spread around the world.

Within this dominant understanding of time, all societies that do not exhibit the characteristics of the West exist in a devalued and static past outside the time of modernity.[18] The division of cultural production, such that certain kinds are amenable to intellectual property protection while others are not, maps onto this organization of temporality. As a result, cultural production that is sanctioned by intellectual property law belongs in the temporal mode of modernity in which the present is ever constant. The political effect of this is to render deficient modes of cultural production outside the privileged time of modernity.

This view of time that values the present of modernity over other realities that are regarded as traditional and permanently in the past is further reflected in intellectual property law when that law conceives of authorship as the work of an individual, since notions of subjectivity within modernity privilege the autonomous individual whose actions (including creative work) can be distinguished from the actions of all other individuals. Persons who do not conceive of themselves and their actions in this way belong to a different temporal mode wherever they may be situated geographically. While groups of such persons can be found in the West, it is those in the non-West who are most strongly defined in terms of living outside the temporality of modernity. The cultural production of the latter, especially when it values principles like sharing and custodianship over individual authorship and ownership, thus becomes "folklore" or "traditional knowledge."

These terms mark such cultural production as belonging outside the time of modernity, and their use often fails to engage critically with the fact that the cultural products they denote and societies they represent in fact exist contemporaneously with modernity.[19] Such terms also reify the ranking of different ways of organizing time, taking their alleged superiority or inferiority as given, without considering the "strategies of power" inherent in different temporal modes.[20] Examining those strategies makes it possible to critically analyze different kinds of temporality in relation to each other in ways that also interrogate their standard ranking relative to one another and undermine the hegemonic functioning of modernity as an organizing principle in cultural production. I propose to undertake such an examination, focusing on two elements in creative work: authorship and authorization.

Authorship and Authorization

I first expand the term *author* beyond its strong association with an individual creator of original work. Despite that association, the word is a useful shorthand term for discussing all creative work, especially given the instability of claims of individuality and originality. In the rest of this discussion, therefore, I separate the words *author* and *authorship* from their narrow definitions in intellectual property law and use them more broadly to refer respectively to people who do creative work, whether individually or communally, and the act of creating such work. This makes it possible to apply these terms to different kinds of creative work and critically compare them. I therefore view adinkra and kente makers as authors whose acts of creativity are different from those of music composers, say, not because they are more or less individual and innovative, but because of those aspects of their creativity that they emphasize and the claims they are able to make as a result of such emphasis.

Authorship within intellectual property law distinguishes clearly between the work of one author and the next. In doing so, as a number of critics have argued, the law obscures the fact that *all* creative work occurs within a tradition, and there is little such work that is completely original and does not build on the work of others.[21] Contrary to the law's emphasis on the individual, and as discussed in the previous section, adinkra and kente weavers express a very healthy awareness of the limits of their own creativity and insist on attention to the traditions within which their own authorship is located. They emphasize the importance of the work of previous cloth producers *as a basis for* the work of present ones. This sense of authorship as dependent on the work of previous authors is one that intellectual property law, almost by definition, is designed to suppress.

Adinkra and kente cloth producers' acknowledgment of multiple authors of their cloth and designs—living and deceased—is reflected in other kinds of traditional knowledge in Ghana. For example, with certain forms of indigenous music, communities of musicians recognize both individual and group authorship of their songs.[22] In being communal, and especially in including both living and dead authors, this system links individual authorship to the tradition in which it belongs in a way that creativity within intellectual property law does not. Authorship therefore operates in a far more fluid manner in this context than it does in the law.

The emphasis in intellectual property law on individual creativity and innovation minimizes the importance of the temporal and social contexts of cultural production. By focusing on individual authors and inventors due to its roots in Enlightenment views of humans as autonomous individuals and in Romantic ideas of creativity as a function of individual genius and inspiration, intellectual property law obscures the social context of cultural production. Indeed, the law exists to specify and police a sharp demarcation around the work of each creator. It is, in effect, a system for organizing knowledge and cultural production so that their social and temporal contexts are deemphasized and devalued in order to uphold the fiction of an individual creator.

Yet those social and temporal contexts are important to any recognition that something is knowledge or a cultural product. One can only recognize a cultural product as such because of its similarity to other such products and the fact that it comes out of a social system that produces such items. This makes it possible to describe it as a piece of kente cloth, say, or a novel. The makers of specific kinds of culture and knowledge share norms of production that make their work recognizable as one kind of product and not another. Whether acknowledged or not, these production norms constitute part of the social context of any cultural product. However original a novel may be, for example, it can only be a novel if it has certain features that are common to all novels. Those features are established over a period of time through the work of successive generations of writers, pointing to both the social and temporal contexts of that particular mode of writing and of each "new" work in that mode.

A key difference between adinkra and kente production and the production of book manuscripts occurs in the way these cultural products are invested with authority, and Michel Foucault's analysis of the "author function" is useful in understanding this.[23] In Foucault's discussion, authorship involves at least two processes. One is the actual production of creative work by a specified individual. However, this is of less interest to Foucault than a second process by which the author's name is used to organize his or her creative work as a coherent whole and to invest that work with authority. That authority becomes the basis for evaluating the merits of the work and making certain kinds of claims over it. For example, the authority of the author's name makes the work more amenable to commercial exchange.

Extending this analysis to adinkra and kente production, there is first the production of a creative work—a piece of cloth. While each piece may be individually produced and contain new design elements created by the individual cloth maker, it also incorporates elements designed by other creators who may be living or dead. At this level, and especially if one takes into account the element of intertextuality, the authorship of adinkra and kente is not so different from the authorship of a book or music composition. In these cases, cultural producers *also* draw on creative elements from past and present creators.

One of the most important differences between these kinds of creative activity occurs at the level of authorization. While it is the name of the writer or composer that invests the book or composition with authority, in the case of adinkra and kente, that authorization comes not from the person who makes the cloth but from the history that makes the cloth a valuable commodity. The cloth maker's name, in this scheme, has little authorizing value. Rather, it is his ability to link his cloth to a particular heritage whose elements include a long tradition of practice on the part of other cloth producers in his spatial and temporal community, the continuing prestige of Asante royalty long after the decline of the Asante kingdom and its incorporation within the nation of Ghana, the power of the Ghanaian state that makes adinkra and kente key elements in cultural nationalism, and the importance of cloth itself as a socially valuable commodity.

Against this background, cloth makers' references to the ancestors can be understood as a strategy of authorization. Such references are part of a well-developed narrative approach that adinkra and kente makers use in explaining their work to the many visitors who come to their communities as tourists, researchers, and clients. Those narratives highlight the prestige and distinction of the crafts and products of adinkra stenciling and kente weaving. Clearly, doing so is a useful and effective marketing strategy, but cloth producers emphasize this heritage of cultural production even when the interaction is noncommercial, as in the case of reactions to the life histories method described earlier.

Cloth makers invest their creative practices with authority by invoking the ancestors from whom they derive those practices and the history of cultural production laid down by previous generations of ancestors. Unlike Foucault's "author function" that invests discourses with authority, authorization here is not bound up with the identity of a single person working at a specific historical moment but with a community of living and deceased producers. Authorship and authorization, in this scheme, are therefore collaborative and temporally indefinite. Authorization of cloth producers' creative labor is bound up with ancestral authorship not just through general claims but sometimes in a literal or direct sense. Yaw Boakye's "the tongue does not rot" statement, in the previous section, is an example of this. Another is a kente weaver, Kwabena, who declared,

> The designs, now, all of those we are making, when you look into it, our ancestors established them. Ours, it is just little bits that we add onto it. Our ancestors did the work for a very long time indeed. So if anyone says that he is designing a cloth and when he finishes it he says, "As for this I sat down and made the cloth to the end without the hand of our ancestors being in it," he is lying, it is not true.[34]

At face value, this statement seems contradictory, since this same person, at a different point in his narration, spoke of "new" cloth patterns that he had designed. Without the authorizing "hand of the ancestors," however, those new patterns have little significance. The authorship of the ancestors in creating designs that living craftsmen use becomes significant when new designs are introduced not because individual creativity is less important than communal creativity but because the ancestors' work authorizes new designs as part of an established tradition. This is contrary to the understanding of authorship in intellectual property law in which tradition is obscured to better highlight the individual author working in that tradition. Among adinkra and kente makers, a new design has the status of adinkra or kente not because of its individual features but because of its incorporation into a pool of ancestral designs. It does not follow, however, that that incorporation erases the designer's individual contribution.

Authorization also occurs in the cloth's association with particular institutions—first, the Asante state, as represented by its royalty. Kente and adinkra production have been recognized as socially and politically important creative labor since the introduction of these crafts into Asante in the eighteenth and nineteenth centuries. In their early history, that importance was signaled by the initial status of these crafts as royal monopolies. With the relaxation of the restrictions around the use of adinkra and kente cloth, their status as royal crafts is no longer inherent but must be constantly reaffirmed—and supplemented. This is what cloth producers do when they insist on attention to the location of their cloth and their own creative work in a particular heritage. They are able to do so by appeal to Asante royalty because of the national policy of formally recognizing indigenous systems of governance (for example, through the constitutionally mandated National House of Chiefs) within the political space of the nation-state and also because of the continuing prominence of the Asantehene among indigenous rulers in Ghana.[25]

Along with the ancestors, therefore, the Asante royal palace is an important means of authenticating the heritage of cloth production. It is not enough that the very attention that adinkra and kente attract is an index of their singular status; craftsmen emphasize that singularity lest anyone regard their cloth as interchangeable with similar commodities and diminish the importance of their own work of cultural production. A second institution that is important to strategies of authorization is the Ghanaian state and its identification of adinkra and kente as elements of a distinctive national culture. One way that Ghana claims distinction from other nations and markets itself as a tourist destination is by claiming a "rich cultural heritage," with adinkra and kente as key elements of that heritage. One adinkra maker, asserting the superiority of handmade adinkra cloth over mass-produced imitations, underscored the difference by declaring, "But ours is the *cultural* one!"[26]

Yet another source of authorization of adinkra and kente is the medium of cloth itself. As discussed in the Introduction, cloth in Ghana is important as a bearer of psychological and social meanings including grief, celebration, status, and wealth. Adinkra and kente are therefore important not only for their design elements but also because those elements, in combination with cloth, constitute the most prestigious examples of an important social commodity. Unlike appeals to ancestors, royalty, and national culture, however, the medium of cloth is almost invisible as a mode of authorization until one engages cloth makers about the use of their designs either in mass-produced fabric or in nontextile forms.

A striking example of this was Nana Baffour Gyimah, who expressed concern over what he considered to be the degradation of the royal status of adinkra and kente cloth by the proliferation of cheap imitations. For him, these were clearly inferior versions of the cloth that he and others produced not only because of their quality but also because they lacked the authorizing links to ancestors and royalty. When asked what he thought about the appropriation of adinkra symbols in jewelry form, he seemed perplexed at the question saying, "But earrings are not cloth." This response is best understood in the context of the social and cultural symbolism of cloth. For Baffour Gyimah, earrings and other forms of jewelry were a completely different kind of product and irrelevant to a discussion of adinkra and kente. His reaction to the subject of jewelry was an indicator of the importance of the medium of cloth as a source of authorization.

Apart from this indirect reference to cloth as a medium, Baffour Gyimah stands apart from other adinkra and kente producers as one who has been able to push the boundaries of what counts as adinkra while managing to gain legitimacy and acceptance of his cloth by drawing on the same authorizing sources as other cloth makers. A cloth producer who works in both adinkra and kente, Baffour Gyimah has merged the cloth-weaving techniques of kente with silkscreen printing methods using commercial dyes to produce a kind of cloth that is regarded by himself and others as adinkra. Yet this cloth deviates from the standard methods of adinkra production and from the aesthetic conventions of adinkra cloth. In addition to the screen-printing method, Baffour Gyimah creates designs that are different from adinkra not only in their appearance but also in their scale. Whereas a typical adinkra motif is about three inches square, his designs are seven inches square. The larger scale is more amenable to the screen printing method and can include human figures, which do not occur in the adinkra pool.[27] Baffour Gyimah's use of this technique and introduction of new aesthetic conventions troubles the boundaries between authentic handmade cloth that follows certain conventions and inauthentic mass-produced cloth that introduces new ones (see Figure 2).

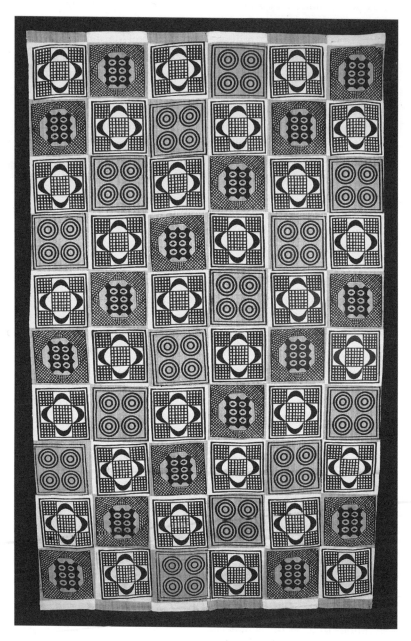

Figure 2. Screen-printed adinkra cloth by Nana Baffour Gyimah.

Baffour Gyimah skillfully manages the tension between authentic and inauthentic cloth, and while he asserts his status as an innovator, he highly values his recognition as a producer *within* the traditions of adinkra and kente. That recognition is based on his success in building an elite clientele that includes members of Asante royalty. The importance of this clientele to his positioning of himself is so strong that he reported having once given up a stall in the main market of Kumasi, the Asante capital, because the surrounding area became muddy when it rained, making it unsuitable for his clients. Baffour Gyimah's patrons' acceptance and use of his screen-printed cloth in situations in which adinkra would be appropriate authorize his cloth as adinkra far more strongly than any claims that he could make as an individual and have led to its widespread adoption by Ghanaians as a new kind of adinkra cloth. Accordingly, like more conventional adinkra and kente craftsmen, he refers to his work as part of a heritage established by the ancestors and, in his case, further legitimated by his distinguished clientele.

Baffour Gyimah's use of ancestors and tradition to authorize his work is even more interesting when one considers that of all the respondents producing adinkra and kente, he was the only one who had tried to use intellectual property law to protect his innovative designs. Unlike most of the other respondents, he was well acquainted with the national legal sphere and had registered a company earlier in his career. When he began producing his new designs, he considered registering them under the textile designs registration decree that protected the designs of mass-produced cloth.[28] He refrained from doing so because he felt it might be perceived as greed on his part ("You are the only one who wants to make money") or as appropriating a commonly held resource. Instead, for a while, he took to printing his company's registered business logo on his cloth in order to distinguish it from imitations by other craftsmen. While working within the tradition of adinkra and drawing on its heritage to authorize his cloth as part of the tradition, he actively resisted the practice of allowing his designs to pass into the communal pool.

The importance of the ancestors and heritage in authorship is even clearer when one considers Baffour Gyimah in relation to the local batik industry. Batik production has been an important cottage industry in Ghana since the 1980s. Several Ghanaian batik producers use adinkra designs in their work. However, they work outside both the aesthetic conventions and the authorizing discourses available to someone like Baffour Gyimah. Without those discourses, he would be one more Ghanaian artist appropriating adinkra symbols and combining them with his own designs. Baffour Gyimah's ability to avoid this characterization is due to the care he has taken to establish himself as a producer of cloth that, while innovative, is still authorized by living and deceased elders.

The most important differences between the context of cultural production in which adinkra and kente makers operate and that in which intellectual property law typically operates have more to do with these strategies of authorization than with the nature of authorship itself. While one can point to similarities in authorship in the two contexts, the strategies of authorization within them are completely different. In one system, authorization is based on the name of the individual cultural producer. In the other, authorization rests on the work of other cultural producers, including those who have died, and also on institutions of power as well as on the medium of cloth itself.

These different systems of authorization enable different kinds of claims. While individual cultural producers in both systems benefit financially from their work, the claims they can make within their respective systems are different. In the system associated with intellectual property law, the importance of the individual cultural producer's name as the source of authorization effaces the social and temporal sources of a person's creative work, making it easier to claim the sole right to be recognized as the author of the work. In intellectual property law, that work has its most value when it is linked to the author's name and diminishes in value when that link is weakened or broken.

In the system of adinkra and kente production, on the other hand, authorization points away from the individual producer to the history and political structures that make his work noteworthy. While acknowledging individual creative genius in the creation of adinkra and kente, authorization practices focus on adinkra and kente as distinctive genres rather than on their individual producers. Although cloth producers make claims over individual designs, those designs derive their greatest importance as part of a symbolic system bound up with the medium of cloth and anchored in a specific context of cloth production. Thus, cloth makers' most important claims are of association with the overall genre rather than over individual elements within it. Cloth makers introduce varying degrees of innovation into the genre, and Baffour Gyimah's new adinkra cloth is one of the most radical examples of such innovation. However, his success as an innovator comes from his ability to insist that he remains within the genre of adinkra cloth rather than standing apart from it. Such use of ancestral authority to authorize new kinds of cloth production has also been noted in Senegal, where weavers producing cloth using broadloom techniques insist that their cloth belongs within older traditions of strip-weaving.[29]

Cloth makers' emphasis on the genre as the source of value also reveals adinkra and kente production as occurring within a specialized commons, and authorization focuses on the commons rather than the individuals within it. That authorization also functions to exclude certain kinds of products even though, on the face of it, they may be related to products within the commons. Thus, jewelry that uses adinkra symbols belongs outside the commons, along with imitations of adinkra and kente cloth produced in textile factories. Yet Nana Baffour Gyimah's work shows that new forms that borrow from mass-production techniques may be admitted into the commons if they can tap into the sources of authorization that delineate the boundaries of the commons. In the section that follows, I discuss the ways in which cloth makers' knowledge transmission norms also function to delineate the boundaries of the commons.

Knowledge Transmission

One important set of cloth makers' practices has to do with the ways that they pass on knowledge of their work. The practice of demanding apprenticeship fees, including drinks for libations to deceased elders, shows that such knowledge is not accessible to all. The standard view of traditional knowledge is that it is not systematically learned but informally picked up. In fact, the level of skill required in both adinkra and kente making is such that it cannot be casually picked up without very privileged access. Those with strongest access are cloth makers' immediate family members who live in close proximity to the cloth production process and can learn a lot from observation, and several cloth makers spoke of learning in this way.

As adinkra maker Kwame described it, "While we were going to school, when the elders were preparing their dyes, on Saturday and Sunday, they would drag you and make you sit down. You couldn't go anywhere. They would continually teach you bit by bit."[30] Similarly, a cloth maker at Asokwa said that he learned adinkra making from his maternal uncle, but when the uncle was not working, "I could go to another elder, anyone. As for this place, the older ones need the children to help them to make the cloth."[31] Other comments showed that the learning process was not simply one of proximity and indirect learning but of active teaching. Adinkra maker Yaw Boakye spoke of teaching his children "as if they were my sister's sons."[32]

The matrilineal inheritance system in Akan society makes the affinity between men and their sisters' sons more important than their relationship with their brothers' sons or even their own. As a result, men play an active role in the lives of their sisters' sons in a relationship that is not adequately captured by the English word *nephew*. For Boakye, therefore, those who were most entitled to learn from him were his sister's sons rather than his own. His words also suggest that being around him was not a sufficient condition for his sons to learn cloth making; they had to be actively taught. He further revealed that he had learned how to weave kente as an adult and had been taught by his uncle after unsuccessfully trying to teach himself. As he described it, whenever his uncle took a break and left the loom unattended, he would take his place and invariably ended up making mistakes and ruining the cloth. "It was later that he caught me at it and said that if I wanted to [learn], I should tell him so that he would teach me and I would learn how to do it rather than doing it when he was away and spoiling it. And I consented and told him I wanted to learn, *and he taught me*" (emphasis added).[33]

Boakye's wife, Maame Tabi, who produces black *kuntunkuni* cloth, described the process by which she learned to make cloth. There is a fairly strong gender division in cloth production, and kuntunkuni is made by women. I provide a full discussion of this gendering and of kuntunkuni production in chapter 2, but Tabi's experience is worth discussing here as an example of the systematic way in which learning takes place in cloth making and of the fact that kinship is no guarantee of such learning. After reaching puberty and being initiated into adulthood, Maame Tabi decided that she wanted to earn her living from cloth making, and she was sent to live with her sister, a kuntunkuni maker. Although the fee was waived and her sister supplied her with the equipment she needed, she reported that she paid in kind by giving up the opportunity to profit from her work while she learned the trade. Her description of the training process also made it clear that even though she was living with her sister, the latter could still withhold knowledge from her.

> I didn't pay, but rather she profited a lot from my work. When I did the work, she would take it away [and sell it]. When she returned, she would give me what [amount of money] she wanted. . . . If you didn't do it like that, *she wouldn't teach you*, so at the beginning I was doing it like that and she was teaching me, "Do it this way, do it that way"; then when I finished, [when] she returned [from selling cloth], then she would sometimes say, here's ten, or twenty [currency units], then I would thank her." (emphasis added)[34]

Later in her narration, when I suggested that she had an advantage in being able to learn from her sister instead of paying an apprenticeship fee, Maame Tabi exclaimed, "But how I toiled, isn't it more than paying? Ah! I worked to her advantage for so long!" All these examples point to the acquisition of cloth-making skills as the result of a systematic process and not solely of proximity. Such proximity may lead cloth makers' children to pick up some skills, but it is no guarantee that they will become expert cloth makers. Further, as Tabi's experience suggests, kinship does not necessarily translate into an advantage even when formal fees are waived because payment can be exacted in other ways. As one adinkra maker put it, "You will continually thank him [the one who teaches you]."[35] Such thanks are offered not only verbally but also in kind.

In instances in which people from outside the community seek to learn cloth making, the barriers to access become even more evident because they must pay a fee before being allowed to learn. At Asokwa, a man whose family belonged to another ethnic group and had migrated to the community reported that he began to learn by observing cloth production like other children in the community. However, because of his immigrant status, cloth makers demanded that he pay a fee before they would allow him to continue observing them. In his case, the lack of ethnic and kinship ties overrode his membership in the community, and for purposes of learning to make adinkra, he was regarded as an outsider. In another example that I discuss more fully in chapter 2, there were strong attempts at Bonwire to raise barriers against a group from within the community seeking to learn kente weaving—this time on the basis of gender rather than ethnicity. The existence of such barriers runs contrary to the conventional wisdom within intellectual property law that the public domain is an obvious or appropriate sphere for such cultural production. Instead, they show that rather than being a part of the public domain, adinkra and kente production are in fact restricted commons.

Public Domain or Limited Commons?

Recognizing the ancestors when knowledge of adinkra and kente production is passed on partly serves to demarcate the boundaries of these traditions of creative work and to set the terms on which others may participate in them. Additional factors delineating those boundaries are gender and ethnicity. Those boundaries establish adinkra and kente production as a kind of commons within which there is a lot of borrowing and sharing and, over time, blurring of individual authorship lines. However, this commons must be understood as distinct from the use of the term (derived from Locke) to refer to resources held in common by members of a society and to which all in that society have rights of access. In that sense of the term, once an individual applies her labor to a portion of those resources, she gains the right to claim ownership over that portion and remove it from the commons.[36]

The Lockean understanding of the physical commons and the means by which resources existing within it are converted into private property has become influential in intellectual property law's protection of intangible property. It is also at the heart of the legal conception of the public domain of creative works whose intellectual property protection has expired—a commons that has typically been held to include uncopyrightable "folk" knowledges and cultural production like adinkra and kente. Under current global economic conditions, this conception of a commons of folklore does little to promote our understanding of indigenous and local cultural production, while legitimizing its rampant appropriation.

The concept of the commons has been revitalized since the mid-1990s as scholars and activists have applied it against what they perceive as the intensified use of intellectual property law to enclose the commons of cultural goods.[37] In the United States, one key piece of legislation triggering this activism was the Sonny Bono Copyright Term Extension Act of 1998, which lengthened the term of copyright protection from fifty years plus the life of the author to seventy years plus the life of the author. This expanded term has become the norm internationally and has made its way into Ghana's copyright law.

If intellectual property law is informed by the Lockean view that those who mix their labor with a portion of the commons have a right to claim ownership of the results of that labor, it is now argued that in the case of cultural production, such ownership claims amount to a "second enclosure movement" that threatens the continued existence of a common pool of cultural resources.[38] Challenging the "tragedy of the commons" that supposedly occurs when the lack of private ownership leads to abuse and destruction through overuse, scholars have noted that private ownership is having precisely this negative effect. They further point to the "comedy of the commons" in which commonly held resources are well managed without recourse to private ownership.[39]

The commons has been described as "the opposite of property" and "property's outside,"[40] while its legal counterpart—the public domain—has been described as "a broom closet in the grand palace of intellectual property law."[41] Such descriptions illustrate that in contrast to the well-developed ideas about property informing intellectual property law, the nonproperty realms of the public domain and commons have received much less attention. As intellectual property laws have expanded in duration and scope at the same time that the rise of digital technology has opened up unprecedented possibilities for creative uses of the cultural commons, scholars and activists have noted the dangers of taking the commons for granted as a free resource that is open to exploitation by all. Recent developments in intellectual property law, such as the extended duration of copyright protection, are being used to privatize the commons and restrict its use, thereby limiting its further expansion and development.

As a result of these developments, the last fifteen years have seen renewed attention to the importance of understanding the nature of the commons and the advantages of structuring cultural production according to its logic of sharing. Rather than simply being the indeterminate "outside of property," the commons has been defined by Yochai Benkler as "a particular institutional form of structuring the rights to access, use and control resources."[42] Benkler argues that this institutional form is the opposite of property in the sense that

> no single person has exclusive control over the use and disposition of any particular resource in the commons. Instead, resources governed by commons may be used or disposed of by anyone among some . . . number of persons, under rules that may range from "anything goes" to quite crisply articulated formal rules that are effectively enforced.[43]

Drawing on the work of scholars like Elinor Ostrom and Carol Rose, Benkler further identifies four types of commons based on whether they are open to anyone or only to a defined group and whether they are regulated or unregulated. This framework offers a more useful alternative to the view that if traditional knowledge is unowned as private property, then it must be in the public domain and therefore free for the taking.

The case of adinkra and kente production draws attention to an aspect of some commons that has received relatively little attention: the existence and nature of boundaries around them. Discussions of the commons of cultural production tend to focus on the importance of eliminating the boundaries imposed by private property regimes. However, that focus obscures the fact that while both adinkra and software production may occur within commons, there are boundaries around these. Acknowledging the existence of these boundaries and understanding their nature can make for a more nuanced understanding of the conditions for participating in different kinds of commons as well as the ways in which they are managed.

Rather than dismissing adinkra and kente production as belonging within an undifferentiated commons of traditional knowledge, such production must be understood as a distinct commons of cultural production with specific rules of entry and access. It is somewhat analogous to the "innovation commons" of the Internet and to what has loosely been called a "tribal commons," and all three have certain kinds of boundaries around them.[44] In the case of the Internet, the boundaries are made up of certain kinds of cultural and material capital, and the delineation of the boundaries around the commons, in this case, depends less on active admission and exclusion and more on the possession of such capital.

Similarly, the boundaries of a tribal commons are composed of the factors that differentiate the "tribe" from other social groups, namely, ethnicity and lineage. Although these factors are also at play in the case of adinkra and kente production, they cannot be reduced to tribal commons because doing so privileges ethnicity and lineage as the primary defining features of the commons. In adinkra and kente production, ethnicity operates in combination with factors like kinship, gender, knowledge, and location to delineate the boundaries of the commons. Further, these boundary markers function with varying degrees of flexibility in allowing and preventing entry. The restricted access to the commons of adinkra and kente production makes it analogous to certain kinds of physical commons that "are better thought of as limited property regimes, rather than commons, because they behave as property vis-à-vis the entire world except members of the group who hold them together in common."[45]

The commons of adinkra and kente production needs to be understood as a sphere of creativity with multiple outer boundaries that are managed by cloth makers. Cloth producers permit entry if certain conditions are satisfied. For those who are related to members of the commons, kinship ties are often (though not always) enough to secure access. For those who are deemed to be outsiders, the cost of admission is formal apprenticeship and the payment of fees. One does not need to reside outside the community as an apprentice or researcher in order to be regarded as an outsider. The category of outsider can also extend to people who have migrated to the community. Similar restrictions apply to children from families that may be of the same ethnicity as the rest of the community but in which there is no practicing adinkra or kente maker. Gender is an additional factor restricting entry to the commons of adinkra and kente production. The principle here, as in the case of ethnicity, is that this restriction can be set aside if the conditions of formal apprenticeship are satisfied or if there is a concerted effort to gain admission for women.

In addition to ethnicity, kinship, and gender, the boundaries of the commons of adinkra and kente production are marked by their status as products of a particular heritage—that is, through the authorization discussed earlier. An artist operating outside the commons may draw from it and appropriate its designs for her work but cannot contribute to the design pool without belonging to the heritage of adinkra and kente production. As a result, it is only those authorship practices that are undertaken within the commons that make its expansion possible. Further, drawing from the commons does not necessarily confer the status of adinkra or kente onto the resulting work. The status of a piece of cloth as adinkra or kente depends on its association with the heritage that craftsmen emphasize. As is evident in the case of the innovative adinkra maker Nana Baffour Gyimah, the authorial practice of invoking that heritage functions as a marker both of authenticity and of the boundaries of the commons.

An important feature of those boundaries is their permeability, which has been important in allowing cloth producers to manage the interface between the commons and external forces. For at least two hundred years, adinkra and kente have been shaped by a changing social and economic environment, and their physical features, as we know them today, represent cloth producers' adeptness in assimilating and adapting to that change. The vivid colors that are typically associated with Asante kente represent one such form of assimilation. When silk fabrics from Europe began to appear in Asante, weavers unraveled them and used the resulting yarns for cloth that they had previously woven only in the locally available colors of indigo and white. Baffour Gyimah's innovations in adinkra cloth production are another example of externally influenced change that goes beyond the appearance of the cloth itself, while his authorizing strategies ensure that his cloth remains firmly within the commons.

Adinkra and kente production therefore does not occur in a hermetically sealed cultural space, and it would be a mistake to reify the creative spaces of their production as bastions of an unchanging tradition. Rather, they are commons with permeable boundaries that have permitted cloth producers to respond to new materials and technologies as they have encountered different aspects of the global economy. Cloth makers therefore do not stand apart from global circuits of culture but operate within them, and for the best part of two centuries, they have dealt effectively with the impacts of globalization in its earlier phases. They continue to operate skillfully within global markets where they encounter them through the tourist industry. With the changes in the value systems guiding adinkra and kente consumption, accompanied by improved technologies for appropriating their cloth, however, the ability of adinkra and kente makers to manage the boundaries of their creative commons is increasingly in question.

As long as producers and consumers agree that only cloth that is made within those boundaries has the status of adinkra or kente and can be used as such, these criteria of authenticity help to keep the commons intact. This agreement is essentially the correspondence between production knowledge and consumption knowledge discussed by Appadurai.[46] When there is a gap between these two knowledges, it creates an opportunity for middlemen who exploit it to their economic advantage. However, the boundaries start to break down when consumers cease to distinguish between products from within the commons and imitations from outside. When authenticity ceases to matter to consumers, the commons loses its power and its relevance in cloth markets. The breaking down of these boundaries is a key factor in the appropriation that has made adinkra and kente the subject of intellectual property law along with several other kinds of indigenous and local cultural production.

Legal Options and Constraints

As this discussion has shown, authorship in relation to adinkra and kente production differs most from intellectual property law in the means by which cultural work is authorized. Further, adinkra and kente producers' active management of access and entry to cloth production marks that production as occurring within a specialized commons rather than an undifferentiated one. An additional difference stems from the medium of cloth in which adinkra and kente are produced. The social value of cloth in Ghana is such that the legal separation of cloth from its designs not only fractures such cultural production but also highlights the fragmentation inherent in intellectual property law.

Nana Baffour Gyimah's comment on jewelry and cloth, noted earlier, points to this fragmentation and shows that adinkra and kente designs lose much of their value when separated from the medium of cloth. Yet, in protecting adinkra and kente designs and not the textiles, Ghana's copyright law makes no distinction as to the form in which imitation occurs. For the Ghanaian state, all unauthorized appropriations, whether in the form of cloth, jewelry, or gift-wrapping paper, are illegal. This is contrary to cloth producers' varying perceptions of appropriation according to the *medium* of appropriation and also ignores the cultural economy of cloth.

This legal separation between cloth and designs highlights the challenge of fitting complex cultural products like adinkra and kente into the categories of intellectual property law. In order to extend protection such that the medium of appropriation is taken into account, industrial property law might be more appropriate, and Ghana has tried this option but so far with little success. Legislation passed in 1973 attempted to protect the rights of local textile manufacturers in the mechanized textile production industry while simultaneously preventing the appropriation of adinkra and kente in textile form.[47] However, the provision within this law that was intended to protect adinkra and kente from appropriation served, in effect, as a loophole that enabled the registration of cloth designs very similar to adinkra and kente. Those registering such designs simply included a disclaimer stating that they did not claim ownership of the adinkra and kente symbols incorporated in their design. The law was repealed and replaced by an industrial designs law in 2004, but it is still too early to tell how the new law will affect appropriation of these designs in the local textile industry.

In another area of industrial property law, Ghana introduced legislation protecting geographical indications in 2004. Geographic indications were originally developed in order to protect distinctive food products associated with particular regions in Europe and are well suited to the protection of products like adinkra and kente.[48] Their effectiveness is derived from the prestige associated with the name and place of origin of a product. These laws bar imitations from bearing the same name as the original product and therefore prevent their being accorded the same prestige. In doing so, they partly address the issue of material form by protecting a specific material product made in a particular place.

The Ghanaian version of this law, while referring to Ghanaian "handicrafts," singles out kente. This means that products other than the handwoven cloth made within the aesthetic conventions of kente may not be sold as kente. As with the industrial designs law, it is still too early to tell how effective this law will be. Potentially, it introduces another boundary around the commons of kente production policed, this time, by the state rather than by cloth producers. In doing so, it may help to preserve the hierarchy of value in which kente is ranked above appropriations, but it will not necessarily eliminate the appropriations.

In conceptualizing protected goods solely in terms of tangible material culture ("any product of handicraft or industry"), the geographical indications law is narrower in scope than copyright law. It therefore cannot function as a comprehensive attempt to overcome some of the shortcomings of the use of copyright law to regulate the appropriation of all forms of local cultural production. It is clear from these examples of legal protection that the nature of adinkra and kente cloth as bearers of cultural heritage and identity, and of distinctive designs, makes it difficult to capture them within any one category of intellectual property law. However, in the short term, geographical indications law seems to offer the best prospect of protecting them as commons of cultural practices and products.

The global currents that threaten to undermine the boundaries of the commons of adinkra and kente production have led to changes in the nature of intellectual property regulation not only nationally (in Ghana, for example) but also internationally. However, the response to these global pressures in the area of intellectual property regulation has tended to intensify the law's orthodoxies (for example, its insistence on certain kinds of legal personhood) and to harness it to the hegemonic operations of capital. Intellectual property law has become an important means by which cultural goods are transformed into commodities, and corporations producing a range of goods from pharmaceuticals to movies have aggressively used the law to expand their control over such goods.[49] This latter trend is most strongly exemplified in the move that led to the inclusion of intellectual property regulation within the purview of the World Trade Organization under the Agreement on Trade Related Aspects of Intellectual Property (TRIPS), and I discuss that move and its implications for Ghana in chapter 5.

As a result of these trends in international intellectual property regulation, the conceptual gap between ideas of creativity and alienability within the law and within indigenous and local cultural production has widened even as the law has gained in importance as a space for adjudicating claims over different kinds of cultural production and appropriation in the global economy. The law has therefore not only been unequal to the task of maintaining creative commons like those of adinkra and kente production; it has been inimical to such commons and those who work within them. The challenge therefore remains of maintaining these as viable creative spaces that stay distinctive and at the same time permeable enough to permit exchanges with other creative spheres without rendering them irrelevant in the process or disempowering those who operate within them.

Ghana's application of the law has also tended to favor the state over cloth-making communities and the ethnic groups to which they belong. While the state acknowledges the fluidity of the authorship norms within which these textiles are produced, ultimately it interprets them in static ways that favor state ownership. The law speaks of custodianship rather than ownership, but for practical purposes, the rights attendant on such custodianship are very similar to those that would pertain if the law explicitly made the Ghanaian state the owner of the different kinds of folklore protected under copyright law.[50] As authors, therefore, adinkra and kente producers have little standing before the law, and as is typical in many other applications, intellectual property law ends up favoring the rights of owners—in this case the Ghanaian state—over authors.

Technically, the law recognizes the authorship of individual adinkra and kente producers but places the burden of proof of authorship on cloth makers, who must demonstrate that the designs they claim as theirs are original and distinct from the larger design pool. In addition, asserting individual ownership claims through the agency of the law would radically change the nature of the commons within which cloth producers work. The freedom of borrowing and adaptation that enriches that commons would be severely curtailed. It is therefore debatable whether a set of legal arrangements that requires cloth makers to pursue such claims is even desirable.

In the next chapter, I examine women's activities in cloth production to highlight a number of contradictions that arise from the fact that while male cloth makers may manage the commons of adinkra production and in doing so exclude women, the women's actions are crucial in the cultural economy of cloth use that gives adinkra and kente their value. Women are often responsible for the sale of these and other kinds of cloth. They also produce and sell imitations that compete with handmade cloth. Further, while male producers have little standing before current intellectual property law, women who produce imitations do so within the space of the law. In the next chapter, I examine this tension between men as managers of cultural commons that exclude women and women as both purveyors of cloth that threatens the male-dominated commons and privileged legal subjects within the masculinized space of the law.

Chapter 2 The Women Don't Know Anything!
Gender, Cloth Production, and Appropriation

He said, "But if you weave you will not give birth," and I said,
"Oh, I have given birth once so even if I don't give birth again it
doesn't matter."

—Akua Afriyie, weaver, Kumasi

Women deceive you!

—Kofi, adinkra producer, Asokwa

IT WAS MY FIRST VISIT TO ASOKWA, and I was explaining my research goals to Kofi. After the initial hostile reaction that I described in chapter 1, he agreed to record his life history and help me contact other adinkra producers. I told him that I would also like to talk to women in the community. His response was, "The women don't know anything! I'll tell you everything." In an interesting shift, his gatekeeping had gone from being total—refusing to have anything to do with me—to being gendered, barring my access to women. It seemed an almost stereotypically male dismissal of the possibility and value of women's knowledge.

Fortunately, this turned out to be a temporary dismissal, and when I later made the acquaintance of Kofi's wife, Ajoa, a kuntunkuni maker, and asked for her life history, he did not repeat his objection. Kofi's contradictory responses can be seen partly as a function of the research situation in which it was in his interests to assert his gatekeeping authority in that initial encounter. Later, as I gained his trust along with access to other members of the community, he readily relaxed that authority. His words also indicate a concern to protect men's position as the authoritative voices on adinkra production (even though women's roles in such cloth production show that they are quite knowledgeable). While it is tempting to see his initial reaction as a dismissal of women's knowledge, it is probably more

67

accurate to understand it as an insistence on keeping separate those things on which women and men can speak.

Kofi's responses are also useful as metaphors for the different ways of understanding gender relations around cloth production. At face value, adinkra and kente production are gendered male because they are produced by men and can be said to represent male control of cultural production. One can therefore think of gender here in the way suggested by Kofi's "The women don't know anything" exclamation and conceptualize gender relations around cultural production as a site of straightforward male dominance and female subjugation.

Or one can look more closely and begin to see how cloth production is gendered in ways that are much less obvious, reflecting Kofi's shift in attitude. Women play roles in cloth production that may be less prestigious than men's roles but are nonetheless important, undermining any claims of complete male dominance. Gender roles become even more complex and contradictory when one considers cloth production by an entirely different group of women—cloth traders, a group that Kofi later referred to with considerable resentment as he noted the decline of adinkra (and therefore male) cloth production at Asokwa. The actions of these women invert standard understandings of gender in relation to cultural production and appropriation and also show how gender extends beyond the identities of actual persons. The case of adinkra and kente provides a basis for interrogating standard analyses by critically examining both the conceptualization of gender and the distinction made by some scholars between male and female knowledge.

The common framework that conceives of gender as the socially constructed meanings of biological sex has been challenged from a number of perspectives. Poststructural feminist scholars have criticized this framework for analyzing gender in terms of a male–female binary that makes it difficult to conceive of gender identities as shifting and "performative."[1] African feminist scholars like Ifi Amadiume and Oyèrónkẹ́ Oyěwùmí have also pointed out the pitfalls of applying the standard framework to societies on the continent. Amadiume has famously shown that gender does not map neatly onto biological sex in Igbo society, making possible the existence of "male daughters and female husbands."[2] Oyěwùmí also argues that in the Yoruba language, there is more social distinction on the basis of seniority than there is between males and females. She states, "Unlike European languages, Yorùbá does not 'do gender'; it 'does seniority' instead."[3] Based on her study of Yoruba language and social practices, she further asserts that taken at its face value, the feminist charge to make women visible is carried out by submerging many local and regional categories, which in effect imposes Western cultural values. Global gender-formation is then an imperialistic process enabled by Western material and intellectual dominance.[4]

While Akan society is by no means identical to Yoruba society, there are parallels and similarities, including minimal linguistic distinction between the sexes. Further, the case of adinkra and kente cloth production makes it clear that male–female differences do not always translate into male dominance and female subjugation. While a certain degree of male dominance exists, it is complicated by male and female interdependence in cloth production and sale as well as spheres of autonomous female production and appropriation.

When applied to cultural production, gender analysis often seeks to recover and legitimize female knowledges that are "subjugated" within patriarchal knowledge systems.[5] When such studies apply to folklore and indigenous knowledge, the concern is often with the loss of female "traditional" knowledge as it is replaced by "modern" knowledge systems.[6] Such traditional knowledge is gendered female because it is produced by women. The case of adinkra and kente shows that if one focuses on the physical bodies of knowledge producers, then tradition can be gendered male. However, as I argue in this chapter, traditional knowledge is feminized in the encounter with the paternalistic state and with masculinized modern knowledge regardless of the gender identities of those who actually produce it.[7]

As a result, in the case of adinkra and kente, even though these fabrics are produced by men, that production is feminized in the encounter with the Ghanaian state. While feminization does not necessarily entail powerlessness, it is frequently equated with vulnerability, especially under conditions of patriarchal dominance. In the encounter between adinkra and kente producers and the state in Ghana, feminization occurs in ways that disempower male cloth producers. Women who are able to carve out a space within that state, however, benefit by operating effectively in a masculinized sphere.

Since feminist scholars also conceptualize formal Western law as masculine, this gendering of indigenous and local cultural production and knowledge is intensified in the encounter with intellectual property law. Well into the twentieth century, the legal sphere was literally male and excluded women as legal subjects. In the area of intellectual property law, authorship was conceived as a male activity.[8] Further, the law has often facilitated the appropriation of female indigenous and local cultural production by pharmaceutical and agricultural companies operating in the masculinized sphere of modernity.[9] The role of intellectual property law in ranking certain forms of knowledge and cultural production over others is therefore not only hegemonic but also gendered.

In this chapter, I examine gender relations around adinkra and kente production in the three ways suggested by Kofi's words and actions: as characterized by male dominance, as interdependent, and as an inversion of the standard gendering of cultural production and appropriation. I argue that while one can certainly speak of male dominance, this does not account for the full extent of gender relations around cloth production. I show that unlike the common model of subjugated female forms of culture and knowledge, the different modes of gendering around adinkra and kente do not result uniformly in female loss of power. Rather, power shifts back and forth between women and men as cultural production moves between different spheres of production and regulation. There are also accompanying shifts in authorship and ownership.

In the sections that follow, I first examine adinkra and kente as male spheres because of men's roles in their production and the ways that male control is actively maintained. I also compare two examples of female entry into these spheres and the extent to which they challenge male dominance. Next, I discuss the interdependent nature of women's and men's roles in cloth production. Following the insights of African feminist scholars who question the relevance of binary gender frameworks in the African context, I argue that this interdependence represents a truer picture of gender relations around cloth production than one of exclusive male dominance. I also argue that changes in such interdependence are partly due to the widespread shifts in gender relations that occurred in the social transformations that began with colonization. I then examine gender as a function of the sphere of production and show that the same social transformations that have eroded some female roles in cloth production have nonetheless opened new sites for female agency and male disempowerment.

If You Weave, You Will Not Give Birth

Like many other kinds of cloth in West Africa, the division of labor around adinkra and kente production is organized according to gender. Those divisions are usually quite stable; Malian *bogolanfini*, for example, is made by women.[10] In some cases, the divisions are permeable, and cloth production shifts back and forth between women and men depending on changes in the wider economic and social context. This is the case, for example, with Yoruba handwoven cloth.[11] In the case of adinkra and kente, the gender division remains fairly rigid despite a few attempts to cross it.

The gender arrangements around the production of adinkra and kente have partly to do with the connection between these textiles and Asante royalty. Several crafts practiced in Asante—particularly those brought to the area by conquest—were directly linked to the palace and sustained by royal patronage. In the case of kente, the brothers who "invented" the craft are said to have presented their cloth to the first Asantehene, Osei Tutu I. The king's response was to institute the position of Oyokomaahene,[12] the official producer of the Asantehene's kente. The holder of this title, in his life history narration, challenged the usual story of discovery of the craft by men. In his version, it was women who invented the craft of weaving and then passed it on to the men, who presented the resulting cloth to the Asantehene.

Since women could not be office bearers, the position of Oyokomaahene was given to one of the two brothers and has always been held by men. However, the name Oyokomaahene, according to the same respondent, acknowledges the role of women in the discovery: it refers to them and literally means "king of the Oyoko women."[13] This account of the origin of kente is interesting in simultaneously challenging the standard accounts of male discovery and exemplifying a classic case of male appropriation of female knowledge. In the two centuries since the emergence of kente weaving in Asante, a complex set of taboos and ritual requirements has been elaborated to ensure male dominance of the craft.

The Asantehene functions as both a political and spiritual ruler, and his spiritual duties require the observance of certain codes of purity. In Asante, as in several other societies, menstruation is associated with impurity, and while the resulting restrictions on women in the wider society have virtually disappeared, they continue to be upheld in matters concerning the Asantehene. One way in which the Asantehene's purity is maintained is through the exclusion of women from duties, like food preparation, that they would normally be expected to perform in an ordinary household. They are also excluded from all aspects of production of the Asantehene's cloth. As explained by Ajoa, a kuntunkuni maker in the community of Asokwa, the official source of the Asantehene's adinkra cloth,

It may be that . . . as you are stenciling it you may be in your menses, so if you are in that state you cannot prepare the dye [for stenciling]. If that happened, in the old days it would mean that you had soiled the chief's cloth so, as for that, they do not allow the women to make it.[14]

Even though an adinkra maker at Asokwa reported having once seen a woman help her father stencil cloth, he noted that in the case of the king's cloth, she would not have been allowed to even approach it. Similar restrictions apply to the weaving of the Asantehene's kente. Women cannot participate in its production, and in order to ensure the observance of these restrictions, the king's cloth is entrusted to a select group of men who weave it away from the public eye.

At the same time, it is important to note that the taboos around menstruation do not translate into an unreservedly inferior status for women in Asante. On the contrary, they have considerable autonomy in marriage and access to property through their maternal lineage even after marriage, and in royal households, important decisions of state cannot be made without consulting the senior woman in the household who is designated as the queen mother. In line with the matrilineal practice of the Asante, that woman is not the Asantehene's wife but his sister, mother, or maternal aunt.

When cloth production for the Asantehene is involved, few question the exclusion of women, as indicated in the words of the Oyokomaahene. After pointing out with pride that women at Bonwire were "weaving nicely," he declared, "but they will *never* weave the Asantehene's cloth!" While the material rewards for making the king's cloth may be minimal, cloth makers greatly value the recognition and status they derive from being associated with the palace. Although it accounts for a small fraction of adinkra production, cloth making for the Asantehene carries with it a high degree of social recognition that women cannot attain—at least not through cloth production.

The gender division of labor around cloth production is upheld even in the case of cloth produced for the wider population, although purity appears to have diminished as a concern. Earlier in the history of kente production, the looms used for weaving were considered sacred.[15] However, the reasons invoked for keeping women away from both adinkra and kente production now seem to center around female fertility rather than the purity of the equipment or its male users. The popular myth is that women will become barren if they stencil adinkra or weave kente. Women therefore produce different kinds of cloth, especially in adinkra-producing communities where they produce kuntunkuni, a black cloth used for funeral wear and also for conducting business at the Asantehene's palace.[16] It is produced and worn plain or stenciled with adinkra symbols. It also serves as a means of recycling old adinkra cloth, which is often dyed into kuntunkuni for reuse and can therefore be seen as a kind of female erasure of male cultural production.[17]

The production of kuntunkuni involves repeated immersion of cloth in dye baths alternated with mud treatment and sun-drying—a process that is said to help fix the dye. While a piece of adinkra cloth can be stenciled in a few hours or, at most, a couple of days, kuntunkuni requires a month for its production. Although kuntunkuni serves functions that are at least as important as those of adinkra, it is clearly more tedious to make. Its symbolism is also less elaborate, and it therefore lacks the same prestige and attracts far less interest outside Asante than adinkra does.

In a few instances, the gender barrier around adinkra and kente production has been broken, but these have remained exceptions and have not radically changed the gender arrangements around cloth production. An early challenge to the gendered production of cloth occurred in the 1970s when a woman was employed as a weaver at the National Cultural Center in Kumasi, a state institution established to promote and preserve Ghanaian culture. More recently, in the 1990s, a project was established at Bonwire to teach women to weave kente in the project referred to earlier by the Oyokomaahene. This was an effort by a church-based nongovernmental organization to provide young women in the community with "income-generating skills"—a common goal of development initiatives aimed at women in Ghana. The Bonwire initiative met with considerable resistance, and it is significant that the woman who crossed the gender barrier two decades earlier under the sponsorship of the "modern" state was also greeted with some surprise. That woman is Akua Afriyie, and her story demonstrates both the strength of association of cloth production with men and her sense of herself as a pioneer in a male field.

In 1972, Afriyie was a young woman living in a small town in Asante and looking for a means to support herself. When she heard that the Cultural Center in Kumasi had opened a textile department and was looking for workers, she decided to apply. She traveled to Kumasi and was introduced to the head of the textile department, who took her to see A. A. Kyerematen, director of the center and a prominent figure in Ghana's postindependence project of cultural nationalism. As Afriyie described the encounter,

> So he [Kyerematen] asked me why there were so many professions here in Ghana and I, a woman, wanted to weave cloth. And I said yes, here in Ghana no woman had ever woven cloth so . . . I wanted to weave cloth so that in

future it would be a sign for Ghanaians and Asanteman [the Asante nation] that a woman had woven cloth, and he said, "But if you weave you will not give birth," and I said, "Oh, I have given birth once, so even if I don't give birth again, it doesn't matter."[18]

Afriyie reported that, unlike Kyerematen, the men who were asked to train her did not express any surprise or objection to her joining them. They taught her to weave on a broadloom and on the narrow loom used in the kente industry. She also learned to make kuntunkuni and adinkra cloth in addition to other textile arts, such as tie-dyeing and sewing. She rose to the level of supervisor in the department and taught these crafts to other women and men. Afriyie also married and had two more children, effectively refuting the common belief that weaving leads to barrenness.

The experiences of Akua Afriyie, who learned to make adinkra and kente outside a cloth-producing community, contrast sharply with those of women who have attempted the same thing within such a community. Ama, a member of a group of women who learned to weave kente in the income-generating project at Bonwire, reported hostility on the part of male weavers in the community:

> There are some men who do not want, they do not want you to be equal with them because if you weave the cloth perhaps . . . some say when women weave cloth and get money they do not respect the men, and also if women weave cloth . . . they don't have time to cook. If a man is weaving and a woman is weaving, no one gets up to go and cook for the man, the woman will not get up to go and cook for the man. That is what the men say.[19]

According to Ama, many of the women who initially signed up to learn the craft were so discouraged by such comments that they left the project. At the time of her narration, she was one of only three women left out of those who had initially enrolled. Clearly, then, crossing the gender divide within a cloth-producing community is extremely difficult even though the initiators of the women's weaving project at Bonwire took care to gain the approval of living and ancestral community leaders. They also sought testimonials from medical personnel and women weavers who, like Akua Afriyie, had not become barren as a result of weaving cloth.[20] While these measures gained women like Ama the formal acceptance of the community, that acceptance was clearly not unanimous.

Despite the strength of the taboos and the hostility toward women weavers at Bonwire, few male cloth producers expressed any faith in the view that kente or adinkra production would make women barren. Rather, they saw it as a strategy that had been devised in order to reserve these occupations for men and to ensure that women supported men through domestic roles like cooking instead of competing with them. As expressed by Manu, one of the adinkra makers at Asokwa:

> Okay, they said if you were a woman and you did it, you would not have children. That is what they told them, just to get them out of the work, so as for Asantes or we Ghanaians, if they don't want you to do something, then they say [make up] something about it. But I don't believe it because one of Papa K. M.'s children, a girl called N. A., she made some [cloth] but she has given birth.[21]

Manu's words and the reactions of male weavers at Bonwire to women weavers indicate that outside cloth production for the Asantehene, barring women from cloth making is intended not so much to protect women's fertility as to ensure male control of the craft. Given the cloth's association with Asante royalty, this means that men monopolize cloth production not only as an income source but also as a source of prestige. This monopoly is secured not by active physical policing but, as Manu and others so astutely point out, through myths and taboos that capitalize on the fear of barrenness in a highly pronatalist context in which childbearing is an important source of female status.

Apart from the taboos, one must also take into account the views of women like Maame Tabi, a kuntunkuni maker married to an adinkra maker, Yaw Boakye. They both reported that Tabi had helped Boakye in adinkra production earlier in their marriage. Even though she was perfectly capable of undertaking all the tasks involved in adinkra production, she had stopped helping with it because it involved crouching low over the cloth, and she found that difficult. As she put it,

> I will not do it! I know how to do it, but I will not do it. I cannot crouch. If I say I will do it, I can do it all, correct, but I will not do it. I have stopped. This is not women's work, I cannot crouch like that. If you are a woman and you stoop a lot like that, you get dizzy, so as for that I cannot do it. Some women will do it, but as for me, I will not do it. It is not my work, I don't like it!

Yaw Boakye, Tabi's husband, gave rather different physical reasons for women not making adinkra:

> You see, [it's] the knees. A woman can't put her knees on the ground. Look! Look at mine. See how hard they've become—even if you cut them, they won't bleed. Women too, with all respect, you can't kneel for yours to become

like that. You see? The knee-work, the work is hard, in the case of stenciling. It is not like where you put them [dyed cloth] out to dry.

Boakye went on to make the doubtful claim that women could not stand prolonged contact with the heat of the fire needed for processing the dye. Given women's responsibility for both food preparation and the preparation of adinkra and kuntunkuni dyes through boiling, his views on the factors limiting women's ability to make adinkra cloth must be assessed against those of his wife.

The result of the strength and persistence of the division of labor around cloth production is that adinkra and kente are gendered male. Through the combination of the continuing importance of the Asantehene within contemporary Ghana and the marketing of cloth-producing sites as tourist destinations, this division of labor translates into a source of considerable privilege for men in cloth-producing communities. While women often play complementary and autonomous roles, such as in the sale of cloth made by their husbands or the production and sale of kuntunkuni cloth, they do not derive the same status from cloth production and sale that men do. While male producers may point to their communities as the rightful owners of their cloth, the authorship of that cloth is male.

Whether communal or individual, the different acts of authorship and authorization—accounting for the origins and pedigree of their craft; serving as custodians of inherited designs and adding to the design pool; determining who may and may not gain access to knowledge of the craft and transmitting that knowledge; and, finally, actually designing and producing cloth—in all these, authorship is gendered male. Under certain circumstances, and in a few cases, women may invert that gendering but not to the extent that they seriously challenge or undermine it. The combination of formal restrictions, taboos, and hostility ensure that the authoritative voices and bodies in adinkra and kente production at traditional production sites are male.

Gender Interdependence and Cloth Production

While adinkra and kente are produced predominantly by men and constitute sites of male privilege, such male monopoly and privilege must be seen as evolving historically rather than as naturally fixed. Women's and men's roles in cloth production were affected in different ways with the introduction of competing products through the encounter with European economies through trade. Within kente-producing communities, women were often responsible for growing, harvesting, and spinning the thread used for weaving in the days when the cloth was produced from locally grown cotton. It also appears that such cotton production was an important female economic sphere among Akan women beyond Asante. For example, Mona Etienne documents the power that Baule women derived from cotton production prior to colonization.[22]

The Baule ethnic group, in the Ivory Coast, is a part of the larger Akan group that includes the Asante. Etienne reports that among the Baule, the shift from locally produced to imported yarns resulted in a decline in the power that women derived from their control of the cotton supply. It is reasonable to assume that similar developments occurred in women's cotton production in Asante. At the same time, in response to colonial and subsequent economic policies that gave priority to male economic activity, women in different parts of Africa carved out new economic spheres for themselves, often through trading in the informal economy. As a result, the erosion of their roles in cotton supply has not meant a complete loss of female influence. Even though women no longer process cotton yarn for kente weaving, they may supply the mass-produced yarns and often sell the finished cloth.

The decline in women's roles in kente production, due to the introduction of mass-produced yarn, contrasts with the effects on men for whom such yarn was simply an alternative raw material rather than a competing product. Similarly, when European silk textiles were first introduced to Asante, kente retained its status as a distinctive product. Rather than competing with kente, silk became an additional source of yarn when weavers converted it into raw material for kente production. They unraveled the silk fabric and used the yarns to produce cloth that remained within the aesthetic and symbolic conventions of kente while expanding its color palette.[23] Thus, the introduction of silk fabric did not undermine kente production and men's roles in it.

Maame Tabi's words in the previous section also point to the important factor of women's volition in maintaining the gender divide around cloth production. Her account suggests that the division of labor may very well work in women's interests, complicating the view of adinkra and kente production as sites of male privilege. While kuntunkuni is tedious to make, women may indeed prefer the tasks involved in its processing to those needed for adinkra production. In adinkra-producing communities, the gender divide may therefore serve women's interests, especially since it does not simply exclude women from one kind of cloth production but also assures them autonomy in another kind. The implications of that divide must therefore be seen as different in adinkra- and kente-producing communities.

Although less prestigious than adinkra, kuntunkuni cloth has its own importance. First, while adinkra is well known as mourning cloth, it is worn only at certain stages in the mourning process, while kuntunkuni is basic mourning attire. Second, kuntunkuni is also the standard attire for conducting business at the Asantehene's palace because of the gravity of such affairs or, as one former palace official put it, "We do not joke there."[24] These uses mean that even though kuntunkuni attracts less attention than adinkra, it serves equally important functions. There is also the factor of male dependence on women (often kuntunkuni producers) in the production of adinkra. The dyes used in adinkra stenciling are produced almost exclusively by women in a tedious process that involves procuring the bark of a particular tree, sometimes from distant sources that require a few days' travel. The bark is then pounded, boiled, and strained to produce dye that is sold to the men who produce adinkra. Clients also go back and forth between men and women as they procure adinkra cloth and return old cloth to be made into kuntunkuni and then restenciled with adinkra symbols. Under such arrangements, male adinkra producers are clearly dependent on women's dye production and on women's recycling of old adinkra into kuntunkuni that can then be made into "new" adinkra cloth.

Both adinkra and kente producers also often rely on their wives or autonomous female cloth traders for the sale of their finished cloth. In such situations, it becomes harder to claim exclusive male dominance of cloth production. Instead, women and men have interdependent roles, especially in adinkra-producing communities where women's roles are more significant than in communities that produce kente. This interdependence is closer to gender roles as analyzed by African feminist scholars who argue that contemporary conditions of male dominance are partly derived from colonial policies that distorted gender relations in ways that undermined women's economic production and reinforced patriarchal tendencies in local communities.[25]

Gender roles in adinkra and kente production show that in spite of those distortions, women continue to carve out spheres of autonomy and influence. While women's influence in kente production has diminished considerably, it remains strong in adinkra production because women continue to be important in the supply of an important ingredient in adinkra production and also because they have retained control over kuntunkuni production.

Like male adinkra makers, however, they are vulnerable to the effects of mass-produced textiles that can be substituted for the cloth they produce.

These Same Women!

Male kente and adinkra producers' power and privilege diminish considerably in the wider Ghanaian cloth market due to a number of factors, one of which is women's control of that market. Another is the proliferation in Ghana of mass-produced imitation adinkra and kente cloth since the late 1980s. Although disdained as inauthentic by some producers of the handmade versions, these imitations have gained wide acceptance among Ghanaians as cheaper and more practical (i.e., washable) substitutes for handmade cloth. As discussed in chapter 1, Ghana's copyright law does not distinguish between different media of appropriation in its protection of adinkra and kente designs, but for the producers of the cloth that bears those designs, it is the imitation of their cloth in textile form that causes the most concern—especially when the imitation can be substituted for the original. The fact that such substitution occurs with factory-printed imitations makes these the most serious instance of appropriation. A significant feature of these mass-produced imitations is the role of women in its production and the ways in which this changes the gendered division of labor around cloth production.

There is evidence that factory-printed imitations of adinkra have been produced for at least three decades.[26] Imitation kente has also been available for about the same length of time. However, the procurement and sale of such cloth by women as well as its widespread acceptance by Ghanaians appears to have begun in the late 1980s. That acceptance occurred much earlier for imitation adinkra than for imitation kente. Whereas such kente was used for less formal purposes than handwoven kente, imitation adinkra quickly became accepted wear at funerals—especially for sympathizers not closely related to the deceased.

Based on popular Ghanaian accounts, the first mass-produced imitations of both kinds of cloth were manufactured in the Ivory Coast and imported into Ghana by female cloth traders. The association of such cloth with the Ivory Coast was so strong that it was generally referred to in Ghana as "Abidjan kente" or "Abidjan adinkra" after the Ivory Coast's commercial capital (see Plate 6). By the late 1990s, women traders were commissioning imitation adinkra from factories in Ghana. More recently, the Ghanaian company Akosombo Textiles Limited has begun production of imitation kente (see Figure 3).[27] The perception of appropriation as a female activity was expressed most strongly by adinkra makers at Asokwa, who saw women traders as a major reason for the decline of their trade. When asked about the proliferation of imitation adinkra cloth, one of them, Kofi, said,

> It is these same women who, when you make a design, while you are sitting there and a design comes into your mind, as soon as it reaches the market, she buys one and takes it to Abidjan. Then she takes it to the factory and gets the price. The next thing you know she has made it and brought it [to Ghana]. That is what they do, but even when they do it, when people wear it, still they like ours. Before long they bring it to be dyed with kuntunkuni. They often prefer the handmade one.[28]

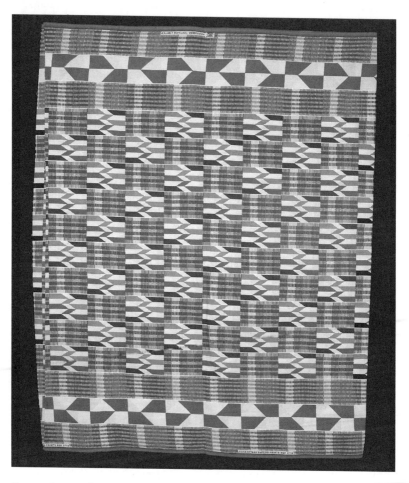

Figure 3. Imitation kente produced in Ghana.

The sense of threat expressed by the cloth makers at Asokwa contrasts sharply with the prestige and privilege that they and other adinkra and kente producers derive from their craft. The threat is felt all the more strongly by the Asokwa cloth makers because of the decline of their community as a center of cloth production compared with the vibrancy of other centers such as Ntonso and Bonwire. Unlike the physical male gendering of adinkra and kente production and its direct inversion through figures like Akua Afriyie and the women weavers of Bonwire, the local appropriation of adinkra and kente is gendered female not because women physically produce them but because of women's influence in the spheres within which the imitations are produced and sold.

The sale of cloth is an important activity for women in Ghana and several other West African countries.[29] In these countries, women control much of the retail trade in food and other consumer products, including cloth. A few of these women operate as wholesalers who procure goods and sell them to retailers.[30] Women who operate at this level exercise considerable control over the goods that they supply, and in Ghana, they are sometimes referred to as "market queens." There is a tendency to romanticize this female control of many West African markets, and it is therefore important to note that most women operating in those markets do so at considerably marginal levels. However, women traders who operate at the wholesale level not only procure cloth for redistribution but sometimes also commission cloth to their own design.

In a practice analogous to craftsmen's naming of adinkra and kente designs, cloth traders name the designs of the cloth that they sell. This is partly a marketing strategy in which market women sometimes change the name of a design that is not selling well, and this can make a difference in sales. In the course of an interview with a cloth trader who operates as a wholesaler, I observed several women who came into the store to buy cloth and often asked for the name of the cloth in deciding what to purchase.[31] Some of the names of cloth in the respondent's store were *otan nni aduro* (there is no remedy for hatred) and *obi nno obi kwa* (one does not love another for nothing) (see Figure 4).

In addition to being a marketing tool, the naming of cloth is also an important means of symbolic expression for women who may have limited access to other forms of public discourse.[32] Women may name cloth to reflect opinions that they might have difficulty expressing openly. Their clients in turn purchase cloth in order to overcome similar difficulties in openly expressing their views. In some cases, the name of the cloth reflects a

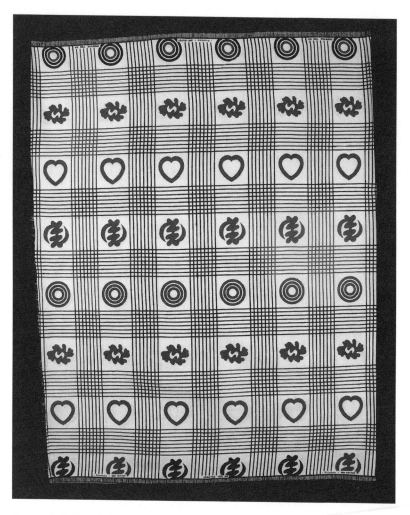

Figure 4. Imitation adinkra produced in Ghana.

commentary on a repressive political system and becomes a silent means by which both women *and* men express dissent.[33]

The cloth trade is thus an important female economic and symbolic sphere that is further feminized because of the status of the cloth concerned as traditional. As noted in the Introduction, Ghanaians distinguish between the fabric they designate as "cloth" and other kinds of textiles. Even though it is produced through the processes of "modern" industry, and even though it has its origins in Dutch appropriations of Indonesian batik, such cloth is widely regarded as African and is used primarily for "traditional" clothing. The result is a product of modern manufacturing that is nonetheless feminized in the traditional sources of its value and the uses to which it is applied.

It is within this female economic and symbolic sphere that adinkra and kente cloth are appropriated for local markets in Ghana. Within this sphere, appropriation is gendered in ways that run counter to standard accounts. In those accounts, one typically finds women's cultural production being appropriated by men or feminized cultural production being appropriated through masculinized forms of appropriation. In the Ghanaian case, such patterns of appropriation are inverted because of women's influence in the sphere of cloth production within which appropriation occurs, their control of the markets where appropriated cloth is sold, and their status as purveyors of a specific kind of cloth that is valued on a continuum with adinkra and kente and therefore lends the appropriations legitimacy and increasing acceptance as substitutes for handmade adinkra and kente cloth.

This gendering of appropriation becomes even more contradictory when the sphere of cloth production is articulated to that of intellectual property law. A decree passed in 1973 as one of Ghana's industrial property laws enabled individuals and factories producing textiles in the country to register their cloth designs if they wanted to secure legal protection of those designs.[34] By the late 1990s, such registration had become standard practice, and those registering designs included both factories and individual women commissioning cloth to their own design.

This procedure meant that if a cloth trader registered an imitation adinkra design, she could claim ownership of the design. Although the law included a clause intended to prevent the registration of indigenous textile designs, an element of the registration process functioned as a loophole that defeated this goal. In registering a design that contained indigenous elements such as kente and adinkra designs, the person registering the design could simply include a disclaimer stating that they did not claim ownership of those design elements. This was pointed out by the woman cloth trader mentioned earlier in defense of her use of adinkra symbols in cloth that she had commissioned. (She also claimed that since the adinkra designs in her cloth were larger than those used in hand-stenciled cloth, her cloth was not really adinkra). The disclaimer therefore provided a loophole that enabled the registration of designs that closely imitated adinkra.

The textile registration decree placed female cloth traders and male adinkra and kente producers in interesting and contradictory relations to

the law. Ghanaian law typically exhibits the gender bias identified by feminist scholars due to the origins of such law in the statutes introduced to the
territory through British colonization. Western laws were originally conceived as the domain of men based on their presumed superior rational
capacity.[35] Well into the twentieth century, therefore, women were relegated
to the status of legal minors. Gender bias in Ghanaian law is also partly a
result of colonial authorities' combined misinterpretation and dismissal of
indigenous norms recognizing and protecting women's rights.[36] Western-
style constitutions granted women nominal equality with men and introduced some civil rights for women, such as the right to vote. However, more
than five decades after the end of colonization, many biases remain in
Ghana's laws, and for the most part, de facto women's rights have lagged
behind de jure rights.[37] At the same time, Ghanaian women have successfully lobbied for increased legal protection of their rights.[38]

With mass-produced cloth designs protected as individual intellectual
property and adinkra and kente designs protected as folklore and therefore
national intellectual property, it is much easier for women in the cloth trade
to claim legal ownership of their cloth designs than it is for male producers
of adinkra and kente. This inverts the standing that women and men usually have before the law. Despite the status of the law as a space of patriarchal dominance, Ghanaian cloth traders have been able to turn it to their
advantage not by changing it but by their influence in a sphere of economic
activity regulated by the law. Women thus effectively harness the masculinized spheres of intellectual property law and industrial cloth production to
the female sphere of the local cloth trade.

In contrast, the paternalistic stance adopted by the state in its copyright
custodianship of folklore, including adinkra and kente designs, feminizes
that folklore regardless of the gender identities of those actually producing
it. It is here that that the gendering of cultural production and appropriation comes close to the common accounts of male appropriation of female
cultural production. In this case, though, it is more accurate to speak of
masculinized appropriation of feminized cultural production. Here appropriation occurs not through the imitation of cultural production but through
state claims over such production. While those claims are characterized as
custodianship, they are more like ownership in their practical effects.[39]

The Ghanaian case is useful for showing how the gender of cultural production and appropriation can be conceptualized as a function of both the
gender identities of the persons involved and the status of the spheres in
which they work as modern or traditional. However, this kind of gendering

must be qualified in order to avoid reinforcing the problematic aspects of the tradition–modernity divide. I draw on ideas of the gendering of modernity and tradition because of the power and pervasiveness of these concepts, especially in relation to the encounter between intellectual property law and folklore. However, I also keep in view the highly contestable nature of these categories that function all too often as one more set of binary oppositions that work more to uphold different interests than to fully explain what they describe. Therefore, in using these categories as a basis for exploring the gender of production and appropriation, I pay attention both to their limitations and to the ways in which women and men in the Ghanaian case frequently confound the tradition–modernity divide.

In fact, both the traditional status of cloth in Ghana as well as the modern status of industrialized textile production and the law can be questioned. How traditional, for example, is adinkra cloth in which the designs are stenciled onto cotton fabric that is mass-produced in China or kente cloth that is woven using mass-produced rayon yarn rather than handspun cotton? Similarly, what is traditional or African about cotton prints that started out as mass-produced imitations of Indonesian batik? The law and industrialized cloth production can similarly be questioned, since their modernity lies primarily in claims about the exemplary status of the Western systems of governance and production from which they emerged.

Given these limitations, my discussion of the ways in which cultural production and appropriation are gendered depending on whether the spheres in which they occur are modern or traditional is based primarily on the strength and pervasiveness of these categories rather than an acceptance of their legitimacy. Indeed, the actions of cloth traders and adinkra and kente producers often undermine these categories. Apart from dealing in traditional cloth produced through modern manufacturing processes, cloth traders and other market women in Ghana routinely cross back and forth between modern and traditional financial sectors.

They may raise funds from traditional sources that include kinship and mutual help associations like *susu* groups (also known in some societies as *esusu*). These are associations whose members contribute money to a fund that rotates among them. In Ghana, they are a common means of raising funds not only among market women but also among junior level female clerical workers who contribute a part of their monthly salary to the fund.[40] Market women who operate at levels that permit the generation of such capital may also save excess capital in modern banking institutions.

Adinkra and kente producers also confound any simple characterization of their work as traditional not only because of their incorporation of "modern" materials into their work. Adinkra makers have been known to incorporate nontraditional elements like the Mercedes Benz logo into their designs as a symbol of prestige.[41] Adinkra and kente producers are also linked to modern markets through the tourist industry and through clients who secure their services for nontraditional uses. For example, kente weavers are often commissioned by entrepreneurs in Ghana and the United States to weave stoles that are then sold to African American students to wear at their college graduation ceremonies.[42]

While female cloth traders' and male cloth producers' actions trouble the tradition–modernity divide, it is nonetheless a useful way of conceptualizing the gender dimensions of their cloth production and appropriation. Women cloth traders' successful appropriation of adinkra also lends itself to a common Ghanaian interpretation suggested by Kofi's identification of cloth traders as a major reason for the decline of Asokwa as a center of adinkra production. Ghana has an unfortunate history of demonizing market women in times of economic crisis because of their control of food and other consumer goods.[43] That control makes women an easy target but fails to take into account their general situation.

Even in matrilineal groups, like the Akan, in which women have higher than average autonomy and access to productive resources, Ghanaian women tend to be disproportionately represented among the poor, and it often falls to them to make up for the withdrawal of state support for social services like health care under economic policies imposed at the behest of the International Monetary Fund and World Bank.[44] A manifesto published in 2004 and based on consultations among a broad coalition of Ghanaian women's groups documents the harsh conditions as well as the gender inequalities that characterize most Ghanaian women's lives.[45] Through their trading activities, however, some Ghanaian market women have been able to carve a niche for themselves that has survived the assaults of harsh governments and economic policies.[46]

Instead of reaching for the old stereotype of women traders as economic saboteurs, therefore, it is useful to consider their actions in the same light as male adinkra and kente producers when the men adapt their production to a changing economic context. Those male producers who are not dependent on royal patronage and have been successful in repositioning themselves as suppliers for tourist markets and continuing local demand seem to be less concerned about women as competitors. Like many Ghanaians, they rank the different kinds of cloth available on the market in a hierarchy in which the handmade versions continue to be preeminent. Thus, gendered cloth production translates into power depending on positioning within markets, responsiveness to changing technology and tastes, and access to capital.

Virgin Knowledge

Cloth, then, is not only gendered on the basis of subjectivity, that is, in being made by men or commissioned and sold by women, it is also gendered on the basis of social processes and institutions. In this case, cloth production and appropriation are gendered on the basis of the spheres within which those women and men work, in particular, the perception of those spheres as traditional or modern. These, in turn, have their roots in the historical and political processes of Western expansion and dominance, which have been analyzed as masculinized enterprises carried out against societies and territories that are feminized in the process.[47] Western law, including intellectual property law, is also a gendered space that for centuries conceived of legal subjects as male. Finally, cultural appropriation, especially in instances in which traditional knowledge is appropriated by Western companies, has been conceptualized as masculine because women are often the custodians of traditional knowledge.

Therefore, while the gender analysis of institutions and practices may be directly linked to the sex of the people involved, it also functions metaphorically. Analytical frameworks that ascribe women's oppression to patriarchy view acts of aggression and control as masculine and subjugation to such control as feminine. The problem with this mode of analysis is that it focuses on one dimension of oppression, ignoring factors like ethnicity, race, class, and nationality. Further, it makes it difficult to conceive of female power and male subjugation under patriarchal conditions. This is evident in the Ghanaian case in which a form of traditional culture is produced by men but does not guarantee male power in all situations. Due to their operation in the sphere of tradition, and due to the gendering of tradition and modernity as female and male respectively, these textiles can also be understood as feminized forms of cultural production. The production and appropriation of adinkra and kente is therefore gendered differently depending on whether one focuses on the subjectivity of those involved or the sphere of production in which they operate.

Adinkra and kente cloth are generally regarded as traditional, and they are promoted as such by the men who make them and emphasize the heritage within which they are made. In promoting these fabrics and the communities where they are made, the Ghanaian state also emphasizes their status as part of Ghanaian tradition and culture. With the exception of Western art collectors and anthropologists who lament the passing of "authentic" kente,[48] this traditional status is generally unquestioned even though mass-produced cloth and yarns produced by factories in Ghana and abroad have been used in adinkra and kente production for a long time. As previously discussed, these modern materials have been successfully assimilated into cloth production partly through authorization strategies that have maintained the status of adinkra and kente as traditional.

By contrast, the textile factories that produce imitation kente and adinkra are modern because of their use of Western industrial technology. Although their products include cloth that is governed by traditional conventions of value and use, these factories are part of the modern sphere of Ghanaian industrialization. The gendered nature of tradition and modernity is worth considering because ultimately it is an important factor in determining how different kinds of cultural production fare before intellectual property law. Tradition is the sphere of an unchanging nature—the sphere of women—while modernity is the sphere within which nature is transformed and progress occurs due to the application of male rationality.

As noted earlier, authorship was generally regarded as male until fairly recently, and therefore intellectual property law has given privileged status to male cultural production.[49] In the area of traditional knowledge, however, gendered subjectivity takes a back seat to the way in which the sphere of production is gendered. The gender assigned to the sphere of production rather than to the actual producers is more reliable as a predictor of how cultural production is likely to fare before the law. What counts is not whether cultural products are made by women or men but whether they are made in the feminized sphere of tradition or the masculinized sphere of modernity. Therefore, traditional adinkra and kente are only minimally protected by intellectual property law even when there is an attempt to accord them such protection. The designs of cloth made in modern textile factories, by contrast, are routinely protected under intellectual property law in Ghana and beyond.

As a result, women have fared better than men as subjects before Ghana's laws dealing with cloth production because of their operation in the modern sphere where products have long been accorded legal protection. Male adinkra and kente craftsmen, conversely, make products that, as part of a feminized tradition, have the status of virgin knowledge—in the same way that uncultivated land is regarded as virgin. As in the case of the "discovery" of the Americas and Africa, the fact that such land may in fact be occupied does not change the perception that it is available for the taking.[50] This is true not only for Ghanaian folklore but also for the folklore and indigenous knowledge production of Third World nations and indigenous peoples.

In sum, the gendering of adinkra and kente production takes place in a number of ways: through the subjectivity of those who produce the hand-made cloth, those who commission and sell imitations, and the spheres in which the originals and imitations are made. At the same time, the inter-dependence between women and men in cloth production and sale shows that gender roles cannot be reduced to the common framework that pits female against male. Of these modes of gendering, the sphere of production has most relevance for the legal status of adinkra and kente cloth. The priv-ilege that male cloth producers enjoy in their communities has little signifi-cance before the law.

In contrast, women's control of the sale and production of cloth is strengthened by the legal status of that cloth. This both reinforces and chal-lenges the characterization of the status of women's cultural production. When women undertake that production in a sphere that is traditional, they may see their cultural production taken over by local men.[51] They may also see their cultural production appropriated for global markets and the appropriations protected by intellectual property laws. In such cases, gen-der operates at the level of subjectivity and sphere of production to leave women doubly disadvantaged. In the case of adinkra and kente, however, the sphere of operation takes priority over subjectivity to give women supe-rior power in local cloth production.

In the interaction between gender and the law around adinkra and kente, therefore, male authorship does not translate into male legal ownership. In the same way that the law makes the state the effective owner of adinkra and kente, it also grants ownership of many of the imitations to women. While this may have occurred due to a legal loophole in the past, it does not change the fact that mechanized textile production enjoys a superior status before the law over adinkra and kente production, and therefore, for as long as women are dominant within it, they have an advantage over men. The loophole was closed in 2003 when the textile registration decree was re-pealed and replaced by an industrial designs law, leaving copyright law as the main legislation governing the appropriation of adinkra and kente designs.

While closing off the legal loophole means that women may be obliged to pay royalties for the use of adinkra and kente designs in the future, it is unlikely that this will result in their abandonment of the cloth trade or of imitation adinkra and kente if these continue to be popular with the Ghanaian public. As legal subjects, therefore, women may change their strategies in dealing with the law but are unlikely to give up their control of cloth and their operation in a sphere that gives them advantages over men in the traditional sphere.

Added to this is the fact that male adinkra and kente producers have a highly pessimistic view of their status before the Ghanaian state and in relation to intellectual property law. It is therefore highly unlikely that any but a few entrepreneurs like Nana Baffour Gyimah, the innovative adinkra maker, will actually seek to establish their ownership rights under intellectual property law. Cloth makers' perceptions of their legal status contrast strongly with those of musicians in Ghana's recording industry. In the next chapter, I examine this contrast in order to further explore what it means for different kinds of cultural producers to be subjects of intellectual property law.

Chapter 3   Your Face Doesn't Go Anywhere
Cultural Production and Legal Subjectivity

It is the MUSIGA people who can bring it.

         —Kwame, adinkra maker, Accra

The musicians are troublesome!

         —Copyright Administration official, Accra

AKUA AFRIYIE was one of the first respondents I encountered, and when asked about copyright, her response established a theme that was to recur with a number of others. She said, "Isn't it what MUSIGA does?" (MUSIGA is the Musicians Union of Ghana). Next was Manu, an adinkra maker, who expressed doubts about the possibility of protecting his community's designs from appropriation with the words, "You see, we are not members of, what is it called, the musical thing." As his narration progressed, it became clear that by "the musical thing" he meant copyright protection. Like Afriyie, he was clearly of the view that matters concerning the legal protection of cultural production were the purview of musicians. Kwame, another adinkra maker, was most forthright in expressing this view when he said, "You see, with copyright . . . it is the MUSIGA people who can bring it. You see? As for . . . adinkra and kente, they can't include those."

Adinkra and kente producers often acknowledged that the appropriation of their cloth designs was a concern. Yet, in these comments about copyright protection as a musicians' issue, they established a clear distinction between their work and music as objects of *legal* protection. In doing so, they pointed to musicians' dominance of copyright as a public issue in Ghana. Ghanaian recording artists and producers began to press for more effective copyright protection of their work in the late 1970s after cassette recording technology became widely available in Ghana. This brought the copying of commercial music within the reach of the average person, threatening the livelihoods of many musicians. The lobby that emerged in response to this has been so active that, as can be seen from cloth makers' comments above, musicians have become the most visible group in the debate on copyright protection in Ghana.[1] Their influence as a lobby is evident in the strong focus on the interests of musicians and the recording industry in the copyright laws of 1985 and 2005. Given this success, it is not surprising that for some Ghanaians, copyright is "what MUSIGA does."

Musicians' vigorous presence within the space of Ghana's intellectual property law stands in sharp contrast to the near absence of adinkra and kente producers in that space. Musicians and cloth makers also perceive themselves differently as legal subjects who can demand state attention to their concerns. This contrast provides a good basis for considering a key issue: the kinds of subjects who are brought into being by the law. While, on the face of it, there is no difference between musicians and craftsmen as citizens, it is clear from their self-perceptions alone that there is a great difference between them as both citizens and legal subjects. This difference is well worth exploring for what it reveals about the nature of legal subjectivity, especially as it relates to intellectual property law in Ghana.

Cloth producers' perception of themselves is also striking because of its contrast with their strong sense of themselves as creators of adinkra and kente, as discussed in chapter 1. However, as their gendered positioning in the space of the law reveals, their status in the social and cultural space of cloth production means little in the legal sphere. Their own words show their awareness of this position—not in relation to women but in relation to musicians. I argue in this chapter that the difference between cloth makers' and musicians' perceptions of themselves as legal subjects is partly a function of intellectual property law—particularly copyright law—and linked to the status of their different forms of cultural production within the law. It is also due to the different ways in which these groups are positioned in relation to the national state. Ghanaian musicians' successful lobbying activities also illustrate the ways in which intellectual property and other laws are shaped as much by social and political forces as by abstract principles.

In this chapter, I first provide a brief history of the emergence of the most well-known and popular Ghanaian music form, highlife, and the way that sound recording technology made it amenable to copyright protection. I then discuss recording artists' dominance of copyright as an issue in Ghana, along with the history of lobbying that led to this dominance, and the ways that the country's copyright law and lawmaking reflect this dominance. I also examine adinkra and kente producers' actions and perceptions of them-selves in relation to intellectual property law and to the state. Next, I com-pare musicians' and cloth makers' perceptions and actions and consider what they reveal about intellectual property law as a set of discourses that produces different kinds of legal subjects.

I also consider the different ways that recording artists and cloth pro-ducers are linked to the state through their cultural production and how these links also shape their status as citizens and legal subjects. I argue that in spite of their lobbying success, musicians ultimately conform to the modes of subjectivity established for them by the law and by neoliberal principles of citizenship, while cloth makers reveal the limits of such subjectivity. I further argue that the different ways cultural producers are linked to the state can provide alternative modes of subjectivity to those possible within the law.

Highlife Music, Sound Recording, and Intellectual Property Law

The musicians discussed in this chapter are recording artists who produce the popular and distinctively Ghanaian music known as highlife and who also work in a wide range of musical genres from other parts of Africa and beyond. The history of highlife is one of local and imported instruments, musical forms, and performance techniques merging into a distinctive genre. It is also a story of the relation between technology and intellectual prop-erty law, as the emergence of sound recording made the popular cultural form of highlife music eminently suited to copyright protection.

According to music scholar and activist John Collins, some of the earli-est roots of highlife can be traced to influences from Sierra Leone, Liberia, and even Jamaica. From Sierra Leone came the gombey drums and drum-ming, one of many forms of African music that were "taken to the Ameri-cas by slaves, transmuted there, and then brought back to Africa."[2] In this case, the return occurred through freed Maroon slaves from Jamaica, who settled in Sierra Leone in the early nineteenth century. From Liberia came "an African guitar plucking technique" developed by sailors from the Kru ethnic group.[3] Other forms soon grew from these influences, most notably "palm wine" music, named for the dockside palm wine bars frequented by local and foreign sailors in West African coastal towns. The earliest forms of highlife emerged in the Gold Coast in the late nineteenth century when musicians added the instruments introduced by European military bands at forts along the coast.[4]

With the addition of these brass band instruments, the humble "palm wine" music went upscale (hence the name "highlife"), especially as it spread in popularity well beyond the social circle of sailors and dockworkers and beyond the coastal towns where palm wine music first emerged. By the early twentieth century, popular highlife bands had emerged, and sound recording technology made it possible to capitalize on that popularity beyond live performances in dance halls.[5] Accordingly, palm wine and highlife music were recorded as early as in the 1920s, and the highlife classic *Yaa Amponsah* is reported to have been recorded during that decade.[6]

The confluence between the popularity of highlife music and sound recording occurred at a historical moment when recording was gaining in importance as a mode of "fixing" music for the purposes of intellectual property rights (copyright law protects creative work when that work is fixed in some form, such as writing). Prior to this, musical creativity was fixed through musical notation. Notation changed music from a purely oral cultural form to a written one that compressed the time required to learn music. In addition, "Musical notation gave rise to the composer, just as print gave rise to the author."[7]

Notation was therefore crucial to proprietary claims over musical compositions from the seventeenth century beginnings of European copyright law to the early twentieth century. However, this changed when sound recording became the basis of the popular music industry, especially in the United States, and recording became "the moment of fixation or completion of the work and . . . therefore . . . the 'primary text.'"[8] While this also made the record producer rather than the composer the most important bearer of rights, it made it possible to extend copyright protection to works for which there was no written notation.[9] Recording technology thus linked oral cultures of music (like jazz improvisation) with the "literate" culture of intellectual property law. This was ideal in the Ghanaian context in the early twentieth century because it meant that musicians did not require formal training in musical notation to fix their compositions. In becoming recorded genres, therefore, palm wine and highlife music took on features that aligned their production with the norms of authorship in copyright law, making them well suited to intellectual property claims.

Highlife music's association with the recording industry makes it distinct from other kinds of indigenous Ghanaian music. Like adinkra and kente cloth, these other forms of music do not conform to the norms of authorship and production of intellectual property law. While their themes may reflect changing times, they are also similar to adinkra and kente in staying fairly consistent in their modes of production and their local sources of authorization. Finally, like adinkra and kente, indigenous music forms are also recognized as elements of national culture and subject to protection as folklore. At the same time, although highlife music is a hybrid and fits easily within intellectual property law, it is also regarded as a part of Ghanaian national culture, along with those local forms of music that have largely remained outside the recording industry. Despite highlife's long history in the recording industry, it was not until the late twentieth century that Ghanaian musicians in that industry began the lobbying activities that led to their strong association with copyright law in the popular imagination.

Marching to the Castle

In 1979, Ghanaian musicians marched to Christiansborg Castle, the seat of government in Accra, the capital, demanding better protection of their work.[10] Built by the Danes in the seventeenth century,[11] Christiansborg was one of several forts and castles built by European powers along the West African coast following the Portuguese introduction of navigational routes around Africa in the fifteenth century.[12] It has served as headquarters to a number of governments from colonial times to the present, and "marching to the Castle" has strong political significance in Ghana. In the course of the country's history, several groups have undertaken this act as a means of demanding government attention to their concerns. With this powerful, symbolic move in 1979, Ghanaian musicians, led by MUSIGA, began the lobby that was to make the name MUSIGA synonymous with copyright protection. As noted earlier, cassette recording had, by this time, become a widely accessible mainstream technology that facilitated the copying of recorded music. A number of entrepreneurs set up businesses that sold cassette copies of commercially produced music.

While these entrepreneurs were regarded as "pirates," other perceptions of their activities point to the contentious nature of the term. In the international context, as a number of observers have noted, piracy is applied unevenly to cultural appropriation in ways that privilege the interests of powerful nations over those of weaker ones.[13] In the case of the Ghanaian music industry, Collins argues that constructing the unauthorized commercial copying of recorded music as piracy destroyed the beginnings of a vibrant local music production industry.[14] At the same time, in producing and selling copies, that burgeoning industry compromised musicians' ability to make a living from recordings of their music.

Using forums like television discussion programs and news commentaries, musicians successfully drew the government's attention to their cause, and the government responded with a number of important measures.[15] The most significant was the passage of the revised copyright law in 1985. The previous law, passed in 1961, was more than due for revision given the technological developments since its passage, and as the copyright administrator put it, "Copyright law follows after technology."[16] However, the 1985 law also provided an opportunity for addressing musicians' concerns and therefore placed strong emphasis on the recording industry and the rights of artists and producers within it. The law also provided for "a society of authors," which came to be known as the Copyright Society of Ghana (COSGA)—a move that proved to be controversial.[17] Later, in another measure benefiting musicians, the government eliminated import duties on musical instruments.[18]

An important factor in musicians' successful lobbying was the "cultural revolution" of the 1980s, which created a favorable climate for their activism. This revolution occurred during the rule of the PNDC (People's National Defence Council) government that came to power in a military coup on December 31, 1981. In official discourse, the PNDC takeover was seldom referred to as a coup d'état but was known instead as the 31st December Revolution. "Revolution" was therefore an important signifier in the rhetoric of the period. Key figures in the government included a number of intellectuals and artists, including Dr. Mohammed Ben Abdallah, and when the government established a National Commission on Culture in 1990, with Dr. Abdallah as its first chairman, the Copyright Office was transferred from the Ministry of Information to the Commission.[19]

The most effective measure against the so-called pirating of locally produced music was the *banderole,* a device introduced in 1992. The *banderole* was a sticker issued by the Internal Revenue Service on the authorization of the Copyright Office and (in the case of imported recordings) the Customs and Excise Prevention Service and affixed to authorized copies of commercially produced music.[20] The introduction of the banderole was accompanied by strong enforcement measures, including the seizure of recordings not bearing the sticker, and the cassette recording companies described earlier soon went out of business. Despite the argument that the elimination of these companies also destroyed a budding spirit of entrepreneurship in the music production business, for many Ghanaian musicians, these measures were a positive move. The active enforcement of the law considerably improved their ability to profit from their work, and between 1987 and 1991, the amount of royalties collected by COSGA increased threefold.[21] Musicians expressed their gratitude to the government in public pronouncements that, along with the more public lobbying activities that preceded them, no doubt helped to establish copyright as a musicians' issue in the public mind.

Musicians' lobbying activities extended to folklore, and the case of the song *Yaa Amponsah* is a good illustration of the complex issues in this area. *Yaa Amponsah* is considered to be the source of the basic melodic pattern of Ghanaian highlife music, and in 1990, singer Paul Simon paid $16,000 in royalties to the Ghana Copyright Administration for the use of the song in his album *The Rhythm of the Saints*. Simon intended the royalties for Kwame Asare (also known as Jacob Sam), who was said to be the song's composer.[22] However, since Asare had died in the 1950s, and since the melody was also closely linked to guitar plucking styles developed by Liberian sailors that formed the roots of palm wine music, the National Commission on Culture declared *Yaa Amponsah* to be "a work of anonymous folklore."[23] On the album itself, Simon skillfully navigated the tension between individual authorship and national cultural claims by describing the song in the liner notes as "a traditional Ghanaian song, Yaa Amponsah, by Jacob Sam."[24]

Simon's royalty payment was used to set up the National Folklore Board.[25] While the 1985 copyright law made provision for such a board, it was this royalty payment that made its actual establishment possible. The board was a site of contention as cultural and legal experts disagreed over the premise that the authors of folklore were unknown. Several folklore specialists argued that it was often possible to identify individual creators of folklore, but they were overruled. Folklore experts also disagreed with other members of the board over whether Ghanaians should pay royalties for the use of folklore, and again, the specialists lost the argument. The requirement of royalty payments for folklore has been actively resisted by musicians, who call it a "folktax." Not only do they regard indigenous culture as their own, but as the example of Yaa Amponsah shows, they both add to it and draw from it as a resource for their compositions.

As the effective copyright protection of locally produced music became a reality, dissension began to emerge among musicians. In a meeting with musicians in late 1989, the Secretary for Information "deplored the lack of unity among members of the musical community due to factions within the Musicians' Union of Ghana on one hand and the emergence of two producer organizations on the other hand."[26] Tensions also developed between musicians and other royalty earning groups. Following its establishment under the 1985 law, COSGA, set up to collect royalties for all protected works, was administered by the copyright office. Explaining this in 1999, the copyright administrator said that it was necessary in a country where the level of royalties collected was low.[27] The goal was to spare artists collection costs that might exceed their resources. A guiding principle was to treat such industries equally and to use at least part of the royalties collected to the benefit of all.

Musicians, however, saw things quite differently. On one occasion, they objected strongly to efforts to elect a member of the Ghana Association of Writers (GAW) as the chairman of COSGA. As one policy advisor put it, musicians argued that "this was *their* association, and they were not going to allow any so-called 'book-long' people to take over."[28] Speaking years later in a 2004 interview, a member of the music lobby confirmed this and directly linked decision making in COSGA with revenue earned. He saw the leadership of COSGA by nonmusicians as an infringement on the rights of the musicians, who also constituted the largest group of royalty earners. Musicians, he claimed, "were contributing about 99% of the revenue of COSGA."[29] While this argument has its merits, it casts musicians as the preeminent cultural producers in the space of Ghanaian copyright law. This position enables them to continue having the main say in the shaping of that law so that it responds more acutely to their interests than to those of other cultural producers in a continuing cycle of dominance. Ironically, this stance also parallels the current culture of international intellectual property regulation in which decision making is based more on economic power than on democratic principles that grant all member states an equal say.[30]

In addition to wanting to control COSGA, some musicians began to raise questions about accounting practices related to copyright enforcement. For example, they claimed a lack of transparency around the introduction of new devices to replace the banderole. They also questioned the neutrality of the Copyright Administration as an arbiter in such matters.[31] By the late 1990s, the conflict caused by these issues had grown to the point of fragmenting the music lobby and straining the relationship between some musicians and the Copyright Administration. A new group of activists emerged to challenge both the Copyright Administration and the MUSIGA establishment. These developments resulted in the creation in 2000 of an alternative collection society, the Ghana Society of Composers, Authors and Publishers (GHASCAP), modeled on the American Society of Composers, Authors and Publishers (ASCAP) in the United States. In 2004, a related organization, the Coalition of Concerned Copyright Advocates (COCCA) was formed to act specifically as a copyright lobby.[32]

In the meantime, starting in the late 1990s and continuing into the early 2000s, Ghana embarked on a comprehensive reform of all its intellectual property laws in order to bring them into compliance with the TRIPS Agreement of 1994. Articles 65 and 66 of the agreement set deadlines for the entry into force of the agreement in member countries, and "Developing" and "Least-Developed" countries were granted extended periods (up to ten years) to comply.[33] As a developing country, Ghana was required to make its intellectual property laws TRIPS-compliant by 2000. Although the musicians' lobby was by then far less unified than it had been in the late 1970s and the1980s, it continued to participate actively in the revision of the copyright law.[34] The reform of this law was the last to be completed, and activists in the music lobby claim that this delay was due to their success in preventing the government's efforts to rush the passage of the law without proper consultation.[35]

While musicians did play a role in the process, there were additional intervening factors in the passage of the copyright law, most notably the electoral cycle.[36] The period for considering the copyright bill, after it was first introduced to parliament in 2000, lapsed at the end of that year, which was also the end of the 1996–2000 electoral cycle. The elections at the end of that cycle were particularly important for Ghana because they presented a unique opportunity to change not only the party whose presidential candidate won but also the party that held the majority of parliamentary seats. This also promised to be the first time in the country's history that a change of government was achieved through democratic rather than military means. The stakes in the 2000 election were therefore exceptionally high and dominated the national political agenda as the electoral cycle drew to a close. The balance of political power did change dramatically in the elections, but the intellectual property law reform exercise remained on the new government's agenda. While all the other laws concerned were passed by the middle of 2004, copyright remained an intractable issue until late that year, almost the end of the new government's first term in office.

Finally, a week after national elections on December 7, 2004, and days before the formal end of the new government's first term in office, the parliament's Committee on Constitutional, Legal and Parliamentary Affairs made one more attempt to secure passage of the copyright law. On December 16, the committee held a public forum to discuss the revised copyright law with interested parties or, in the term commonly used in Ghana, stakeholders. Representatives from different parts of the entertainment industry attended the meeting, along with book publishers and software developers, but they were outnumbered by participants from different sectors of the music industry, including representatives of both MUSIGA and COCCA.

Although the bill under discussion continued the 1985 law's attention to kente and adinkra designs, there were no representatives of producers of such material folklore at the meeting. While musicians raised the issue of folklore as one of their concerns, they did so mainly in terms that reflected their interests and in relation to the kinds of folklore in which they were most interested: indigenous music, proverbs, and other oral traditions. Representatives of the different groups proposed a number of changes, and a day after the forum, parliament finally passed the copyright law.[37] Formal gazette notification and publication followed early in 2005.

While factors such as the cultural revolution of the early 1980s and the electoral cycle were important in the legislative processes that led to the 1985 and 2005 copyright laws, there is no doubt that those laws were also influenced by musicians. The 1985 law devoted considerable space to the rights of performers (given the importance of the fixed performance as "the primary text") and music producers. The 2005 law retained this strong emphasis on the rights of musicians, and in one important triumph for the latter, it provided for the establishment of collection societies by copyright holders. As such, they testify to the effectiveness of the music lobby in Ghana. As one policy advisor noted with reference to the 1985 law,

> You know it was something that came out of intense lobbying from *one* particular section of those who could be considered to collectively be owners of intellectual property . . . it was an intense lobby from the Musicians Union of Ghana. So that kind of bias was built into the framing of the law itself, but even more so in the implementation [referring to musicians' dominance of COSGA].[38]

As noted earlier, Ghanaian musicians' lobbying activities have often placed them in an oppositional stance to the Ghanaian state, as represented primarily by the Copyright Administration. A former official in that administration, when asked why the 1985 copyright law paid so much attention to the music industry, responded, "The musicians are troublesome!"[39] If musicians' accounts are anything to go by, this antagonism continued into the last round of intellectual property law reform as some segments of the music lobby questioned the neutrality of the Copyright Administration. By the end of 2004, relations between those segments of the lobby and the copyright administrator were very tense.

In viewing musicians as a problem, government officials play into the hands of groups like COCCA and GHASCAP that construct themselves as a healthy sector of Ghanaian civil society, keeping the state and its representatives accountable to the interests and needs of citizens. The language of

Carlos Sakyi, one of the leaders of these new groups, is particularly telling in this respect when he describes the COSGA and the Copyright Administration as infringing on musicians' rights of citizenship. Contrasting the PNDC era with the constitutional period that began in 1992, he said,

> COSGA was imposed on us. Because, well, we were operating under military rule then, and all that, and . . . when the constitution came into being in 1992, several provisions in COSGA's setup became contrary to the provisions in the constitution. For instance, the constitution talks about freedom of association, right? That's the right to free association, but as far as COSGA is concerned, whether you like it or not, once you are in the creative arts, you *have* to belong to it, you *have* to belong, you don't have a choice. And . . . we saw that as autocratic, we saw that as . . . taking our rights away, you know, and we started complaining about that.[40]

This discourse of democratic rights casts members of the music lobby not only as active subjects, as is evident in the responsiveness of the copyright law to their concerns, but also as exemplary citizens of a democratic state. They take to heart the civil rights (like freedom of association) granted by the liberal democratic state and actively insist on those rights as their due. This could not be more different from the way cloth producers perceive themselves, as the following section shows.

Your Face Doesn't Go Anywhere

Although adinkra and kente producers' perceptions of themselves in relation to the state are not entirely uniform, they are still strikingly different from the way musicians see themselves. With cloth producers perceiving copyright as a musicians' issue, it is not surprising that they tended not to associate their work with either the legal sphere or the state until asked what they thought about state custodianship of adinkra and kente designs and the prospect of seeking legal protection for "their" designs. However, it is noteworthy that once the possibility of such protection was raised, their responses showed that they saw the legal sphere and the Ghanaian state as, at best, indifferent to their interests. Commenting on the prospect of cloth producers from his community seeking and gaining legal protection for their designs, adinkra maker Kofi said

> They [government officials] will treat you with disrespect. If someone [else] states their case right now, they accept it, but as for you when they look at your face, your face doesn't go anywhere.[41]

Kofi's use of the term "face" is somewhat analogous to the common understanding of the word in reference to the state of being honored or shamed. As he uses the term in this case, *face* also translates into class, and the apprehension he expresses is over discrimination on the basis of class. In his local community, Kofi might enjoy some social advantages on the basis of his involvement of adinkra production for the Asantehene's palace and his status as a leader in his community. In the world of lawyers and government officials, however, these count for relatively little. He thus saw the national state (or its representatives) as responsive to people primarily on the basis of class and influence, and in his view, cloth producers like him lacked the status necessary to attract the state's attention to their concerns.[42]

An additional source of Kofi's skepticism was his belief that state support was conditional—specifically, that in order to gain protection of their designs, craftsmen must first be "registered" and pay taxes. Another respondent, Kwabena, a kente weaver at Bonwire, was even more mistrustful of the state. His response to the possibility of state custodianship of kente designs was a strong protest in which he pointed to abandoned infrastructural projects as evidence of the state's longstanding neglect of his community. While he cited this neglect specifically as an argument against state custodianship of kente designs, his response also suggested that, in his view, the state could not be trusted to promote the interests of the weavers who produce the cloth that bears those designs. Kwame, another adinkra maker, while seeming to support the official view that adinkra designs belong to all Ghanaians, along with the principle of state custodianship, also echoed other cloth makers' skepticism toward the state when he added, "And the compensation too . . . when it goes to the government, even those of us to whom it belongs, they won't give it to us."[43]

Kofi and Kwabena expressed a different kind of skepticism when they pointed to cloth producers' lack of organization, suggesting that they felt they were more likely to succeed in pressing for their interests in groups rather than as individuals. In Kofi's words, "If we could get some people to send or if we had some real unity and were focused, then we could petition the chief [Asantehene] and ask him to support us and help us." He further noted that although he and other cloth producers in his community had tried to organize themselves into a group, those efforts had failed. Kwabena, the kente weaver, also referred to group organization and noted that weavers were dispersed—several in small forest hamlets—and for this reason, it would be hard to organize them into a group. He said,

Even if you call a meeting, there is no one who will bother to come to a meeting, it is not something that will work. But if when it [cloth production] was new, we had said "This cloth was made by such and such a person so see to it that no-one copies it," then even if you were seen carrying it [a copy], you could be arrested.

For Kwabena, protective measures should have been established locally with the introduction of the craft, and it was now too late to institute such measures, especially given the difficulty of organizing weavers.[44]

These observations about communal effort and its futility in their communities are interesting because apart from what they show about cloth makers' views on seeking protection for their designs, they are an indicator of their awareness of such effort as a desired mode of citizenship in Ghana. Communal effort is a longstanding principle in Ghana, such as in the *nnoboa* system in agricultural communities where farmers help each other harvest their crops. Kofi's words linking communal effort with petitioning the Asantehene show that this principle also pertains to the indigenous Asante state. The principle of communal effort has periodically been appropriated and reinvigorated by the Ghanaian state as an important means of achieving development goals such as new or improved water supplies and the construction of medical clinics and schools.

Communal effort has become especially important since the mid-1980s when the government of Ghana began to implement a series of economic recovery and structural adjustment programs as conditions for World Bank and International Monetary Fund assistance. Such programs have been a key means of exporting U.S. neoliberalism to the Third World.[45] Apart from promoting trade liberalization, such policies urged the reduction of government responsibility for a range of social services, shifting the burden onto individual citizens and local communities in an "attack [on] the social contract."[46] At the same time, multilateral and bilateral agencies like the World Bank and the U.S. Agency for International Development began to co-opt the concept of civil society in ways that helped to justify this shift.[47] In noting the necessity of group effort in order to address the appropriation of their work, cloth makers were therefore signaling their awareness of this shift as a preferred mode of subjectivity. They showed that they recognized the conditions necessary for addressing issues of concern to them in the same way that groups like MUSIGA and COCCA have done.

Yet adinkra and kente producers raised the possibility of organized group action only to reject it either because their organizing efforts had failed or because they expected such efforts to fail. At best, they saw group effort as effective if harnessed to the leadership of the Asantehene. They expressed concern about the appropriation of adinkra and kente designs, and some, like Kofi at Asokwa, the original center of adinkra production, saw such appropriation as a key source of the decline in demand for their cloth. However, unlike musicians in the 1970s, they did not see appropriation as something against which they could take effective action on their own. They also saw the Ghanaian state as untrustworthy or biased in favor of those of higher status, and they further rejected the mode of subjectivity required of citizens seeking to gain state attention to their interests. Ultimately, adinkra and kente producers did not give much credence to the possibility of the national state serving their interests in the appropriation of adinkra and kente designs, especially if those interests were expressed individually.

While these perceptions of the Ghanaian state are somewhat similar to musicians' views, there is an important difference. For musicians, state indifference or hostility is an obstacle to be tackled in order to gain rights that they consider to be theirs. For cloth producers, state indifference is a factor over which they have no influence or control either because they lack the appropriate status or because of the longstanding nature of what they perceive as state neglect. In pointing to such neglect of his community, Kwabena not only cited the current situation but also linked it to the broken promises of different governments going back almost three decades.

Although several cloth producers were aware of their importance to the tourism industry, and therefore as players in the national economy, this sense of value did not necessarily translate into an equally strong sense of importance as citizens who could insist on attention to their rights in the formal space of the Ghanaian state. Their feeling of inadequacy in relation to the state and the law contrasts with cloth makers' status within their communities, where, as discussed in chapter 1, they tended to have a strong sense of their importance as makers of a valued cultural product. When they could claim an association with the Asantehene's palace, their status was further enhanced. Cloth makers' identification of the Asantehene as a possible leader of their efforts to gain protection of their rights as cultural producers also showed that in addition to the prestige derived from royal patronage, they were surer of their place in the Asante state and of that state as a sphere more supportive than the national state of their interests. With the continuing legitimacy of indigenous states within the national state,[48] and given his status in both political spheres, the Asantehene was the perfect link between the two as an advocate for cloth makers in the civic and legal space of the national state.

Cloth makers' statements about copyright as a musicians' issue, the national state as untrustworthy, and their own lack of organization point to a number of deeper issues around the meaning of both legal subjectivity and citizenship in the space of the nation-state of Ghana. Within the latter space, when it comes to gaining state attention to their interests as cultural producers, the extent of their citizenship is considerably limited both by their own self-perceptions and by the different sources of effective citizenship in their communities, the Asante state, and the larger nation-state.

In his comments about "face," Kofi points to these different kinds of subjectivity that adinkra and kente producers have in different social and political spheres. A cloth producer whose skill and royal connections assure him a respected position at the local level cannot assume that those skills and connections will assure him any advantages in the national space of the state and its laws. In the national space, class advantages may accrue from indigenous sources where the person concerned is a major figure like the Asantehene. Otherwise, one's social position is closely tied to factors like wealth and formal education and the ability to translate these into an advantageous position within the formal economy. Within this set of arrangements, skill in an important craft is not, by itself, a particularly useful resource, and this is what Kofi was alluding to when he said, "Your face doesn't go anywhere." As he correctly assumed, in order to gain the serious attention of professionals and bureaucrats like lawyers and government officials, one would need to possess class advantages derived from factors like education and wealth rather than skill in the production of a nationally important cultural form.

The one cloth producer who did not appear to share this sense of inadequacy relative to the state was Nana Baffour Gyimah, the innovative cloth producer discussed in chapter 1. Of all the cloth makers in the study, he was the most visibly wealthy and the only one who had dealt with the formal legal system. Not only did he describe his designs as "copyright" even before the subject was raised, but he had also taken steps to protect those designs using a kind of trademark. His success as a cloth producer had led him to formally register his business as early as 1976, and when he began producing his distinctive screen-printed adinkra, he printed his registered business name and logo as an informal trademark symbol on each piece of cloth that he made to distinguish it from imitations by competitors. He considered formally registering his designs under intellectual property law but decided, instead, to borrow from the legal principle of trademark protection in order to stake his claim over his cloth.

These practices suggested a willingness on Baffour Gyimah's part to use laws and state agencies to protect his interests as a cultural producer. Yet he ultimately aligned himself with other cloth producers in choosing not to do so. When it came to measures to prevent the appropriation of adinkra and kente designs, he was also similar to other cloth makers in two respects. He spoke of the need for such measures to be initiated through the collective effort of cloth producers, and he saw the Asantehene as the person who should prevent appropriation. He justified this view by making a distinction between things that belonged to Asante royalty and those that belonged to Ghana:

> We have what belongs to the nation of Ghana that everyone can buy and some buy and take abroad. Then we have what we make for our own royalty that you must not make for the market. You see? That is how it is.[49]

Even though Baffour Gyimah did not appear to share other adinkra and kente makers' suspicion of the national state or their hesitation in seeking state attention to their interests, he did not view the state as the appropriate sphere for seeking protection of adinkra and kente designs. For him, adinkra and kente were, above all, part of Asante royal heritage. While he distinguished himself from other cloth producers, he still saw his cloth as a part of this heritage, and protecting the latter was as important to him as protecting his own innovations. Further, he saw such protection as a matter of more than his own individual interests and efforts despite his emphasis on his individuality as a cloth maker.

Beyond Efficacy

Musicians' and cloth producers' relation to the state around intellectual property law can be explained in a number of ways based on their comments and actions. In those comments and actions, efficacy appears to be an important aspect of subjectivity—musicians demonstrate such efficacy, cloth producers do not, and this is evident in the degree to which the law responds to their interests. Closely related to efficacy is the element of ignorance in determining how different kinds of cultural producers fare in relation to intellectual property law. Adinkra and kente makers, for the most part, are ignorant of intellectual property law as a sphere in which they can seek protection for their work—much less one they can influence in determining the nature of that protection.[50]

A focus on knowledge and efficacy can obscure other important factors, however. It is certainly true that groups that actively demand attention to their interests—through such actions as marching to the Castle, attending public forums where pending legislation is discussed, and challenging legal and policy measures with which they disagree—are likely to have their interests addressed by the state, while groups that do not engage with the state in this way risk being ignored. The history of the music lobby and the passage of the revised copyright law by a military government in 1985 also suggest that even in conditions under which the government cannot be held to the principles of democracy invoked by the musician quoted earlier, certain kinds of citizen action can still be effective.

While citizens can be effective both in getting legislation changed and using existing laws to their advantage, focusing on their efficacy places the burden of responsibility on them when the state does not meet their interests. In such a situation, adinkra and kente producers like Kofi become responsible for their own invisibility before the law because they are "not part of the musical thing" in failing to demonstrate the ability or willingness to engage the state as musicians do. Such a focus plays into the neoliberal moves that have shifted responsibility for citizens from the state to citizens themselves. Equally problematic is that the agency of groups like the music lobby may be exaggerated when one focuses solely on their self-representation or on how they are perceived by other cultural groups and by government officials.

"The musicians are troublesome" may signal public officials' exasperation at musicians' lobbying activities, but it also casts them as active citizens who keep the government accountable to the needs of the people. As musicians see it, they are simply exercising their rights and holding the state accountable to their interests. In their accounts, they are the heroes of Ghana's copyright law reform process. When one examines musicians' actions as subjects produced by the law, however, that heroism is somewhat tempered. A focus on musicians' active citizenship makes cloth makers appear passive by contrast, when they are, in fact, very active in promoting their interests within their own communities either in vying for recognition as cloth producers for the palace or in accessing tourist networks.

In addition to efficacy, therefore, it is important to consider more structural factors in order to avoid a mode of analysis that makes groups and individuals exclusively responsible for their legal standing. One can consider, for example, the argument that certain points in history lend themselves more to policy and legislative change than others. If one applies Susan Sell and Christopher May's model of triangulation to the Ghanaian case, it becomes clear that musicians' lobbying must be considered along with other factors.[51] In proposing this analytical framework, Sell and May argue that intellectual property law has developed through a history of contestation that occurs when three key elements coincide to create conditions that permit changes in the law.

Those elements are ideas about intellectual property, technological change, and institutions, and triangulation occurs when they converge, allowing for the possibility of contestation. The law reflects certain sets of ideas that have become enshrined as the outcome of these interrelated processes. In the case of Ghana's 1985 copyright law, for example, the cultural revolution, changes in recording technology, and changing ideas about what should be protected under the law (including ideas about the protection of folklore) converged to create a climate in which musicians' lobbying activities could be effective. The TRIPS-induced legislative reform of the early 2000s created another such climate.

In order to understand recording artists' and cloth producers' differing perceptions of themselves in relation to copyright law, therefore, it is important to go beyond internal qualities like knowledge and efficacy. Those perceptions also have to do with more structural factors, including cultural producers' differing relations to the state both as legal subjects and as citizens, along with the nature and legal status of their modes of cultural production. In directing attention away from an exclusive focus on cloth makers' and musicians' effectiveness as individuals and interest groups, these factors offer a more nuanced understanding of the sources of legal subjectivity, and examining them can yield insights that are obscured when one focuses on the degree to which musicians and cloth makers are active or passive.

Subjects in the Discourses of Intellectual Property Law

An important factor in Ghanaian cultural producers' subjectivity is intellectual property law itself as a set of discourses that is productive of subjects. In making this argument, I follow the line of reasoning that Michel Foucault offers when he poses the questions: "How, under what conditions, and in what forms can something like a subject appear in the order of discourse? What place can it occupy in each type of discourse, what functions can it assume, and by obeying what rules?"[52] He further suggests that we "analyz[e] the subject as a variable and complex function of discourse."[53]

From this perspective, intellectual property law is not only a social and political mechanism through which the "author function" operates to legitimize certain discourses but is in itself a set of discourses whose main authors include thinkers of the Romantic and Enlightenment eras in European history. The views of these thinkers underpin the norms of alienability and human subjectivity that combine in many areas of intellectual property law—particularly patent and copyright law. The legal subjectivity of cultural producers is thus a function of these discourses, and the subject that emerges from the discourses of intellectual property law is the individual. Only individuals can claim to be authors or inventors; thus, cultural producers who work as individuals have legal standing, while those who operate in groups do not unless they individually claim authorship of discrete parts of the group's production. Alternatively, if those groups are formally constituted such that they can claim the status of "legal persons," then the group becomes a kind of honorary individual that can claim authorship.[54]

A person who fails to establish a clear distinction between her work and that of the tradition on which she draws cannot be a subject under these conditions. These discourses also exclude any creativity that originates from a group unless that group is clearly defined or formally constituted as a legal entity. This makes musicians in the recording industry ideal subjects of intellectual property law. As performers and producers of music that is fixed through sound recording, they produce in accordance with the norms recognized by intellectual property law. Those norms go beyond the mode of "fixing" their work to the ways in which they function as individuals, as clearly identified groups (like choirs), or legal corporate entities (recording companies) in accordance with the law. These map neatly onto the kinds of subjectivity recognized by the law.

The kinds of subjectivity privileged by the discourses of intellectual property law exclude cultural producers like adinkra and kente makers. Although the designs they use have individual creators, those individuals are not easily separated from the community as authors because the norm is for their designs to pass into the communal pool. Individual creativity is recognized through the right to name designs, but that does not necessarily translate into a formal right to prevent others from using those designs. In cloth production, the acts of borrowing that are suppressed in the Romantic author mode of intellectual property law are freely acknowledged as being bound up with acts of individual creativity. In most cases, therefore, the separation required in order for cloth producers to become legal subjects of intellectual property law is far from routine and familiar. This merging of individual into communal creativity conflicts with the clearly delineated individual subjectivity produced by the discourses of intellectual property law, and adinkra and kente producers therefore cannot be legal subjects. Cloth makers' authorization practices further increase their distance from the law because they authorize their cloth by appeal to the social and temporal contexts of cloth production and use rather than to the persons who produce them.

Strictly speaking, Ghana's copyright law provides scope for folklore producers to operate equally before the law as subjects. The 2005 version of the law makes the state the custodian of "kente and adinkra designs, where the author of the designs [is] not known."[55] This means that, in principle, individual creators of specific adinkra and kente designs can protect their designs under copyright law—especially creators of more recent designs who are still alive to press their claims. In order to do so, however, such persons must give up one kind of subjectivity to occupy another, separating their creativity from the contexts that give meaning and value to their individual work. Alternatively, they must constitute themselves into formal legal groupings that conform to the kinds of collective subjectivity produced by the law.

Musicians' activism, as well as Ghana's protection of folklore within the inhospitable framework of intellectual property law, suggests that the discourses of the law can be changed or at least modified. Indeed, one advantage of looking at the law as a set of discourses is that discourses are not static, and musicians' impact on the discourse of Ghana's copyright law is evident in the provision for individual claims over folklore in the 2005 version of the law. However, both musicians and the Ghanaian state have remained within the established discourse—even with respect to folklore protection. While musicians have challenged the provisions of copyright law, they have not radically challenged its premises. Similarly, while the state's use of copyright law to protect folklore seems progressive on the face of it, it has not changed the boundaries of subjectivity within the law. By assuming the position of custodian of folklore, the state assumes the status of a legal person—this is especially evident in the wording of the 2005 law, which vests the rights to folklore in "the President of the Republic." Although a nation is a completely different entity from a corporation, the position that the state assigns itself within the law, in this case, is similar to that of a corporation or other formally constituted group.[56] Ultimately, therefore, adinkra and kente producers are written out of the law through its discourses.

The discourses of intellectual property law, then, establish the kind of subjectivity available to different kinds of cultural producers. As long as those discourses remain unchallenged, they constrain the degree to which personal efficacy and activism can be effective in promoting the interests of different kinds of cultural producers. Individual and group qualities may be used effectively when those individuals and groups conform to the kinds of subjectivity established for them by the law, and this is clearly the case with musicians. For groups and individuals who fall outside those kinds of subjectivity, however, the struggle to promote their interests is unlikely to have much effect while the discourses of the law remain intact.

Despite their importance, legal discourses do not exhaust the full range of subjectivity available to cultural producers. Apart from intellectual property law, musicians and adinkra and kente makers interact with the state through its policies. Cloth producers may be marginal legal subjects in the space of intellectual property law, but they are linked to the Ghanaian state along other axes, such as economic and cultural policy. For cloth makers, these come together most strongly in national tourism policies. Within this sphere, they may have wider scope for pursuing their interests than they do in copyright law, and apart from the law, these are possibly the most important spheres within which adinkra and kente makers interact with the Ghanaian state.

Managing Tradition

Even as Western-style systems of governance are important to Ghana's identity as a modern nation, cultural *traditions* are important to its assertions of distinctiveness. As noted in chapter 1, Ghana claims a "rich cultural heritage," and adinkra and kente are important elements in that heritage. The tradition–modernity binary is, of course, a false one that obscures a lot of exchange, overlap, and interdependency between the two spheres. At the same time, the binary is an active one that is invoked to support different kinds of claims. The status of kente as traditional, for example, is an important selling point that cloth producers use to their advantage, even though the yarns used in weaving the cloth are no longer locally grown and handspun.

In the case of music, the older genre of highlife takes on the status of tradition when Ghanaian music lovers deplore newer artists' corruption of established forms (as, for example, in purists' preference for traditional highlife music over the "hip-life" that began to emerge in the 1990s). Conversely, while invoking the tradition in which their cloth is embedded, producers promote new designs on the very modern basis of their newness, setting them apart from that tradition.[57] Thus, even though cloth makers and musicians' cultural production is often treated as though it were unquestionably modern or traditional, these categories operate more as bases for making different kinds of claims than as indicating fixed or definitive characteristics. Both modernity and tradition are strategically deployed for different ends by the nation and its citizens.

Tourism policy is a key site for managing tradition and applying it to the assertion of a distinctive national identity. It is at this site that tradition is organized for the consumption of the outside world, for example, in the network of key cloth-producing centers that appear on tourist maps. As noted in chapter 1, some centers appear on those maps in a sign of recognition by the national state. Such recognition makes tourism policy important as a space in which adinkra and kente producers are situated far more advantageously in relation to the state than they are in intellectual property law. Apart from organizing tradition, such recognition is also important in mediating yet another set of distinctions with implications for cloth makers: the rural–urban divide.

If one follows the argument that rural–urban inequalities in Africa are a result of modern nation-states' failure to overcome structural inequalities established during colonization, then the legal status of adinkra and kente craftsmen, particularly those in small semirural towns like Bonwire and Ntonso, can be seen as being partly due to this failure.[58] From this perspective, such communities represent an emphasis on the interests of urban populations to the neglect of rural areas where the majority of the population live. Comments like Kwabena's about the failure of successive governments to provide basic infrastructure and amenities for Bonwire provide some support for this view.

However, the opposition of a privileged urban sector to an underprivileged rural one does not hold up in all instances. The project of modern nation-building in Africa has not uniformly benefited urban populations, as can be seen in the large numbers of urban-dwellers who live very marginal lives. Despite their urban location, such groups cannot be said to be fully integrated into the modern nation-state when they experience it mainly in terms of neglect similar to that identified by Kwabena at Bonwire.[59] It is also necessary to consider the diminished capacity of the Ghanaian state to address citizens' needs given the weakened nature of that state, partly as a result of the structural adjustment policies of the 1980s and 1990s.[60]

In addition, the boundary between rural and urban is very permeable and regularly crossed such that neither category fully contains nor completely defines the lives of those within it. Take adinkra maker Yaw Boakye, who was born in the community of Ntonso, worked in an urban area as a mason, and then returned to his home town to take up adinkra production and farming. Apart from having gone back and forth between rural and urban contexts in the course of his life, he is tied simultaneously into both spheres through his participation in the rural economy of farming and the national tourism industry. That industry makes his community into a key node in a national network that links Ntonso with both urban-based tourism businesses in Ghana and wider global tourist networks. The degree of integration into modern systems of governance is therefore not straightforward and cannot be perfectly predicted on the basis of location in rural or urban areas.

The ways in which cloth producers' practices confound categories like modern–traditional and urban–rural suggest that their structural relationship to the state cannot be understood only in terms of those categories. It is also important to consider how their practices—as well as different areas of national policy and law—link them to the state in ways that destabilize those categories. As producers of key goods for the tourism industry, many adinkra and kente producers benefit from state policies in the tourism sector, while some are excluded by the same policies. Asokwa, for example, although it is central to the history of adinkra production in Asante and is the official source of the Asantehene's cloth, does not appear on the national tourism network. Cloth makers' relationship with the state therefore needs to be understood in relation to the specific axes along which they interact with it. Viewed in this way, they are marginalized in some areas, like intellectual property law, yet may be empowered in others, such as tourism policy. These relationships, more than individual or group efficacy or even their urban–modern or rural–traditional location, determine their standing before the state. The most passive Ntonso-based adinkra producers are therefore structurally at an advantage in relation to the most active cloth producer at Asokwa, while all are disadvantaged with respect to intellectual property law.

Looking at adinkra and kente producers' relationship to the state on the basis of these connections also helps to explain the marginalization felt by those like Kofi at Asokwa. In the case of these cloth producers, the center of power to which they are most closely connected as cultural workers is not the modern national state but the indigenous Asante state. Although Nana Baffour Gyimah also saw matters concerning adinkra and kente as belonging under the jurisdiction of the Asantehene rather than the national government, his combination of personal success and strategic location along a major highway linking different centers of interest in the tourist network also meant that he did not share Kofi's feelings of inadequacy in relation to the national state.

Civil Society beyond Neoliberalism

Since 1979, Ghanaian musicians have captured the political space of activism around intellectual property law to the point that adinkra and kente producers interviewed in 1999 and 2000 regarded copyright as something that musicians do. Even though cloth makers were concerned about the appropriation of their work, for the most part, they did not see copyright law as a sphere in which they could challenge such appropriation. It would be easy to read this as evidence of musicians' active citizenship and cloth producers' passivity, but this interpretation is insufficient for explaining the difference between these two kinds of cultural producers within the legal and political spaces of modern Ghana. Such an explanation risks serving the neoliberal project of making citizens responsible for their own welfare, absolving the state of its duties. It also contradicts the fact that people who appear passive in one civic sphere may be very active in another.

Adinkra and kente producers' apparent passivity in relation to intellectual property law must be understood partly as a function of the discourses of the law itself, which requires modes of subjectivity inadequate to the kinds of subject positions that cloth makers assume in relation to their work. Those positions locate cloth producers in networks that exceed the conceptual space of intellectual property law, making the law unsuited to the full expression of cloth makers' experience. The situation is different when one factors in tourism policy, which provides more advantageous links between cloth producers and the Ghanaian state. Adinkra and kente makers' identification of the Asantehene as a possible mediator between them and the national government points to yet another axis: the link between the modern state and indigenous states within it. This link confounds standard frameworks of modern political action, since such frameworks make no provision for indigenous political systems.

Those frameworks also privilege the role of "civil society" as a counter to the state, and the rhetorical strategies of Ghanaian musicians match this conceptualization of civil society. Yet with civil society increasingly co-opted into neoliberal projects, the activism of musicians can end up merely conforming to, rather than radically challenging, intellectual property law. In the Ghanaian case, while they have gained significant advantages in copyright law as a result of their activism, musicians have not fundamentally altered the premises of the law in ways that accommodate the modes of subjectivity and production of cultural producers like adinkra and kente makers.

This should serve as a cautionary note in organizing cloth producers into constituencies that can take on the state in the way that musicians have done. The Centre for Indigenous Knowledge Systems (CEFIKS) is one possible arena for such organization. Established as a nongovernmental organization (NGO) in Ghana in 2000, it is engaged in efforts to help adinkra and kente producers protect their designs.[61] While this may be a means by which cloth makers can begin to push at the boundaries of the law, it is clear from the discussion so far that it is not enough to protect designs in the manner currently provided for in Ghana's copyright law. This is because the value of cloth is located not only in the designs but also in the genre of cloth itself as well as the social and temporal contexts of production. In addition, the discourses of the law limit the subjectivity available to cloth producers.

Further, CEFIKS's goals may harness cloth production and other forms of indigenous culture to ends that reinforce rather than challenge other aspects of the status quo. For example, center states that it is "committed to the utilization of indigenous knowledge systems and other forms of information for capacity building as a way of accelerating socioeconomic development in rural and urban areas of Ghana and throughout the West African region."[62] The question that arises is whether in doing so CEFIKS will challenge current models of development that advance the neoliberal project discussed earlier, or whether it will simply be co-opted into that project as has been the case with so many NGOs. Ultimately, this is not solely a local issue but also a global one with scope for transnational activism. I explore these dimensions and possibilities in the next chapter.

Chapter 4 **We Run a Single Country**
The Politics of Appropriation

> If we have to really nitpick, the adinkra symbols didn't come
> from the Ashantis, [they] came from the Ivorians. . . . I would
> think of the adinkra symbol as Ghanaian, and not Ashanti
> or Akan.
>
> —Mansah, artist, Accra

> They say kente is from Ewe people, the earliest kente is from
> Ewe people.
>
> —Kwasi, kente weaver, Accra

KWASI IS FROM THE EWE ETHNIC GROUP and grew up in the town of
Agbozume, a center of Ewe kente or *adanudo*, where he learned to weave.
When he moved to the national capital, Accra, and realized that Asante
kente was more popular than the Ewe version, he found a group of Asante
weavers who readily taught him how to weave Asante kente.[1] This interethnic
sharing belies the rivalry between the Ewe and Asante people of Ghana,
who both claim to have originated the craft of kente weaving. In a parallel
version of the Asante account of kente's origin, Kwasi's grandfather, a
weaver, told him that "a hunter saw a spider . . . weaving something like a
net . . . then the man came to his house and . . . started [to imitate] how the
spider was weaving. From that day we [the Ewe people] started weaving
kente." Kwasi's grandfather also told him that kente weaving was introduced
to Asante by migrant Ewe weavers who taught the craft to their Asante
apprentices.[2] Like Asante kente, the origins of Ewe kente weaving probably
lie beyond the region, and one source traces it to Western Nigeria, which is
also known for its strip weaving and from where the Ewe people originally
migrated.[3]

Kwasi's story points to the multiple identity-based claims around cultural
products like adinkra and kente. Other claims of this kind include the

assertion by Ghana's copyright administrator that "we run a single country," while an African American woman responded to the copyright protection of adinkra designs with the words, "A fool is sold his own tomatoes." In the case of the former, the identity in question is national, and national unity trumps ethnic diversity, while "a fool is sold his own tomatoes" signals diasporic African rights to continental African culture. These statements can also be understood as assertions of the right to appropriate and, where appropriation is successful, the right to own. Appropriation here is understood as taking something that can be claimed by, or proved to belong to, someone else. Bruce Ziff and Pratima Rao provide one definition in this vein that describes cultural appropriation as "the taking from a culture that is not one's own."[4] They explore the questions raised by this definition, asking, for example, "What do we mean by 'taking'? What values and concerns are implicated in the processes of appropriation?"[5]

While these are important questions and inform the discussion in this chapter, the approach taken here varies in a number of respects from that of Ziff and Rao and from much of the literature on appropriation of indigenous and local cultural production. In that literature, appropriation tends to be viewed as occurring when a more powerful group takes the cultural production of a less powerful group.[6] What is often left out of the discussion is how less powerful groups come to acquire that culture in the first place. Also excluded is consideration of the political importance of acts of appropriation that may not be backed by laws and other instruments of state.[7] Such cases show that appropriation can and does occur without ever translating into formal or legal claims of ownership. Longstanding practices of appropriation can therefore become ownership claims that are backed by the tradition of appropriation itself rather than by formal authority. One can therefore lay claim to adinkra and kente without asserting the right to restrict access by others who also claim them.

The approach taken here interrogates the ownership claims of the group with which the culture originates—or is said to originate. It also gives greater attention to the appropriative acts of subaltern groups when such appropriation constitutes resistance to, rather than assimilation into, the dominant culture. Ziff and Rao's approach works well in cases in which appropriation occurs within the context of imperial or colonial dominance. However, it is less helpful in cases of cultural nationalism in which the kinds of claims made over culture have to do with changes in the nature of political and social organization within a given territory that occur apart from (or are only partly mediated by) Western colonization. The approach taken here also distinguishes between the kinds of power backing different acts of appropriation. For example, the moral authority backing diasporic African appropriation of continental African culture is very different from appropriation backed by state power and expressed through policies and laws.

Questioning *all* ownership claims over cultural products like adinkra and kente undermines any naturalized notions of origin or ownership. Rather than being inherently Asante or Ghanaian, adinkra and kente are among a wide range of cultural products that have been *made* Asante and Ghanaian. The intellectual property protection of adinkra and kente designs must therefore be understood in the context of a series of cycles of appropriation that has been going on since, at least, the early eighteenth century when the Asante federation was established. In this process, cultural appropriation is an essential feature of nationalist projects—a feature that points both to the political nature of culture and to its instability as a marker of nationalist and other identities. Against this background, intellectual property law becomes a means of formalizing and legitimizing one set of appropriating practices over others. It is important to point out that the Asante model of appropriation does not necessarily apply to all indigenous cultures within Ghana. At the same time, while other cultures within the territory may not have the same history of institutionalized appropriation found in Asante, few can be said to be free from all borrowing and mixing of elements from other cultures. Asante is therefore useful as an extreme case that highlights such mixing and borrowing.

The appropriation under consideration here also occurs in the context of globalization in its changing forms. Globalization is understood here primarily as a historical process of capitalist expansion. However, groups and individuals engage with this process on the basis of local conditions such that globalization does not always manifest itself in predictable ways. Globalization is also seen here as a multidimensional process that cannot be reduced to economic and financial conditions—especially in the current phase that has to do with the flows and exchanges made possible by advances in information technologies (including the ethnic, media, technological, financial, and ideological landscapes identified by Appadurai).[8]

As previously noted, the saturated colors of Asante kente originated from the introduction of European silk textiles to Asante in an earlier stage of globalization. Asante weavers' response to these fabrics was to unravel them and use the yarn in weaving cloth according to the technical and aesthetic conventions in which they worked. These appropriating practices expanded both the meaning of European silk cloth (from being valued in itself to also being valued as raw material) and of kente. In the current phase of globalization, the appropriating practices of Africans in the diaspora constitute an important factor in the global circulation of African cultural products like adinkra and kente.[9] These practices are also examples of long-standing appropriation for nationalist purposes, which translates into widely accepted claims over culture but without the backing of formal laws.

The appropriation of cultural goods like adinkra and kente for nationalist projects is thus also bound up with processes of cultural and economic globalization. Local, national, and global circuits of production supply cultural goods that have value not only for their aesthetic features but also for their political symbolism. The Ghanaian case therefore offers an opportunity to examine the power dynamics of cultural appropriation while also taking into account the processes of cultural and economic globalization that support some appropriating practices while undermining others.

In this chapter, I examine the intellectual property protection of adinkra and kente in the context of this recurring politics of appropriation that converts products like adinkra and kente into national culture. I examine this not only in Asante and Ghana but also in the African diaspora, especially in the United States. I argue that claims over culture are not always a function of location of origin. They also have to do with the power to make such claims "stick" long enough that their association with specific locations appears naturalized. At that point, they become indicators of the success of the nationalist project concerned. Ghana's use of intellectual property law to protect adinkra and kente is of interest not simply because of the presumed lack of fit between these products and intellectual property law or because the law makes the state into the effective owner of these cultural products. It is also significant because of the reason behind that state ownership. Ghana, like all nations, is a work in progress, and the intellectual property protection of "national" folklore is a means of legitimizing the claims over culture that are essential to that work.

Since adinkra and kente continue to be Asante and are also claimed by Africans in the diaspora, Ghana's claims over these and other cultural elements exist concurrently and in tension with others. I discuss these claims in relation to each other and consider what they suggest for the relationship between Ghanaian and diasporic nationalisms as well as for ethnic claims over culture within the space of the nation. I also consider what these claims add to our understanding of different modes of appropriation. Apart from indexing different nationalist projects, these claims also point to the relationship between cultural appropriation and different social identities—in this case, ethnicity, citizenship, and race. I consider what these identities and the political projects in which they are anchored suggest for using intellectual property law to mediate between different claims. In doing so, I seek to answer the question: If cultural origin is as much a function of political action as of location, on what basis does one adjudicate between claims over culture?

In the discussion that follows, I first outline the nationalist projects within which adinkra and kente have been appropriated in Asante and Ghana. Against this background, I examine the views and appropriating practices of Ghanaians within and outside cloth-producing communities. I consider how Ghanaians negotiate the state's project of cultural nationalism as they assert claims over culture based on both national *and* ethnic identities. The words and practices of adinkra and kente producers and those who draw on their work are interesting here because of what they suggest about the nature of Ghanaianness half a century after the creation of the nation. They point both to the successes and limits of Ghanaian nationalism; some seem to endorse the state view that adinkra and kente are elements of national rather than ethnic culture, yet challenge the principle of state ownership, while others insist on the status of adinkra and kente as Asante.

Next, I consider cultural globalization mainly as it relates to African American consumption of African culture, since this gives Ghana's protection of folklore an important part of its global dimension. I argue that considering African American use of African culture helps to illuminate globalization as a multifaceted process. If the current phase of globalization is marked by increased opportunities for the consumption of a wider range of cultural products, that consumption is not simply evidence of a homogenous desire for the "exotic" but is informed by a range of factors—in this case, racial politics. Against this background, I examine black cultural nationalism in the United States and the use of African material and symbolic culture in that nationalism. I end the chapter by considering Ghana's intellectual property protection of folklore in relation to this range of appropriating practices and the politics underpinning them.

Media, Culture, and Imagined Communities

Most of the ethnic groups that currently make up Ghana were linked by trade and migration prior to their merger as one nation. Several of those ethnic groups also shared the experience of Asante dominance during the peak of the Asante federation in the early and mid-nineteenth century.[10] However, it was British colonization that provided the impetus for these groups'

unification (along with the remnants of the Asante state) in the nationalist struggle that led, in 1957, to the creation of the modern nation-state of
Ghana out of the British colony of the Gold Coast. The arbitrariness of the
country's boundaries, initially created in the nineteenth-century division
of the territory between France, Britain, and Germany in the infamous
Scramble for Africa (and later in the division of spoils after the First World
War) means that those boundaries cut through a number of those ethnic
groups instead of completely including and encompassing them.[11]

This history is one of the underpinnings of Benedict Anderson's "imagined communities" perspective that views nations like Ghana, proceeding
as they do from an "artificial" basis, as being constantly imagined and
reimagined in order to sustain the artifice.[12] Against this perspective, the
Ghanaian state's claim that ethnic cultures are first and foremost Ghanaian cultures can be seen as part of the work of imagining the nation and
therefore perfectly legitimate. It is also given legitimacy by the widely accepted
view that culture is essential to establishing a nation. The ways in which
Ghana has used culture in building the nation may be challenged (following Fanon) as reflecting more of a nativist trend that seeks to artificially
preserve "tradition" rather than as an organically emerging culture that
reflects the concrete struggles of the people.[13] However, the premise that
culture—whether nativist and bourgeois or organic and revolutionary—is
essential to nation-building is generally unquestioned. Culture does not play
a major role in Anderson's discussion of the nation, however, except in the
forms of language and modern mass media. Following Anderson's framework, in Africa the nation is simply a template applied in prescribed ways:
a territory is colonized, an elite emerges from the educational system established by the colonizers, and the "power-language" acquired in the course
of that education becomes a key element in imagining the nation and wag-
ing the political struggle that converts colonies into modern nation-states.

Where the territory is multiethnic (and therefore multilingual) with limited access to Western forms of education and literacy, the electronic media
become central to disseminating the idea of the nation. Anderson's account
has been criticized for its Eurocentrism and its emphasis on literacy.[14] It also
privileges modern mass media over other modes of meaning-making and, in
the Ghanaian case, attenuates the history of nationalism. By some accounts,
nationalist thought did not emerge in the Gold Coast in the twentieth century when British colonization became an established fact, but a century
before that, as British interest in the territory began to take shape.[15] While the
print media were an important resource, indigenous cultural symbols and

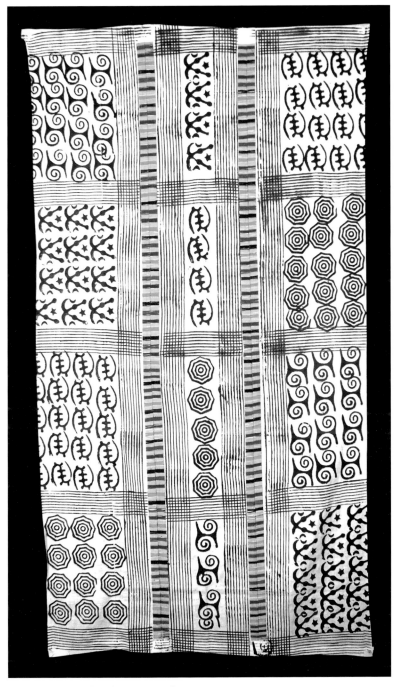

Plate 1. Adinkra cloth with *nhwemu* stitching.

Plate 2. Kente cloth in *aberewa ben* design.

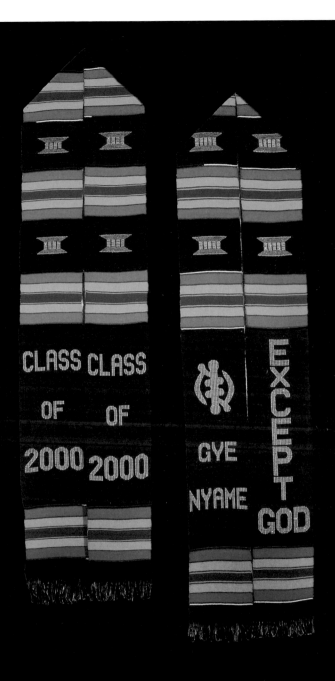

Plate 3. Kente stoles.

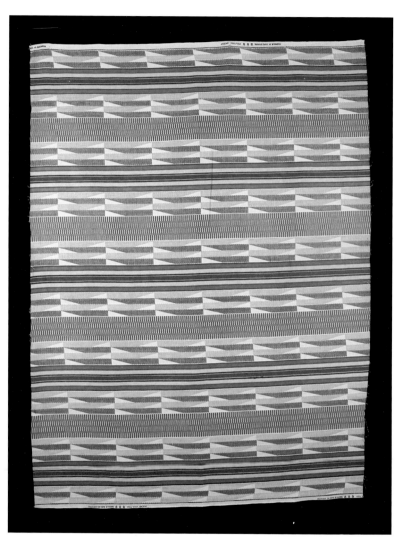

Plate 4. Mass-produced imitation kente cloth.

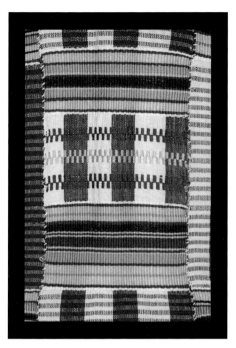

Plate 5a. Detail of handwoven kente cloth showing texture and stitching.

Plate 5b. Detail of mass-produced imitation kente cloth.

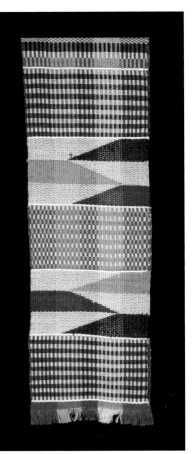

Plate 5c. Detail of handwoven kente cloth in *Oyokoman adwenasa* design.

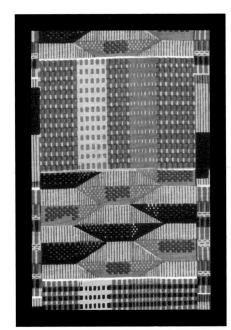

Plate 5d. Detail of mass-produced imitation of *Oyokoman adwenasa*.

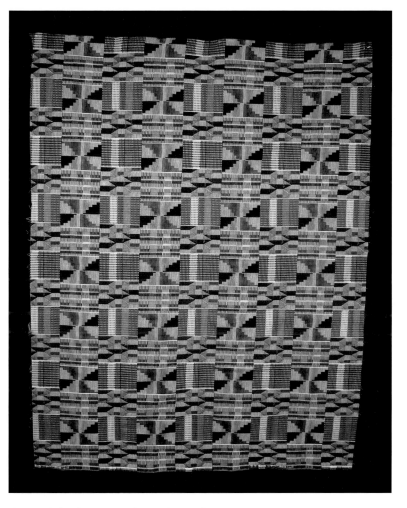

Plate 6. "Abidjan kente" in *Oyokoman adwenasa* design.

Plate 7a. Ethnic fabric purchased in the United States, featuring *Gye Nyame* adinkra design.

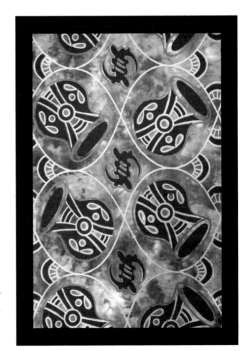

Plate 7b. Ethnic fabric purchased in the United States, featuring *Gye Nyame* adinkra design.

systems were also important to imagining Ghana in the twentieth-century phase of nationalist struggle when the electronic media were still controlled by the colonial authorities.[16]

The imagined communities thesis can also lead to an emphasis on fragmentation as an ever-present danger in African nations. While this view is bolstered by ethnic conflicts from the Biafran War in Nigeria in the 1970s to the Rwandan genocide in 1994 to the postelectoral upheaval in Kenya in 2008, it obscures other realities. Ethnicity and nationality in Africa do not always represent competing affiliations. Rather, as the Ghanaian case shows, they are sources of identification that are given more or less emphasis—separately or jointly—depending on the context and the claims being made.[17] Similarly, the Ghanaian state emphasizes multiethnicity in some spheres and national unity in others. Against this background, the emphasis on national culture in Ghana's copyright protection of folklore is not necessarily an imperative, as the imagined communities perspective might suggest, but a strategic choice.

In the following section, I outline Asante and Ghanaian nationalisms and their attendant processes of cultural appropriation. These two nationalisms cannot be equated, since in the case of Asante, the nation concerned was not an example of the modern form but was rather the nucleus of a federation that, at its peak, was imperial in its power and modes of governance. However, culture was very deliberately deployed in creating the nation at the core of that empire. Asante was not only a political system but a set of cultural symbols and myths that provided a point of identification for the Asante people. The nation that was constructed using those symbols remains to the present as both an ethnic group and a political unit within Ghana, and members of the ethnic group continue to refer to Asante as a nation or state—"Asanteman." This is the term, for example, that Akua Afriyie, the female kente weaver in chapter 2, used when she stated that she wanted her entry into the profession to be seen as an important symbolic act. Asante nationalism in this discussion is also different from the twentieth-century movement that briefly resisted incorporation into Ghanaian nationalism.[18]

Nationalism and Cycles of Appropriation, from Ghana to Asante to Ghana

Akan culture played an important role in imagining the nation of Ghana, and different elements of Akan society and culture were important to the conversion of the British colony of the Gold Coast into the independent nation of Ghana and the project of maintaining that nation as an integral whole. (The Akan are the largest ethnic group in Ghana and include the Asante, Fante, Akyem, Akuapem, and Kwahu subgroups). Some of this use of Akan social and cultural forms was initiated by the British as they modified local institutions to suit their own ends.[19] For example, a number of ethnic groups that were led by priests were required by the British to adopt the Akan system of rule by "chiefs" or kings. This meant that when independent Ghana recognized the institution of "chieftaincy" as a legitimate means of indigenous governance, that institution had, in several instances, been previously shaped into an Akan norm during British rule.

The name "Ghana," a key rallying point for nationalist consciousness in the anticolonial struggle, was chosen by the nationalist leader J. B. Danquah because of the purported links between the ancient West African kingdom of that name and the Akan people.[20] The significant gold deposits that gave the colony its name also gave it an additional important feature in common with ancient Ghana, which was reputed to have been very wealthy. If the name "Ghana" functioned ever so vaguely as a symbolic continuation of Akan hegemony in the territory, it also referred to a society that was distant enough in time and place to be more acceptable than any allusions to more immediate and potentially divisive Akan political groups, particularly Asante. In an interesting parallel with Afrocentrist thought and practice that focus more on past African kingdoms than on contemporary African societies or ethnic groups, the Ga, Ewe, Dagomba, and other subjects of the British Empire in the colony of the Gold Coast all came to embrace the geographically and historically distant kingdom of Ghana as their heritage.[21] While indexing a specific wealthy and powerful kingdom, the symbol "Ghana" was also open to the new meanings with which nationalist leaders imbued it in imagining not just any nation but an exemplary one.

As the preeminent Akan subgroup within the territory, Asante was an important repository of the Akan culture that served to imagine the new nation of Ghana. Akan culture, as exemplified by Asante, was not only ethnic, however, but also political. It was partly the result of practices of appropriation that converted products from various sources into Asante culture. Adinkra and kente, for example, were introduced into Asante along with other arts through a combination of conquest, migration, and settlement.[22] A key factor in these forms of cultural production becoming Asante was a deliberate policy of royal patronage as craft communities sprang up around Kumasi, the Asante capital, partly with the purpose of serving the palace.

As noted in the Introduction, initially, adinkra and kente were produced exclusively for the Asantehene. Thus they quickly gained an association not only with Asante in general but also specifically with the seat of Asante power. Ties to the palace were further formalized as specific groups and individuals were designated as producers for the king. In the royal monopoly of adinkra and kente, appropriation was buttressed by deliberate policy that made the Asantehene the effective owner of these cultural products. This history shows that cultural goods like adinkra and kente were *made* Asante rather than being inherently Asante. In addition to building a kingdom based on military and economic power, therefore, Asante leaders also established a set of cultural symbols that underscored their wealth and power and, as the royal monopoly was relaxed, the cultural distinctiveness of the Asante nation. Even as Asante diminished in economic and political influence, until its defeat by Britain and eventual incorporation into the nation of Ghana, it remained a site of cultural distinction.

Despite the emphasis on Akan culture in imagining modern Ghana, the Ghanaian state has often paid attention to ethnic diversity in crafting a national culture. For example, the national dance company's repertoire includes dances from the country's major ethnic groups.[23] This recognition is important for countering what is often seen as continuing Akan hegemony. Indeed, if there is one compelling argument to be made for treating ethnic culture as national culture under intellectual property law, it is that under this set of arrangements, when it comes to the ability to claim royalties for their cultural production, all ethnicities are equally dispossessed. When no such claims are involved, the state recognizes multiethnicity. At the symbolic level, therefore, the state can claim adinkra and kente as Ghanaian without challenging their status as Asante.

Indigenous textiles and clothing were crucial to the postindependence project of building a culture that could be the focus of national identity. Kwame Nkrumah, the country's first prime minister, used the clothing of different ethnic groups both as a unifying symbol during the nationalist struggle and a marker of pride in Ghanaian identity after independence. One of the most famous photographs of Nkrumah was taken on the eve of Ghanaian independence and shows him standing with other members of the Big Six clothed in the smocks of the people of northern Ghana.[24] This part of Ghana lacked the mineral and agricultural resources of the forest zones to the south, and its people had been marginalized and exploited before and during colonization. Wearing clothing from this area on possibly the most important night of their political careers underscored the inclusiveness that had led to the mass appeal and success of Nkrumah, the "Big Six," and their Convention People's Party.

In the years that followed, Nkrumah and other Ghanaian dignitaries frequently made it a point to depart from Western norms on state occasions by wearing kente, particularly *Asante* kente—the clothing of the country's most powerful indigenous leaders.[25] Notes on dress code in formal state invitations listed "evening dress" and "traditional attire" as equivalent options.[26] This practice went beyond national limits, and from the outset of the country's independence, Ghanaian dignitaries wore kente in major international venues, including the United Nations General Assembly. When Ghana followed the example of other countries in presenting gifts of material culture for display at the U.N. headquarters, its gifts were in the form of kente cloth.[27]

Kente, the royal cloth of the Asante, was therefore very quickly established as the royal cloth of Ghana. Given its connection with mourning, adinkra cloth was worn much less frequently. However, adinkra *symbols* were widely used to signal not just Asante but also Ghanaian values—and more. The country's oldest university, the University of Ghana, for example, has the adinkra symbol for strength, *dweninimen*, in its crest, and Ghanaian Christians have appropriated the most well-known adinkra symbol, Gye Nyame, referring to the power of God, as a symbol of their faith. One striking example of this is the Ridge Church, in Accra, an Anglican church that has a large Gye Nyame symbol in its altar.[28] The linguist's staff, another important element of Akan culture, was also incorporated into Ghana's state insignia. The linguist, in Akan society, mediates in communication between the king and the people and carries a staff of office with a carved figure at the top.[29] That carved figure has a symbolic meaning, and possibly the most well known is *sankofa*, which also appears in the adinkra symbolic system. The figure is a bird with its head turned so that it looks over its back, symbolizing the value of returning to the past to retrieve what has been forgotten.

Against the background of this history, the use of indigenous culture in establishing the modern nation of Ghana can be seen not only as an essential part of the task of building a modern nation-state but also as repeating the appropriating practices by which products like adinkra and kente became Asante. These products' longstanding conversion into Asante culture through deliberate policy has resulted in their status as Asante being taken as given. Half a century after independence, their status as Ghanaian culture is also widely accepted. This conversion of ethnic culture into national culture is reinforced by the principle of state ownership in the intellectual property protection of folklore.

Through a combination of deliberate policy and longstanding practices of appropriation by state, groups, and individuals, therefore, adinkra and kente are now generally regarded as being both Asante and Ghanaian, and Asante officials and Ghanaian state representatives collaborate in the state's custodianship of kente (though not in the state's legal ownership via intellectual property law). The artificial basis of these products' incorporation into Asante and Ghanaian culture comes to the fore, however, in the face of questions about formal ownership rights raised by their legal protection. As the following section shows, the comments of adinkra and kente makers and other Ghanaian artists both challenge and confirm the nationalist projects by which these products have become Asante and Ghanaian.

Taking Snuff by the Seashore

Cloth producers in adinkra- and kente-producing communities in Asante varied in their identification of the rightful "owners" of their cloth. Specifically, they were asked to whom their tradition of cloth production belonged and who should have the right to give or withhold permission to produce or reproduce it. In some cases, they mentioned their community; in some cases, the Asante ethnic group or state; in others, the Asantehene—the latter especially in the case of those who produced his cloth. Some cloth producers pointed to two or more of these in combination. Few identified Ghana as the owner of the rights to the craft, and the most vehement rejection of this possibility came from kente weaver Kwabena:

> No! No! It is not Ghana's kente; those who write the history of kente, if they do not mention Bonwire then I don't see . . . it is like someone who . . . is standing at the seashore and taking snuff [a useless venture]. You are talking about kente, which kente? Say Asante kente, Bonwire kente. Even if you say Asante kente, you have said nothing. *Bonwire,* Asante Bonwire kente. That's when you will have said something![30]

Kwabena supported this view by contrasting the poor infrastructure of his town, Bonwire, with its value to the national government as a source of tourist revenue:

> Look at our road that goes from here to Ejisu, just two miles, [it] is still there, in its old, untarred state. This town is a town that gives the Ghana government great revenue; it is no joke![31]

For Kwabena, the lack of amenities like roads and safe drinking water showed that the state had consistently proved (through several different governments) that it was an untrustworthy custodian of his community's interests and could not be trusted with ownership rights over kente. He also protested strongly any notion that kente might have originated among the Ewe people. He marshaled the support of a prominent Ghanaian musician, Ephraim Amu, in making this argument, pointing to a famous Amu song in which the composer marvels at the skill of "Asante Bonwire kente" weavers. If kente weaving originally came from the Ewe, Kwabena argued, how was it that an Ewe composer had written a song praising not weavers of his own ethnic group but those of Bonwire in Asante? He added that the distinction between the two kinds of kente must be maintained in any copyright arrangements.[32] Occasionally, this rivalry between the two ethnic groups as originators of kente weaving becomes a national issue, as evident in a 1999 letter to the editor in *The Daily Graphic*, Ghana's leading newspaper. The writer discussed a recent rise in competing claims of the two ethnic groups as originators of kente and offered a solution: kente was in fact Dangbe, and Ewes and Asantes would do well to follow the Dangbe people's modesty in not pressing any claims to the textiles.

Akua Afriyie, the female kente weaver referred to earlier, seemed to endorse the Ghana nationalist view when she told the story of some young Ewe weavers who wove kente in the Asante style and brought it to the place where she worked, hoping to sell their cloth there. She said that she and other weavers at the center had shown the young men how to improve the quality of their cloth. When asked why they had done this—whether they minded that the Ewe weavers had produced Asante cloth—she said "No, after all, we're all in Ghana."[33] This attitude on the part of Afriyie and her colleagues is perhaps not surprising given that they worked outside the traditional weaving sites, and as discussed in chapter 2, Afriyie herself had crossed one divide—gender—in order to become a weaver. However, one well-known weaver at the Asante kente weaving center of Bonwire is Ewe and weaves in both traditions, suggesting the possibility of both interethnic sharing *and* rivalry within weaving communities.[34]

Then there is the ambivalence of adinkra maker Kwame, who had migrated to the Ghanaian capital, Accra, from the adinkra-producing community of Ntonso and made adinkra cloth in Accra. As noted in chapter 3, Kwame seemed to support the principle of government custodianship on behalf of the people of Ghana; however, he did so with a certain resignation and even cynicism. When asked whether copyright permission should be sought from his hometown, Ntonso, or the people of Ghana in order to use adinkra designs, Kwame said, "The people of Ghana." But then he added,

"And the compensation too . . . when it goes to the government, even those of us to whom it belongs, they won't give to us."[35]

Even though he chose the people and state of Ghana over Ntonso as the owners of the rights to adinkra designs, Kwame also distinguished between the state as the entity to manage royalty collection and the actual owners of such royalties. His identification of the people and state of Ghana as the owners of adinkra therefore seemed to be based not on what he thought should happen but on what he considered inevitable—the state collecting and keeping royalties that really belonged to adinkra makers. His initial response seemed to contradict Kwabena's outright rejection of the state, but his conclusion was the same: the state could not be counted on to share royalties from cultural producers with those producing it.

These views were dismissed much later by the executive secretary of the National Folklore Board, which administers the folklore provisions of the copyright law.[36] He was of the opinion that the national benefits from the revenue generated from state ownership of adinkra and kente outweighed individual community interests. He added that the poor state of Bonwire's infrastructure was partly the fault of community members who had failed to invest the wealth they gained from kente to provide themselves with the basic services that weavers like Kwabena considered to be the responsibility of the national government. In this, he appeared to endorse the view discussed in chapter 3, that community efforts are an important basis for development. However, the view that local folklore-producing communities (and individuals) must benefit from state ownership is not limited to a few cloth producers. One scholar refers to state ownership of folklore as a "folkloric copyright tax," and this is the general view of a section of the musicians' lobby, which has adopted this language of taxation.[37]

Another source of contestation is the town or community that can claim to be the source of folklore. As Kwabena's words show, for some, kente is not only Asante but specifically from Bonwire. There is considerable basis for this claim—Bonwire is the official source of the Asantehene's kente, particularly kente woven in the vivid colors associated with Asante kente. In the myth of the brothers who "discovered" kente, those brothers were from Bonwire, and the head of the king's weavers has traditionally been appointed from that town. Bonwire is also promoted as the center of kente production by the Ghanaian state in its official tourist literature. These factors have combined to produce Bonwire in the popular imagination as the center of Asante kente production, bolstering Kwabena's claim.

This status is contested, however, as evident in comments from weavers at the neighboring community of Adanwomase, which has been granted the formal status of the source of the Asantehene's white kente (kente woven in the original color scheme of white and indigo). A weaver at this town, Nana Ntiamoah Mensah, claimed to have been one of the weavers for a previous Asantehene, Nana Agyeman Prempeh II, and was of the view that the designation of the town as the source of the king's white kente obscured the real history of kente weaving: that Adanwomase and not Bonwire is the actual source of kente weaving, and weavers at Adanwomase have, in the past, produced the full range of kente for the king.[38] The official view from the palace, however, is that Adanwomase is the source of white kente and Bonwire the source of "silk" kente (named for the silk yarns that changed the color palette of Asante kente weaving).[39] This recognition of Adanwomase alongside Bonwire has the potential for defusing the tension over competing claims, but as the words of some Adanwomase weavers show, the rivalry remains.

In yet another set of views, and perhaps unsurprisingly, formally designated producers of the Asantehene's cloth saw the latter as the person in whom rights to adinkra and kente should reside. Officially, the palace makes no such claims and, as noted earlier, works with the state in treating such folklore as national heritage. Despite this official stance, the views of people like the Oyokomaahene and the Asokwa adinkra makers must be taken into consideration as another source of contested ownership claims. While these cloth producers identified the Asantehene as the rightful owner of adinkra and kente, these views are properly interpreted as claims for Asante state ownership. As noted by the Oyokomaahene, the Asantehene's kente "is woven around the seat [of office]."[40] Cloth producers' identification of the Asantehene as the holder of the rights to adinkra and kente can therefore be seen as analogous to the arrangements under copyright law whereby the law invests the rights to folklore in the president of Ghana—the symbolic representative of the state of Ghana.

State ownership of folklore is contradicted not only by adinkra and kente producers on the basis of communal and ethnic identity but also by some Ghanaians on the basis of citizenship. Some Ghanaians have challenged Asante claims over adinkra, in particular. Two respondents who expressed such views were women, one a textile artist and the other a jeweler, both based in Accra. They use adinkra designs in their work, and both expressed the view that as Ghanaians, they should be entitled to do so without paying royalties. Akosua, the textile artist stated,

I feel that if I am a Ghanaian and I'm using adinkra designs and what not, I don't think it should be copyrighted. . . . I don't think so, I don't think the government should come out and say we have to come and pay some money for using . . . after all, it's for all of us, it's not for one person. And even . . . when you really think about it, adinkra doesn't belong to us. You know that? Adinkra really came from Abidjan.[41]

A jeweler named Mansah, making a similar point, challenged not only state ownership but also Asante ownership, saying,

If we have to really nitpick, the adinkra symbols didn't come from the Ashantis, [they] came from the Ivorians. . . . I would think of the adinkra symbol as Ghanaian, and not Ashanti or Akan.[42]

She pointed to several adinkra symbols, which, she said, had been appropriated from other ethnic groups, thereby weakening any Asante claims of ownership. Interestingly, these respondents' insistence on claiming adinkra designs as a right of citizenship demonstrates the success of Ghanaian cultural nationalism. This is evident in the following statement by Mansah:

I wouldn't buy from [a] foreigner selling adinkra symbols, I never would. I wouldn't patronize anything like that from any other person other than a Ghanaian. So if I found something in America being done by . . . adinkra symbol being done by some American firm, I would never buy it, I would never patronize it. Because I think that it's the Ghanaian's identity, it's part of us. It shouldn't be done by anybody, I mean, nobody else should be making money out of it but us. That's how I feel about it, I'm sorry![43]

In these comments, Mansah expressed not only a strong sense of personal identity as a Ghanaian but also a sense of holding that identity in common with others—"It's part of *us*"—in the same way that Akosua asserted that adinkra symbols were "for all of *us.*" When it came to the use of cultural symbols that are strongly associated with the Asante ethnic group, national identity was an important basis for rejecting any ethnicity-based claims of ownership. Since neither of these artists were Asante, Ghanaian identity was, for them, a far more effective basis than ethnic identity for making claims over adinkra designs. It is also striking that Mansah asserted her Ghanaian identity against others and rejected the appropriation of "Ghanaian" culture by non-Ghanaians almost as a matter of civic duty. Contrary to the law, she made a very clear distinction between the use of adinkra designs by Ghanaians and by foreigners.[44] In her view, Ghanaians could use adinkra as a right of citizenship, while such use by foreigners was illegitimate. Given her reference to the origins of adinkra in the Ivory Coast, "foreigners" here must be understood as those who are so far from Ghana and the Ivory Coast that they cannot lay claim to adinkra on the basis of ethnicity or nationality.

These views align Ghanaian cultural producers like Mansah and Akosua both *with* and *against* the position reflected in the copyright law. They agree that indigenous culture is Ghanaian first and ethnic second. However, when state custodianship of such culture threatens what they perceive as their rights of access, they point to the tenuous basis of Ghana's claims over forms of culture that can also be claimed by neighboring countries. If Ghana's project of promoting ethnic culture as national culture has been successful, therefore, this does not necessarily translate into citizens' acceptance of the principle of state ownership of national culture. Some artists who draw on design sources like adinkra in their work are quick to point out that, strictly speaking, adinkra cannot be identified with either a particular ethnic group or with the nation of Ghana. The likelihood of competing claims from the Ivory Coast over adinkra is minimal but serves as a useful basis for contestation.[45] While affirming the status of such culture as Ghanaian, Mansah and Akosua use the Ivory Coast argument to reject the use of that status in ways that restrict Ghanaian citizens' access to such culture.[46]

The views discussed here also show that in claims over adinkra and kente, at least, ethnicity is not always prior to national identity. At the same time, citizens' assertion of Ghanaian identity is no guarantee of agreement with the state over the regulation of "national" cultural products like adinkra and kente. In addition, as with other kinds of social identity, the relative importance of ethnic and national identities is highly contingent, as is the status of different cultural products as ethnic or national.[47] The views and practices of Africans in the diaspora are similar to those of Ghanaians like Mansah and Akosua. However, they factor somewhat differently into the issue of intellectual property protection of Ghanaian folklore. In the United States, while African Americans claim adinkra, kente, and other forms of African culture as theirs, the basis for those claims has little to do with state power. Further, it is their importance as a market that gives African Americans' claims over such culture their greatest implications for the protection of cultural products under Ghana's intellectual property law. I discuss these claims and their implications in the next section.

In discussing the African diaspora, it is important to note that this is not a unitary group but actually a number of different diasporas with the earliest created by the slave trade.[48] A more recent diaspora that dates back only to the second half of the twentieth century is made up of Africans who have migrated partly as a result of the contraction of many African economies under conditions of globalization. Among the members of this diaspora, culture is an important psychic resource in the face of alienation when class advantages and social networks at home fail to translate into advantages abroad.[49]

The means by which it is formed—through voluntary rather than enforced migration—means that this diaspora differs from the earlier one in its relation to the host state in its new location. Although both diasporas are the result of related historical processes, newer diasporas retain the hope, however illusory, of migration as a temporary rather than a permanent stage.[50] This tempers their relation to the host state in ways that are not possible for Africans in the older diaspora. For the latter group, culture is not just a source of psychological resistance to alienation but also a means of active political resistance to both alienation and dispossession. Because of my interest in the nationalist uses of African culture, my primary focus is on this older diaspora rather than newer, less overtly politicized ones.

A Fool Is Sold His Own Tomatoes

Africans in the diaspora have sought—in symbolic and material ways—to maintain their ties to their continent of origin ever since their forced transportation to the Americas. In different parts of the "New World," diasporic Africans have tried to preserve their religions, languages, and clothing. More direct physical links have included back-to-Africa migration movements since the United States' declaration of independence from Britain in the late eighteenth century as well as political and economic collaboration between Africans and African Americans in the African nationalist struggles of the first half of the twentieth century, black nationalist struggles in the United States in the 1960s, the antiapartheid struggle in South Africa in the 1980s and 1990s, and the economic summits instituted in the 1990s.[51]

In the United States, African textiles and aesthetic sensibilities have figured significantly in African Americans' expression of a unique cultural and political identity. In the race and class arrangements that existed in North America from the early 1600s to the mid-twentieth century, there was very little scope for transported Africans and their descendants to assert an overtly African identity.[52] Upon their arrival in America, slaves' African clothing was almost immediately replaced with Western. However, African Americans put their own imprint on Western clothing in a variety of ways, wearing it in unique color combinations or defiantly wearing clothes of a higher quality than those prescribed for people of their class.[53] Scholars have also noted the "African textile traditions, handed down and adapted by African American women, that helped to shape the appearance of the antebellum slave community."[54] Those traditions were evident in the use of color in the cloth these women wove and in the patterns of the quilts they made.

The open expression of an explicitly African identity through the use of clothing arises from much more recent developments: the civil rights movement, which reached its peak in the 1960s, and the militant black nationalism of the same period. The latter challenged not only the injustice of racism but also the Eurocentrism of mainstream U.S. society and the legitimacy of the U.S. state. In addition to its radical political platform, the black nationalist movement was striking in its use of African clothing and hairstyles to defy Eurocentric norms. During this period the US organization emerged as the result of a rift between its leader Ron Everett, a member of the Black Panthers, and other members of the Panthers.[55] Everett made cultural nationalism the hallmark of his group and established the principle of *Kawaida*, which "stressed that black liberation could not be achieved unless black people rejected the cultural values of the dominant society."[56] Members of US adopted African clothing and learned the "African" language, Swahili.[57] Everett also adopted the Swahili name Maulana Karenga and established the festival of Kwanzaa, based on African harvest festivals. Kwanzaa emphasized the *nguzo saba*, or seven core "African" principles: *umoja* (unity), *kujichagulia* (self-determination), *ujima* (collective work and responsibility), *ujamaa* (cooperative economics), *nia* (purpose), *kuumba* (creativity), and *imani* (faith).

The 1960s were also "the decade of Africa" during which many former colonies on the continent gained independence, while the period from the 1940s to the 1960s also saw the peak of the pan-African movement, which was led by figures from both continental and diasporic Africa. This movement was aimed not only at uniting Africans on the continent but also at linking their political goals with those of Africans in the diaspora.[58] Diasporic Africans like W. E. B. Du Bois and George Padmore were mentors to African nationalist leaders like Kwame Nkrumah, and when those leaders became the heads of independent nations, they served in turn as an inspiration to black nationalist and civil rights leaders in the United States. These political links helped to bring African material culture to the attention of a wider African American audience.

An additional and important factor in this awareness can be found in the journeys made to Africa by African Americans seeking to reconnect with their origins.[59] One prominent African American who was drawn to adinkra symbols through such a trip was Audre Lorde. In a visit to Ghana in 1974, the feminist poet and activist is reported to have been

> particularly fascinated with the adinkra cloth of the Asante: traditionally hand-stenciled symbolic designs were individually named and were proverbs encoding historical, allegorical or magical information. Many of the stamped messages were variations of phrases she remembered hearing from her mother and other Grenadian kin.[60]

This fascination led Lorde to incorporate an adinkra symbol for unity, *funtumfunafu denkyem*, and a *sankofa* symbol from a linguist's staff in the cover design of her collection of poems, *Between Ourselves*.[61]

Due to the connections forged by black political and cultural nationalism, pan-Africanism, and journeys to the continent, the African American community is an important market for continental African material culture. African American appropriation of products like adinkra and kente must also be understood as occurring within the larger context of cultural globalization in which capital expands through the commodification of a widening range of cultural goods. In the current phase of globalization, expanded and intensified communications networks and technologies make possible a greater volume of cultural flows than before.

In the case of the African American market, however, the circulation of African material culture is not solely due to the constant search for new instances of the exotic that can be turned into economically profitable goods in a global marketplace. It is mediated by the racial politics of consumption in the United States, where African American appropriation of adinkra, kente, and other African culture occurs within the context of black cultural nationalism rather than an undifferentiated consumerism. That nationalism may have lost much of its mid-twentieth-century political force, but it is still an important framework for examining African American uses of African culture in the context of cultural globalization.

While militant black nationalism was crushed by the U.S. government, Kwanzaa, the preeminent black cultural nationalist festival, gained widespread acceptance in the African American community and in mainstream U.S. society. Along with Kwanzaa, the official observance of Black History Month and the birthday of Martin Luther King Jr. have imprinted African American achievement and culture onto the annual calendar of the United States. The use of African material culture features prominently in the assertion of black identity on these occasions and makes the African American community an important market for such culture as well as a potential source of ownership claims.[62] Those claims are routinely made at the cultural levels of symbolism and identity, though not as yet at the legal level.

Although the core principles of Kwanzaa are expressed in Swahili, the celebration of the festival draws on African cultural sources well beyond East Africa. As a result, adinkra and kente have become important to this and other annual expressions of black identity in the United States, and although adinkra is not as well known in this market as kente and Malian bogolanfini (or "mud cloth"), it is valued for its symbolic system, and its motifs appear in greeting cards and jewelry designs. Where adinkra is reproduced in textile form for this market (often in the "ethnic" sections of fabric stores), it is usually in combination with other designs and color schemes that are quite different from those of both handmade cloth and imitations made in Ghana for the local market (see Plate 7).

In this regard, imitation adinkra varies from imitations of kente and bogolanfini, which are often found in versions that closely mimic the originals as well as versions that mix their motifs with other designs.[63] These fabrics are used for a variety of purposes, including clothing, accessories, toys, and soft furnishings targeted mainly at the African American community. An important section of the market is made up of African American quilters, who spent $40.3 million on fabric in 2001.[64] Such quilters reported that the fabrics they most frequently purchase are "African prints, batiks, and hand-dyed cloths."[65] This level of demand for African prints, which include the imitations and adaptations described previously, suggests that the overall African American market for adinkra, kente, and other African fabrics is quite large.

In its use of adinkra and kente and other African culture, the African American community presents yet another example of cultural appropriation for political purposes, but in this case, such appropriation is backed by power that is not institutionalized in state laws or policies. Rather, it has its origins in radical challenges to the state. As such, its power remains at an ideological level and derives considerable moral force from the widely acknowledged need to make up for centuries of systematic cultural dispossession. It therefore has more in common with appropriation as a subaltern act of subversion.[66] In this case, however, it is not the dominant culture that is appropriated from below and imbued with new meanings. What is appropriated, instead, is the "forgotten" culture of Africa, and cultural appropriation here becomes an act of both restitution and resistance to mainstream culture.

It is therefore not surprising that *sankofa*, the adinkra symbol for retrieving what has been forgotten, features prominently in African American culture.[67] At the same time, the state's creation of avenues for expressing black cultural identity (such as the institutionalization of Dr. Martin Luther King Jr.'s birthday as a national holiday and the less formal recognition of Kwanzaa) is also a means by which black cultural nationalism has gone mainstream and, as a result, is as much marketing opportunity as political action. As discussed in the following section, this creates avenues for appropriations that challenge Ghana's claims over folklore, particularly the ability to convert such claims into revenue through royalty payments.

Economic and Cultural Appropriation

The demand for African fabric in the African American market must be considered in relation to the average person being unaware that there is such a thing as handmade kente and adinkra cloth, as illustrated in the following anecdote. An African American vendor of African cultural goods told of a client who came into her store asking for kente. The vendor showed her a suitcase full of handwoven cloth, to which the client responded, "No, I want real kente." That "real kente" turned out to be factory-printed imitations.[68] There are some spheres in which handwoven kente is the norm, and the most common of these is in college graduations, where African American students wear kente stoles depicting the year of graduation. Some African American fashion designers and vendors of African prints also use and stock handmade cloth imported from the continent. However, the high overheads involved mean that such entrepreneurs are the exception rather than the norm.[69] As a result, most of the "African" textiles purchased by African Americans are imitations rather than handmade originals. The predominance of imitation African textiles in the African American market is alternatively disparaged, defended, or celebrated by different commentators.

In his study of African street vendors in New York City, for example, Paul Stoller notes these entrepreneurs' success in exploiting African American customers' ignorance about African textiles. Those entrepreneurs are supplied by equally enterprising textile manufacturing companies in East Asia— and more recently, Africa. Stoller reports and seems to echo the vendors' disdain for African Americans who are so easily duped into buying imitations in their search for "authentic" African cultural goods.[70] A wider range of responses is reported in Doran Ross's landmark volume *Wrapped in Pride*, about the use of kente in creating a distinct African American identity. Different contributors to the book in turn defend African Americans' use of "inauthentic" cloth, pointing to Ghanaians' own acceptance and use of imitation cloth; point to the limited opportunities for African Americans to learn about African culture and thereby become more discriminating in their purchase and use of African cloth; challenge the ownership claims of Ghanaian kente weavers who appropriate each other's designs; and celebrate the globalization of culture that makes authenticity claims irrelevant. Generally, these responses contrast the African American view of kente as "anything I want it to be" to Ghanaians' perception of it as a royal cloth.[71]

There is more than ignorance at play in the widespread acceptance of imitations of African cloth in the African American market—especially since those imitations are also accepted by continental Africans. "Authentic" handmade kente, for example, is very expensive and beyond the purchasing power of the average person—Ghanaian or American. The idea of authenticity itself also needs to be interrogated because it can function as a means of unduly setting up hierarchies of taste and, in effect, social status.[72] In the case of kente, there are the regimes of value set up by the Western art world and those that pertain among Ghanaians. The application of these frameworks in judging African American consumption practices is as important for what it reveals about the frameworks themselves as for what says of African American knowledge or ignorance.

For one thing, the frameworks of art collectors do not map onto those of Ghanaians or, for that matter, Asantes. As one kente weaver put it, "The Westerners like the old ones."[73] For a Western art collector (or anthropologist), earlier pieces of kente represent the best of the craft, and Stoller expresses this when he deplores the inferior quality of contemporary kente cloth.[74] It is certainly true that there is a lot of poorly woven kente on the market, and experienced weavers are well aware of this. One pointed out, for example, the practice of weaving cloth loosely in order to skimp on the amount of yarn used. Poorly woven cloth is not necessarily the norm on the part of all weavers, however, and weavers may save their best efforts for more discriminating clients who are willing to spend more on cloth. It is therefore still possible to obtain contemporary cloth of a high quality. Thus, for an Asante weaver, as for many Ghanaian consumers of handwoven kente cloth, antiquity does not necessarily translate into high value, and for them, the earlier pieces prized by collectors are merely "old."

This is not to say that Ghanaians never buy old pieces, since selling one's kente is a way of raising money in times of hardship. However, old kente seems to have most value for Ghanaians when it is acquired through inheritance. In such cases, the cloth is valued both for itself and for the relationship it symbolizes. Random pieces of old kente that do not represent a significant connection with the previous owner do not appear to be as highly valued and sought after by Ghanaians as they are by art collectors, and such kente tends not to be marketed to Ghanaians by weavers and kente dealers. Thus, while at the local level, ideas of value are bound up with the social context of use, collectors strip such social considerations away from aesthetics, and what a piece of cloth represents in the life of the person who wore it is secondary to the cloth's value as an exemplar of certain aesthetic principles and of generalized rather than specific social contexts. As a result of these differing regimes of value, the same piece of kente cloth can embody very different kinds of commodity and different kinds of cultural capital.

This distinction roughly corresponds to a key feature of the gift economy discussed by John Frow in his examination of scholarship that develops Marcel Mauss's concept of the gift.[75] For example, Frow notes, "The force of the gift . . . has to do with the transmission of qualities bound up with the person of the giver."[76] He further states, "Gifts are . . . not *objects* at all, but transactions and social relations."[77] It would be an oversimplification to characterize the circuits of kente acquisition and use in Ghana exclusively as those of a gift economy (rather than a commodity economy); besides, as Frow notes, it is mistaken to draw a sharp distinction between the two kinds of economy. However, the values guiding the circulation of old kente among Ghanaians, on the one hand, and among Western art collectors, on the other, can be distinguished by the ways in which they exhibit this aspect of a gift economy.

That there is such variation in the frameworks used to judge the value of kente cloth undermines any insistence that African Americans should adhere to them in their consumption of African culture. The changing nature of adinkra and kente as cloth makers have incorporated materials and design elements from different parts of the world also undermines any claims that these products are purely or authentically Asante, Ghanaian, or African. Under conditions of globalization in which cultural goods flow in a range of channels and according to values other than those determined by the art world and collectors, authenticity becomes a means of staking out and policing social boundaries.

Despite the problematic nature of authenticity claims, the attendant differences in kente use in the Ghanaian and diasporic markets have important implications for Ghanaian cloth producers. Those differences are evident in the systems of economic and cultural value within which those fabrics are purchased and used in the two markets. Ghanaians rank handmade kente with imitations in a hierarchy in which the handmade versions are reserved for special occasions and the mass-produced imitations used for more mundane purposes—such as street clothing, furnishing, and accessories. Despite the prohibitive cost of handmade kente, a Ghanaian, embedded in the local value system of cloth, is more likely to strive to acquire it as a symbol of status and wealth. For Ghanaians, therefore, there are some purposes that the imitations cannot serve, and this helps to sustain local demand for handmade cloth.

Based on my personal observation and interaction with younger Ghanaians, the distinction between handwoven and mass-produced kente may be blurring, as imitations are increasingly used in settings where only handwoven cloth used to be acceptable. The real difference between the acceptance of imitation cloth in local and diasporic markets may therefore be the kind of revenue loss entailed. In the diaspora, that revenue amounts to scarce foreign exchange, while at home, the loss is in less valuable local currency. At the same time, the Ghana government's inclusion of key adinkra- and kente-producing communities on official tourist maps also means that cloth production in these communities is sustained by the their location in tourist networks.

When it comes to supplying the African American market, however, these communities are at a distinct disadvantage. Adinkra and kente makers are active in global markets, and in one small indication of this, each year kente weavers attract commissions for stoles to be used in black student graduation ceremonies around the United States.[78] Within both old and new African diasporas, there is also some demand for handmade cloth.[79] However, the pace and costs of adinkra and kente production do not match the level of demand. African American cultural appropriation is therefore sustained by business entities that are best able to operate in global markets and whose stake in the culture concerned—and its appropriation—is purely economic. This is where the distinction between economic and cultural appropriation is most useful. Even though the two are intrinsically bound up with each other, separating them helps one to examine more closely the component parts of cultural appropriation under conditions of globalization. While African American appropriation of African culture occurs as part of the project of asserting a distinct identity and expressing pride in that identity, the goods used in that project are supplied predominantly by parties that appropriate African culture for purely economic means.

There is a small portion of the African American community that is knowledgeable about African material culture and seeks to promote African-made versions of such culture. The vendor quoted earlier has described it as the "cultural community,"[80] and it includes vendors of Afrocentric products who import their wares from Africa as well as teachers of African culture—including religions and arts. This group also includes African American fashion designers and artists who draw on adinkra and kente and other icons and products of African culture in their work. It was a member of this cultural community who responded to Ghana's copyright protection of adinkra and kente with the words, "A fool is sold his own tomatoes."

For many of these members of the African American cultural community, their relationship with Africa goes beyond the level of symbolism into concrete economic and political relationships. However, the high costs of doing business with African artisans undermine the best efforts of those African American entrepreneurs who seek to translate their symbolic affinity with the continent into economic collaboration.[81] This means that there are practical limits to meeting the demand for African culture with goods produced by African artisans. At this point, the ability to operate in global markets becomes the most important determinant of supply and opens up very lucrative opportunities for players who appropriate African culture for purely economic reasons.

Nationalist Visions and Global Markets

An examination of the processes by which cultural products become associated with specific groups helps to destabilize the view of such products as naturally occurring within a particular group. While it is true that many cultural practices and products within Ghana may have originated within the ethnic groups with which they are associated, this is not universally the case, and the Asante example helps to keep in view the fact that cultures are not necessarily "natural" in origin but also political. In assessing different claims over culture, therefore, it is important to consider not only the origins of culture but also how claims over culture translate into different kinds of power. The question then becomes not who owns or should own adinkra or kente, but what are the political stakes behind claims over adinkra and kente, and what are the political implications of assigning ownership.

The privileged status of the modern nation-state as a mode of social and political organization means that national claims over local and indigenous culture can easily gain preeminence, especially when the nation concerned is established by people who are indigenous to a territory rather than by foreign settlers. The figure of the nation as imagined community further helps to justify national measures that focus on cultural cohesiveness by evoking the danger of fragmentation even when citizens' acceptance and assertion of national identity suggests a high degree of cohesion. These factors help to obscure the fact that treating local and indigenous culture as national can constitute an act of appropriation as problematic as any such acts by groups and individuals from outside the communities concerned, especially when such appropriation is backed by intellectual property law.

The comments of Ghanaian artists like Akosua and Mansah, and especially of cloth producers, concerning ownership of the rights to adinkra and kente and other folklore serve to highlight these problems. They also show that Ghana is not only what the state says it is but also what Ghanaians say it is, and a key problem with the treatment of indigenous culture as national cultural property is that it fails to engage seriously or creatively with this fact. While the state's cultural policy in this area suggests a unified imagined community, Ghanaians' perceptions show that it is more accurate to speak of "national imaginaries" or "the multiple and often contradictory layers and fragments of ideology that underlie continually shifting notions of any given nation."[82] In practice, it is unlikely that artists like Mansah and Akosua will be penalized by national authorities for their appropriation of adinkra designs in their work.[83] In principle, however, their use of these elements of national culture is rendered subversive, while the groups and individuals whose work sustains that culture are effectively legislated out of the picture, as discussed in the previous two chapters. The power of the state therefore trumps that of citizens in claims over national culture except when, as in the case of musicians, citizens are able to assert themselves effectively against the state.

In the case of African American appropriation of African culture, again, it is unlikely that this will encounter any challenges from the Ghanaian state—partly because of the incontrovertible moral power behind such appropriation and also, quite simply, because of the national scope of the law. In addition, recent Ghanaian policies seek to capitalize on diasporic interest in the country and therefore encourage claims of cultural connections between diasporic and continental Africans—especially Ghanaians.[84] Diasporic claims over continental culture become an issue, however, when it comes to the question of who is best able to supply that culture. In the case of the African American market, despite the existence of entrepreneurs who are concerned with translating their symbolic connections with the continent into support for African cultural producers, the prime suppliers of "African" textiles for this market are Asian factories. It is with these suppliers that Ghana must contend in order to maximize its legal protection of adinkra and kente and translate African American demand for these forms of African culture into benefits for the national economy and for folklore producers. The challenge of doing so is the focus of the next chapter.

Chapter 5   **This Work Cannot Be Rushed**
Global Flows, Global Regulation

KENTE WEAVER KWABENA told the following story about an attempt to produce handwoven kente in the quantities needed to supply global markets:

> I remember once, Mandela, they say he went to America and he wore kente, he wore a kente jumper and wore it there. So when he got there the Americans were so happy and wanted some. A certain Ghanaian came and placed an order in Ghana. He waited for a large quantity to be made. This work, too, cannot be rushed. By the time he returned [to the States], some country had taken a picture and sent it, and the Abidjan people had made about three containers full and sent it there. His enterprise failed.[1]

Whether South African statesman Nelson Mandela was indeed responsible for a spike in U.S. demand for kente is uncertain. But Asante's story helps to reveal the challenges that adinkra and kente producers face in competing in the global economy. If identity-based claims over adinkra and kente are bound up with Asante, Ghanaian, and African American cultural nationalisms, the circulation of these fabrics and their designs beyond Ghana is linked with cultural and economic globalization. That circulation can be seen as an example of the cultural flows that some celebrate as bringing disparate parts of the world in closer contact with each other.[2] It also links adinkra and kente producers in "local" sites like Bonwire and Ntonso with global markets, highlighting the importance of paying attention to the local in discussions of globalization.[3] However, that same focus on the local shows that global cultural flows are uneven and do not equally benefit everyone. Asante cloth producers may be linked to the global economy through the tourism industry that brings part of those markets to their doorsteps and also through commissions from entrepreneurs who operate globally, but there are practical limits to their ability to participate in those markets.

Kwabena's story also provides another example of the impact of mass-manufacturing methods on cloth producers, especially given consumer acceptance of mass-produced imitations of handmade cloth. Where it is no longer important that adinkra and kente be hand-stenciled or handwoven in Asokwa or Bonwire, Asante, or even in the Republic of Ghana; where it no longer matters that they follow the aesthetic conventions of adinkra and kente designs, then they might as well be mass produced in India or Korea and their motifs combined with other markers of Africa, such as Malian bogolanfini designs. This is what has happened with adinkra and kente and countless other examples of indigenous cultural products ranging from textiles to music.[4] Their production has shifted from local communities to sites that can optimize labor and markets. Along with the loss of revenue to the original producers, there are changes in symbolic power and cultural expression. An adinkra symbol that means "unity" in Asante becomes, simply, "Africa" in its new context. While such changes in symbolism are an inevitable aspect of any dynamic culture and important to the working out of cultural identities, they also have significant economic ramifications.

In the case recounted by Kwabena, those exploiting the situation were "the Abidjan people," namely, entrepreneurs from the Ivory Coast, which was the initial source of mass-produced imitation kente in Ghana. It is also clear from the gendered nature of appropriation, discussed in chapter 2, that female Ghanaian cloth traders are perceived by some adinkra and kente producers as complicit in the production of "Abidjan cloth." Increasingly, however, the most effective producers of "African" cloth for global markets are not African at all but Asian. As noted in the Introduction, the November 1996 edition of the Ghanaian newspaper *Public Agenda* cited East Asian appropriations of kente cloth as part of the concern in protecting folklore under copyright law. If globalization brings different cultures together, therefore, it is not always in ways that can be universally celebrated. To some extent, globalization amplifies structural inequalities that have existed for centuries, and while it may provide some opportunities for local actors, it also widens the scope for exploiting them.

The appropriation of kente and adinkra for markets outside Ghana is partly due to the increased circulation of cultural goods in global markets. In the world-systems view, the world capitalist economy must constantly expand and does so by drawing ever-more products into its orbit. This helps to explain the increased appropriation and commodification of cultural products like adinkra and kente as well as their circulation in social and economic contexts beyond their original communities. Under these conditions, the norms of production that pertain within those communities become inadequate to the task of maintaining control over them. That control effectively passes into the hands of those with the capital necessary to appropriate and produce them for wider markets.

While the previous chapter focused on appropriation that occurs primarily for reasons pertaining to different kinds of cultural nationalism, appropriation also occurs for purely economic reasons, and this is the kind of appropriation under consideration here. Clearly, cultural and economic appropriation are closely interrelated, and both come into play when Ghanaian women commission imitation adinkra as part of their trading activities but, in doing so, provide cloth that serves important social and cultural uses. Similarly, African American use of imitation African cloth to express pride in a distinct African or black identity is often supplied by Asian factories seeking to maximize their profits in global markets.

Among the most important factors mediating in those markets are international regulations that have expanded to include intellectual property, most notably with the 1994 Agreement on Trade Related Aspects of Intellectual Property (TRIPS). Along with these developments, the North–South axes of global power have been modified with the emergence of what some have termed "the global East," reflecting China's economic ascendancy.[5] The structural inequalities that counteract the advantages of globalization have therefore also changed from their earlier patterns.

The question that arises, then, is how well nations like Ghana can intervene in global markets to regulate the appropriation of their culture. This question is especially important given the view that the nation is diminishing in relevance under current conditions of globalization. The advances in technology that enable the instant transmission of information have also made possible interactions across national boundaries that bypass national governments while facilitating the growth of transnational corporations whose economic strength is sometimes at par with or greater than that of several nations, particularly those in the Third World. These corporations' influence in shaping national and international policy has grown to unprecedented levels.[6] The repressive tendencies of some modern nations have also undermined their legitimacy as representing the best interests of all the peoples contained within their borders. The promise that global information technology networks offer disempowered minorities for transcending national constraints in their emancipation struggles is yet another reason for the discredited status of the nation under current conditions of globalization.[7]

Despite the rise of significant nonnational players in the global arena, nations still shape many of the circuits through which global flows occur. While local groups can also act transnationally to direct those flows, nations continue to be the privileged actors in regulating cultural and economic globalization.[8] The challenge for Ghana and nations in similar situations is gaining international recognition for the premise that products like traditional knowledge can and should be protected either by intellectual property regulation or through other internationally recognized regimes. That challenge is especially daunting given Ghana's position in an international regulatory context in which economic power has become an increasingly important prerequisite for effective participation.

In this chapter, I discuss some of the issues raised by the circulation of adinkra and kente in global markets. I first outline the context of economic globalization within which these and other forms of indigenous culture circulate. This is closely linked to *cultural* globalization, discussed in the previous chapter. However, separating these two forms from each other and from other dimensions of globalization helps to illuminate the processes of globalization within which the appropriation of adinkra and kente designs occurs. As discussed in chapter 4, some of those processes have to do with the politics of race in the United States, while others are the result of an expanding global economy that supplies the cultural goods used in such political projects. In that economy, however, identity-based claims are not always enough to secure control over cultural production. Ghana's task is therefore one of restoring the link between Ghanaian production sources and global markets or at least intervening in those markets in ways that reduce some of the losses caused by consumption practices that undermine the importance of people like adinkra and kente producers as sources of cultural goods for global markets.

I then provide a brief account of the nature of the international regulatory framework for intellectual property, the significant changes that have occurred in that framework over the past few decades, Ghana's position in that framework, and the country's prospects for regulating the appropriation of cultural products that it claims as national heritage. I also examine the ascendancy of China in global textile markets. While China is not the only producer of imitation adinkra and kente, its influence makes it a useful example for considering the challenges that Ghana faces in global markets. In addition to considering China's place in the global textile industry, I consider how this opens up an additional axis to that of North–South relations of power around appropriation: a South–South (or East–South) axis.

I end the chapter by considering what the Ghanaian case suggests about the place of the nation under conditions of globalization and the implications of that place for making claims over local and national cultures in international regulatory frameworks. I argue that rather than having become completely irrelevant, the nation is more or less important depending on location, history, and its relation to similarly situated nations and to marginalized groups within its borders. Nations also have privileged access to the international policymaking spheres that determine many of the channels through which globalization occurs. At the same time, current conditions of globalization mean that transnational links provide greater scope for effective activism that keeps nations like Ghana accountable to local constituents like adinkra and kente producers.

Economic Globalization and the Dislocation of Source and Supply

One of the most important and most discussed aspects of globalization is its economic dimension. The complexity of economic globalization means, however, that there is no agreement on what it is exactly, since views differ on how to analyze the current phase of globalization.[9] Some analyses focus on the rise of transnational corporations that operate in multiple locations and are therefore not as easily regulated through national economic policies. Along with this is the interconnection of major financial markets such that the shrinking credit supply in the United States, for example, compromises credit supply in all major markets.

While my focus here is on its economic aspects, I recognize that globalization cannot be reduced to one of its multiple dimensions (whether economic, cultural, or political) or to its recent history. I understand globalization to be the sum of several interrelated processes, well captured in Appadurai's framework of ethnic, media, technological, financial, and ideological landscapes.[10] Historically, I also follow the reasoning of scholars who trace the roots of contemporary globalization to the fifteenth century when European mercantile capitalism began to expand its reach around the world. Globalization since then has been closely linked both to the changing and expanding nature of capitalism as well as the widening networks of European political influence that have accompanied it.

Keeping both the history and inequities of globalization in mind serves as a check on the view that globalization is a new phenomenon or that it offers unlimited opportunities and equal benefits to all. Rather, it is a new, expanded, and intensified phase of a process that is at least four centuries old. This is the approach taken by world-systems theorists and is useful for understanding how globalization came about and the place of different players within it. In drawing on world-systems theory, however, I am aware of its dangers—particularly the risk of economic reductionism. The actions of women cloth traders in Ghana show that even in a restrictive world economic system, relatively marginal actors are able to create spaces of opportunity that cannot be explained solely in economic terms. I therefore consider useful those approaches that, while acknowledging the analytical value of world-systems theory, point to the importance of noneconomic factors and also to the unpredictable ways that different factors come together to shape national and local realities under conditions of globalization.[11]

Anchoring globalization in a broader historical framework is especially important for understanding the emergence of nations like Ghana, the world regions in which they are located, and their place in today's global economy. I therefore consider inadequate those frameworks that trace the history of globalization to European industrialization in the nineteenth century and the emergence in the same century of a network of nations linked by international institutions.[12] In both historical perspectives, however, it is clear that certain players have always had a greater capacity for shaping the global economy, while others have merely been integrated into that economy on terms set for them. While locating Ghana in the longer historical framework, I focus on the recent history of the country's experiences with economic globalization. The last thirty years have been particularly adverse economically for many Third World nations, especially in Africa. This period has also coincided with the drive to convert international intellectual property regulation into a predominantly economic issue.

For countries like Ghana, the ability to operate in the global economy is a function of the ways in which, and terms on which, they are integrated into that economy. Several commentators point to modes of economic production and global economic participation established through processes of colonization and empire.[13] A more recent structural factor shaping many Third World economies comprises policies instituted at the direction of the Bretton Woods institutions (the World Bank and the International Monetary Fund [IMF]). For the most part, these policies have constrained African countries' ability to shape their economies in ways that enable them to participate in the global economy on favorable terms.

Economist Thandika Mkandawire offers an extended analysis of the adverse effects of economic reform and structural adjustment policies that many African countries have been forced to implement at the direction of the World Bank and IMF. Under those policies, he argues, the economies of African countries have regressed rather than advanced. In some cases, those economies have gone back to their colonial forms as producers of primary products that are mostly uncompetitive in world markets rather than competing as producers of finished goods. As a result, "Ghana is back as the 'Gold Coast.'"[14] This regression is especially significant given Ghana's status in the late 1980s and early 1990s as a poster child for IMF-led economic reforms.[15]

Factors like political instability and failures of leadership cannot be discounted as additional causes of limited and even negative growth in many African economies. In half a century of independence, Ghana has had several military governments and is now in its fourth period of constitutional rule. The military regime that preceded the current constitutional order also provides an example of the interaction between internal and external factors, since it presided over the most intense and purportedly successful phase of IMF reforms in Ghana. It further suggests that the mode of governance is not, by itself, a key factor in determining the nature or success of economic policy—a fact that is also borne out by China's successful combination of communist rule and capitalist economic success.

Although the system of government may not be a predictor of economic success or failure, the abrupt entrance of military regimes and the equally abrupt shifts in vision and policy that they introduce translates into a dissipation of focus and energy in the project of building both a nation and a strong economy. Internal factors have therefore contributed to the weakened state of the economy in Ghana, as in many other African countries. However, external structural conditions have also constituted a major factor in shaping the nature and terms of Ghana's participation in the global economy. To ignore those conditions is to give credence to the ahistorical and self-serving view that social and economic problems in Africa are due to a kind of innate pathology.[16]

The specific ways in which Ghana experiences economic globalization mean that the circulation of cultural products like adinkra and kente in global markets does not necessarily translate into economic advantages for either the Ghanaian state or adinkra and kente producers. The intensified commodification of culture that is a feature of economic globalization transfers control of that culture from small, local, and indigenous producers to those with superior capital and mobility within global markets. This is both facilitated and accelerated by the technological advances of the last three decades that have made it possible to transmit any content (including cultural and economic information) around the globe instantaneously.

Under these conditions, identity-based authorship and ownership claims have little force. The supply of adinkra and kente is dislocated from these fabrics' original sites of production when consumers accept imitations produced by entrepreneurs in other locations. There is the real possibility that if such dislocation persists, those places of origin can start to become irrelevant. Extending the production knowledge and consumption knowledge framework offered by Appadurai, this is not only a matter of enterprising middlemen exploiting the distance between production and consumption knowledges.[17] Instead, the gap between those knowledges and the scale of external exploitation are such that the very sites of production knowledge are threatened.

This dislocation and the possibility that it could displace indigenous cultural producers in a globalized world is an important reason for mediating in the appropriation of products like adinkra and kente in global markets. Clearly, the concern to protect cultural integrity is another concern, and this is especially evident in Ghana's inclusion of kente in its new geographical indications law. As noted in chapter 1, such laws originated in Europe and prevent the name of a product that is specific to a particular region from being applied to similar products made in other locations. The premise is that the product's distinctiveness is diminished when its name is indiscriminately applied. In that respect, geographical indications laws preserve cultural integrity by maintaining the link between cultural goods and their communities of origin while also ensuring that producers in those communities can profit from the exclusive status of what they produce. They also retain the link between the material forms of distinctive cultural products and their names—a link that is severed in Ghana's copyright protection of adinkra and kente *designs* and not the specific material forms in which those designs are produced or appropriated.

The rupture of location of origin from supply that occurs with the large-scale appropriation of adinkra and kente for global markets not only threatens cultural integrity (to the extent that such integrity can be claimed) but also represents a dislocation from revenue. Despite the popularity of adinkra and kente and other African fabrics in the diaspora, that popularity means very little economic gain for countries such as Ghana, Mali, and the Ivory Coast when "their" adinkra, kente, bogolan, and korhogo cloth are appropriated for consumption in the diaspora by producers who are located thousands of miles from the continent. The widespread acceptance of imitations of these and other African fabrics means that the ability to operate effectively in global markets trumps identity-based claims in determining who profits from the global circulation of these products. In the case of handmade kente, identity-based claims of ownership may converge with the cloth supply to the advantage of cloth producers in local markets. As discussed in chapter 1, adinkra and kente producers' ability to position themselves as the keepers of a royal tradition is a key marketing strategy, and identity, in this case, becomes an important selling point. Such claims become almost irrelevant, however, when consumer acceptance of imitations translates into markets for the most effective rather than the most "authentic" supplier.

Against this background, Ghana's intellectual property protection of adinkra, kente, and other folklore can be seen as an attempt to reconcile this dislocation of identity from supply and from profit in global markets (although the state displaces cloth producers and their communities as the immediate beneficiaries of that reconciliation). Rather than seeking an outright ban on appropriation practices that harm the cultural integrity of Ghanaian folklore, the country claims a share in the profits that accrue from such appropriation. Intellectual property law thus becomes an additional means, along with tourism, by which cultural heritage is converted into an economic resource. If the heritage represented by imitation adinkra and kente is a somewhat diminished or diluted one, intellectual property law at least imposes a tax on that dilution. The fact that a few foreign artists, like singer Paul Simon, have paid royalties for the use of Ghanaian folklore is an indication of this economic potential.[18]

While the ability to profit from local cultural production is an important reason for protecting the latter as national folklore, such profit remains largely potential rather than actual. This is partly because local and indigenous cultural production is not recognized in international regulatory regimes as subject to intellectual property protection. Therefore, in addition to trying to reconcile the dislocation between supply and origin, the Ghanaian state must also regulate the activities of a range of actors who operate at different levels within the local and global economies and therefore within and outside the scope of national laws. The players whose impact is most directly felt by adinkra and kente producers are those who operate closest to home, such as the women traders discussed in chapter 2.

Those whose activities have the greatest implications for national revenue generation, however, are the Asian companies that produce for markets in the United States and other parts of the world. Effectively regulating the activities of these players presents Ghana with an uphill battle because it must act in a global economy in which it operates at a disadvantage due to the ravages of World Bank/IMF-led economic integration into the global economy and also due to changes in the international regulatory framework.[19] Those changes and their consequences for Third World nations are outlined in the next section.

The International Regulation of Intellectual Property

In the 1970s and 1980s, as information-based industries became increasingly important to the economies of major industrialized nations, those nations pressed for intellectual property to be regulated as part of international trade and outside the purview of the United Nations. The result of these efforts was the establishment of the TRIPS Agreement in 1994. It was drawn up in the context of the former General Agreement on Tariffs and Trade (GATT) that was replaced in 1995 by the World Trade Organization (WTO).[20] TRIPS represented the success of the industrialized nations in converting international intellectual property regulation into a trade issue.

Prior to this agreement, most international intellectual property conventions were administered by the World Intellectual Property Organization (WIPO). WIPO had its origins in the merger in 1893 of the offices administering the Paris Convention for the Protection of Industrial Property and the Berne Convention for the Protection of Literary and Artistic Works. The result of this merger was the United International Bureau for the Protection of Intellectual Property. The bureau became WIPO in 1970 and a specialized agency of the United Nations in 1974.[21]

The United Nations' system of decision making, which is based on the premise of equality among member-states, made WIPO a forum in which Third World nations could effectively pursue their interests because of their numerical strength.[22] One set of interests arising from such nations and also from indigenous peoples was the protection of local and indigenous cultural production. In 1982, in response to this concern, WIPO and UNESCO formulated the *Model Provisions for National Laws on Protection of Expressions of Folklore against Illicit Exploitation and Other Prejudicial Actions*. These provisions ran counter to the standard view in intellectual property law that folklore belonged in the public domain and was therefore free for the taking. The model provisions lent valuable support to the premise that such cultural products *should* be subject to protections similar to those afforded by intellectual property law to other kinds of cultural production. When Ghana decided in 1985 to include folklore among the works protected by copyright law, it was guided by the model conventions in a number of respects, for example, in the law's broad definition of folklore.

In a different set of developments, as computer technology developed and grew in importance, industrialized nations pressed for the inclusion of software in protected works. In contrast to works like folklore, software was successfully "shoehorned into the rubric of 'works of authorship,' which remains resolutely closed to so many collaborative manifestations of creativity."[23] Similar developments occurred at the urging of pharmaceutical and biotechnology industries that successfully advocated the patenting of genetic material.[24] While this pressure came from several industrialized nations, the United States was particularly influential. International and national intellectual property regimes have therefore come under different kinds of pressure in the last three decades and have changed as a result.

At the international level, however, those changes have mainly been in line with the interests of industrialized nations. Even as intellectual property law has gained in importance as a means of regulating global cultural flows, and even as concepts of intellectual property have expanded, the international regulatory sphere has remained rather hostile to certain kinds of claims—particularly those over local and indigenous cultural production. This is not only because of the difficulty of reconciling the different principles of authorship and alienability involved but also because such cultural production often originates in communities and countries whose bargaining power in international regulation is considerably curtailed.

The TRIPS Agreement signaled a watershed in the international policy-making framework for intellectual property. The agreement upholds the major conventions administered by WIPO but with some significant exceptions. For example, TRIPS does not uphold the provision in the Berne Convention that protects the "moral rights" of authors (the right of an author to have a say in how a work is used even after the economic rights to it have been transferred). TRIPS also upholds the expansion of intellectual property laws to include plant and animal material and computer software, while excluding the protection of local and indigenous cultural production. In doing so, it upholds the legitimacy of certain modes of cultural and knowledge production and not others. Most importantly, as an agreement of the WTO, and unlike the previous set of arrangements under WIPO, TRIPS is legally enforceable. This increases industrialized nations' ability to police the "pirating" of their cultural production while leaving much of the cultural production of Third World nations and indigenous peoples open to appropriation.

Another feature of TRIPS that is particularly significant for Third World nations has to do with the nature of decision making within the WTO. Unlike the relatively democratic one-nation-one-vote system used in the United Nations, decision making in the WTO is tied to economic power in a system of "linkage bargaining."[25] In this system, developing countries are granted certain concessions in international trade in exchange for consenting to agreements proposed by industrialized nations. It is important to note that this is not a one-way street, and Third World nations can also push for bargains that promote their interests in return for concessions. However, they bring much less to the table, especially in the case of African nations, and as a result, their ability to pursue their interests within the international regulatory framework is weaker than that of industrialized nations.

This disadvantaged position has not stopped Third World nations from pressing for their concerns within the international regulatory agenda. In this respect, WIPO is probably a more hospitable forum than WTO/TRIPS, and in 2004, the General Assembly of WIPO adopted a Development Agenda in response to a proposal put forward by Brazil and Argentina. Some of the proposals of this agenda are the creation of a standing committee on intellectual property and technology transfer and increased civil society participation in the activities of WIPO.[26] Despite resistance to the agenda from countries like the United States and the United Kingdom, the Development Agenda represents an important sign that Third World countries have gained some ground in introducing their priorities into an international regulatory framework that has worked to the advantage of industrialized nations in the WTO/TRIPS era.

In October 2009, at the urging of African and other Third World nations, WIPO's Intergovernmental Committee on Intellectual Property and Genetic Resources, Traditional Knowledge and Folklore also reached an agreement on traditional knowledge protection that could become the basis for an international legal instrument.[27] However, since WIPO has been effectively superseded by WTO/TRIPS, what really counts is what happens in the latter forum. Industrialized nations' acceptance of a development cycle (the Doha Development Round) in the discussions of the WTO promised to be a significant step, but the apparent failure of Doha seems to have borne out the skepticism of those commentators who doubted the value of this round for achieving any major gains for African nations.[28]

As a member of the WTO, Ghana is obliged to align its intellectual property laws with the provisions of TRIPS and, as noted in chapter 3, did so in a comprehensive legal reform process that began in the late 1990s and ended in 2005. While member nations are required to implement only the provisions of TRIPS, they may include additional provisions as long as these do not directly contravene TRIPS. Thus, Ghana also used the reform process to bring its intellectual property laws more in line with national priorities. As a result, folklore is still protected under the new laws even though TRIPS does not recognize such cultural production as intellectual property. In effect, the requirement to comply with TRIPS does not prevent individual WTO member states from using their national intellectual property laws to afford a wider range of protections than those within TRIPS, but only those national provisions that are upheld by TRIPS can be enforced internationally.

In order to use the WTO/TRIPS regime to intervene in the global economic appropriation of adinkra and kente, Ghana would need to seek reforms within TRIPS that recognized folklore and related forms of cultural production as intellectual property. This might seem perfectly reasonable given that TRIPS includes protections that did not exist in intellectual property regimes forty years ago, such as protection for plant and genetic material. The premise that such products should be subject to protection is widely contested on a number of grounds. These include the threat to the livelihoods and knowledge of farmers when they are pressured to use seed stocks produced, patented, and therefore monopolized, by large U.S.-based agricultural companies. Not only do these replace stocks that have been developed in farming communities over several generations and threaten the knowledge that they represent, but farmers are also banned from generating new stocks from those purchased from the agribusiness industry, thus ensuring their continued dependence on the latter.[29] Another set of arguments is based on the premise that patenting plant and human genetic material represents the ownership of life and is therefore morally reprehensible.[30]

Yet, as previously noted, these kinds of knowledge are protected within TRIPS, while local and indigenous knowledges, such as those included in Ghanaian folklore, are not. While philosophical arguments about the nature of authorship are adduced against the intellectual property protection of folklore, ultimately, the reasons that matter most, in practice, are economic and political. Countries and groups that seek protection for these kinds of knowledge are also countries and groups that have been historically disadvantaged internationally and whose goods and knowledges have long had the status of raw material. Even where such knowledge is produced in line with Western conventions, it is still often treated as raw material, a point made by African feminist scholar Obioma Nnaemeka in her discussion of the exploitation of African scholars' knowledge by Western "experts." Paulin

Hountondji makes the same point when he argues that African knowledge production is "exogenous."[31]

International intellectual property arrangements therefore operate to facilitate the extraction of that raw material while strictly policing Third World extraction of knowledges originating in the Global North in what James Boyle describes as "a one-way valve for property claims . . . [that] favors the developed countries, not entirely, but disproportionately."[32] The lack of recognition of alternative norms of authorship and ownership leads to a certain duplicity when traditional knowledge is denied protection on the basis of its presumed communal authorship and ownership while according legal protection to its appropriated versions.

Within the international regulatory order, Third World nations have been most effective when acting in regional or other groups. For example, the WIPO Intergovernmental Committee on Intellectual Property and Genetic Resources' 2009 agreement on traditional knowledge protection was reached with the leadership of the African *group* of nations rather than individual African countries acting in isolation. Under those circumstances, Ghana's best option for advancing its interests in this international intellectual property and trade environment is to place those interests on the agenda of such groups that have proved to be more effective than individual nations in challenging the international regulatory status quo.

It may also need to use the language of the current trade-focused environment to its advantage by making folklore protection more explicitly a trade issue rather than exclusively one of cultural heritage. There is some indication that the country has done this to a limited extent, such as in its use of the widely accepted premise of geographic indications protection to regulate the appropriation of kente. Bilateral trade agreements may also provide an even stronger means for achieving such regulation, and probably no country is more important here than China.

From Global North to Global East

The rise of China as a global economic power and China's dominant position in the global textile industry are two important factors in considering the possibilities for regulating the appropriation of Ghanaian folklore, particularly adinkra and kente, beyond Ghana. While imitation African textiles are produced in a number of Asian countries, China is often mentioned as a source of such imitations.[33] China is also seen as a challenge to mechanized textile production well beyond Ghana and has been viewed as a threat to the fabric and apparel industries of Western nations.[34] In 2000, the manager of a Ghanaian textile factory reported that his factory's production had been undermined by imports from China. Adinkra maker Kofi also reported in 1999 that he and other adinkra makers had gone from using cotton fabric produced in Ghanaian factories to using cotton imported from China. This dominance of Chinese textile products in the Ghanaian market has only increased and can be viewed as part of a wider phenomenon, that of the "Chinese 'Textile tsunami'" that has recently hit Africa.[35]

To the extent that China is a part of the global South, the economic appropriation of African textiles by Chinese factories has a South–South dimension. At the same time, China's place within the category of the South has long been contradictory. Although Western industrialized nations regard China as a part of the global South, some commentators argue that it is more accurate to view China as a new pole that shifts the center of global economic gravity from the "global North" to the "global East."[36] While China's economic power has only recently reached a scale that makes the limits of the category "South" apparent in relation to the North, it has long had the status of a superior economic power in relation to countries like Ghana.

The importance of Africa to China has gone through a number of shifts, however, reflecting changes in Chinese priorities and interests. In the post-Mao period of the 1980s, for example, China's sharply ideological stances against Western industrialized nations and Japan were replaced by more moderate positions in the interests of fostering economic growth. In this context, Africa was marginal to China's interests, and aid to the continent stagnated during that decade.[37] Interest in the continent increased again in the fallout after the Tiananmen Square crackdown of 1989, when African nations offered more "muted" responses than the expressions of outrage in much of the international community.[38]

With the rapid growth of China since the 1990s, Africa has become important to China not only as an ideological ally but also as a source of raw materials for the latter's industries.[39] This makes the relationship between the two more like a variation on the old North–South structures of domination, although in some contexts, China may strategically define itself as a developing nation. One such context is the United Nations Security Council, where China can claim leadership of the developing world. "If this image is to be sustained and carried off, Beijing feels compelled to maintain an active and visible interest in areas such as Africa, which act as a support constituency to add political and numerical back-up to China."[40]

It has been argued that while China's relations with Africa are somewhat exploitative and exhibit a certain degree of racism, they are less so than the region's relations with industrialized nations—particularly the United States. In its trading relations with Africa, it is claimed, more of China's investments benefit the continent than is the case with Western nations whose economic assistance is often "tied" such that much of the money pledged returns to the West to pay for goods and services. According to Sautman and Hairong, this means that 80 percent of U.S. aid is tied in this way, as is 90 percent of aid from Italy and 60 to 65 percent of aid from Canada.

The authors do not provide the statistics for China but claim that "PRC [People's Republic of China] aid to Africa, while not totally 'untied,' manages to attenuate any negative consequences to the donor."[41] Further, China's trade agreements with African nations are more permissive of technology transfer than is the case with Western nations.[42] Ultimately, however, China seems unlikely to differ significantly from the North in its extractive approach to African products—from primary products to knowledge. Indeed, one of the elements of "China's geo-economic strategy in Africa" is "to source knowledge workers in Africa to support Chinese economic transformation."[43]

Along with the shift from WIPO to TRIPS, therefore, China's economic rise means that while industrialized countries remain dominant in international intellectual property regulation, a new axis has opened up in the global economy. China's status as the "global East" has implications for nations at both ends of the old North–South divide. Its ideological distance from the North means that China's current economic importance does not automatically align it with the old power structures of Europe and North America. In the area of intellectual property law, China is often targeted as a threat to the cultural production of Western nations, particularly the United States. At the same time, while China has been ideologically close to Africa and the rest of the Third World in the past, and even though it identifies itself internationally as a developing nation, there is no guarantee that this will translate into advantages for the Third World. As a result, while Ghana must pursue its interests in a regulatory framework dominated by industrialized countries, mostly of the global North, it must also contend with a major economic force that confounds the North–South divide.

Given the differing histories and features of power relations along the axes of North–South and East–South, it is unlikely that strategies used by Third World nations with some success in the former axis will have much effect in the latter. Western industrialized nations' history of global domination makes it fairly easy to identify new instances of that dominance as they emerge. It is much harder to claim and resist dominance when the source is a nation that strategically locates itself in the South while sharing few of the South's economic features. At the same time, China's concern to avoid the perception that it is Africa's latest colonizer may provide openings for promoting African agendas in the era of the "global East."[44] It may also be possible for Ghana to leverage Chinese interests in order to gain concessions in the area of textile production, particularly appropriations of adinkra and kente.

Local–National Alliances

How does anyone—local community or nation—intervene in a complex and fast-paced global economy to regulate the appropriation of "work that cannot be rushed" when such intervention entails contending not only with an inhospitable regulatory climate but also with one of the biggest forces in the global economy—China? For Ghana, as the preceding discussion has shown, economic globalization has meant integration into the global economy on largely adverse terms. While Africa, as a region, has been able to gain some concessions within the WTO/TRIPS framework, it is, for the most part, a minor player within that framework. The economic conditions that marginalize the region mean that Africa offers very little to counteract the emergence of China not only as a key determinant of economic options on the continent but also as a competitor in the global economy. Within this context, influencing the international regulation of both trade and intellectual property law to effectively counteract the appropriation of adinkra and kente in textile form is an uphill battle for countries like Ghana.

That challenge is worth undertaking, nonetheless, because apart from generating revenue for the Ghanaian state, effective intervention in this global level of appropriation could raise the cost of producing such appropriations and thereby reduce the difference in price between imitations and handmade cloth. That would improve, however slightly, cloth producers' chances of competing in global markets. The fact that Africa and other Third World groupings have gained some concessions in the international regulatory sphere also means that the possibility still exists for some gains to be made. Developments in appropriating practices around plant knowledge also suggest additional options besides direct regulatory action. In this area, challenges to the treatment of indigenous and local cultural production as part of the public domain have begun to change industry practices. Even without being legally obliged to do so, companies seeking to exploit such cultural production are increasingly collaborating with local communities and ensuring that the latter benefit from the exploitation of their knowledge.[45]

Since bodies like the WTO are made up of nation-states, there is clearly a continued role for the latter even if they are more effective acting in concert rather than individually. However, it is also important to note that the challenges that have led to changes in practices of appropriation have come from nations, indigenous peoples and communities, and activists.[46] This suggests that an exclusive focus on the role of the nation in challenging appropriation may be misplaced. For one thing, such a focus legitimizes the premise that the cultural products in question should be controlled primarily by the state. It also obscures the agility of activist groups taking advantage of the enhanced information and communications networks that are a key defining feature of the global economy to give greater visibility to the problem of appropriation and represent local interests in doing so.

In the Ghanaian case, if challenging the appropriation of adinkra and kente for global markets is a major concern, the state may be far more effective if it is responsive to activist voices against exclusive state custodianship of products like adinkra and kente and collaborates with such activists. While the WIPO/UNESCO model provisions support the principle of state custodianship, Ghana's application of that principle places it in an adversarial position to groups and individuals that could support the state in resisting appropriation. Confronting and addressing the messy issue of balancing individual, ethnic, and national claims over local culture would give people like adinkra and kente producers a stake in actively challenging appropriation and give greater legitimacy to such challenges. The basis for such activism exists in several locations around the world. To give just one example from Africa, Kenyan activists have been fighting the trademarking of the name *kiondo* (a popular basket produced by Kikuyu and Kamba women in Kenya) by Japanese and other Asian countries.[47] As noted in chapter 3, the Centre for Indigenous Knowledge Systems (CEFIKS), a Ghanaian nongovernmental organization, could play a similar role not only nationally but also transnationally.

A strategy that is attentive to and inclusive of local voices would maximize both the nation's privileged access to international regulatory spheres and the organizing potential of transnational activist networks. In the last two decades, nongovernmental organizations have gained the status of moral conscience of nations, representing "civil society" positions. This has been formalized in the granting of observer status to such organizations in the forums of the United Nations. However, this privileging of civil society risks a certain amount of co-optation, for example, by the Bretton Woods institutions, which showed a willingness to work with decidedly anti–civil society governments such as Ghana's last military regime and yet later discovered civil society as a means of achieving economic development.[48]

While the success of the musicians' lobby, discussed in chapter 3, shows that the military government was receptive to certain civil society demands, that receptiveness did not extend to demands that questioned the legitimacy of the regime itself. This was apparent, for example, in the suppression of dissenting voices in the late 1980s and early 1990s. The Bretton Woods institutions' emphasis on "the private sector as the engine of development" and their discovery of the role of civil society in governance must also be considered in the context of the neoliberal delegation of state responsibility for social services to these sectors in the United States and beyond.

Despite the risk of co-optation, an approach that takes seriously the interests of folklore producers has the potential of keeping the state accountable. With Ghana currently under democratic rule, there is greater scope for demanding such accountability. Aligning itself with folklore producers in this way will gain the Ghanaian state greater legitimacy in its protection of local cultural production. This, in turn, may make it more effective, in the long run, in gaining international support for regulating the appropriation and circulation of local and indigenous culture in ways that are more beneficial to the communities and nations that produce them.

Conclusion **Why *Should* the Copyright Thing Work Here?**

GHANA'S USE OF INTELLECTUAL PROPERTY LAW to protect elements of local cultural production, like adinkra and kente designs, is not simply an interesting case study of an attempt to fit non-Western cultural forms into Western legal regimes. More importantly, it has to do with the place of nations like Ghana in the current global order and the processes by which they have come to occupy that place. In 2007, Ghanaians proudly celebrated the fiftieth anniversary of their independence from Britain. This anniversary also marked fifty years of endorsing modernity as the globally sanctioned form of political and social being and modernization as the means of attaining that form. Yet by 2007, Ghana's economy had regressed to a level very similar to its state under colonization, partly the result of accepting neoliberal policies as a means of economic growth.[1] With a "hollowed-out"[2] state, weakened economy, and integration into the global economy on adverse terms, Ghanaian modernization seems permanently aspirational—a destination that is constantly elusive.

Ghana's intellectual property protection of folklore provides a good basis for understanding the ways in which this elusiveness is built into the paradigm of modernization itself. This has become clear as I have sought to answer the three sets of questions with which I began: What are the differing principles of authorship and alienability in the production of adinkra and kente and in intellectual property law, and what happens when these two systems meet? What kinds of legal subjects are brought into being in the encounter? What kinds of appropriation practices are found around adinkra and kente, on what kinds of claims are they based, and what implications do they have for Ghana's copyright protection of folklore at home and abroad?

These questions are essentially elaborations of a simpler one: Why doesn't "the copyright thing" work here? My goal so far has been to show that if the copyright thing doesn't work with respect to adinkra and kente, it is because of problems with both intellectual property law and the way that Ghana has chosen to apply it to traditional knowledge. To the extent that the copyright thing doesn't work in Ghana, it is because intellectual property law is part of a normative modernization framework that leaves very little space for alternative modes of social, economic, political, and legal organization. It is also because the Ghanaian state has not fully explored those spaces that do exist for considering those alternatives and infusing them into its policymaking.

In this Conclusion, I underscore these points by posing the question differently: Why *should* the copyright thing work here? Specifically, I draw on my arguments in the preceding chapters to explore two main questions: First, how do structural relations of power help to explain why the spatial and temporal modes of organizing cultural production represented by adinkra and kente, rather than the modes of such organization inherent in intellectual property law, are the ones rendered problematic in the attempt at protecting their designs? I argue that the overarching power structure within which the status of traditional knowledge must be understood is a hegemonic modernity that is manifested in laws, the nation-state, and legal subjectivity.

Second, what are the different sources and forms of power underpinning different kinds of claims and practices around adinkra and kente and their production and appropriation? Further, how do these reveal the limits of structural power and point to ways that the latter can be challenged? In particular, I consider how cloth makers' management of the creative spaces of adinkra and kente production expands our understanding and analysis of the commons and what this might suggest about alternatives to the management of, control over, and access to cultural production both within and beyond intellectual property law.

Strategies of Power and the Time of the Ancestors

The continuity of adinkra and kente producers' creative practices with those of the ancestors, as well as their insistence on locating their work within networks of kinship, ethnicity, and political power, mark that work as belonging within a distinctive mode of organizing the temporal and social contexts of cultural production. Viewing creative practices around cloth production in terms of those contexts makes it possible to understand their difference from the practices sanctioned by intellectual property law as more than a simple distinction between individual and communal creativity or between traditional and modern knowledges. Rather, the encounter between intellectual property law and indigenous and local cultural production is one between different ways of conceiving of time and society in relation to cultural production.

Intellectual property is based on understandings of the temporal and social contexts of cultural production that are bound up with modernity. These include the liberal concept of the autonomous, rational individual as the basic unit of society and the actions of that individual as distinct from the actions of all others. As a cultural producer, this individual is the essential subject of intellectual property law—the male or masculinized author or inventor whose ability and right to separate his work from all other such work and make proprietary claims over it is a function of his status as a modern subject. This separation is also temporal in demarcating the creative work of the individual from that of not only living authors but also deceased ones.

Adinkra and kente production features both individual *and* communal creativity. Individuals not only make claims over their own designs but also acknowledge the creativity of other individuals, sometimes long after the latter have died. Further, they work in communities but, far from being an ideal model of cooperation, communal production features both collaboration and rivalry. At the same time, it is by appeal to the collective that craftsmen authorize their work. This is true even for cloth producers who move away from core production sites such that the social nature of their work extends across geographical space. That work also extends across time, and rather than emphasizing their individual creativity as the means of authorizing their work, it is that work's connection to deceased creators that gives it its distinctiveness.

These differences in organizing creative work in space and time would be merely curious if they were generally viewed as equivalent alternatives, but they are not. One mode is bound up with a hegemonic modernity whose understandings of time and society render other modes deficient. Since different societies are ranked by the extent to which they are "modern," they are also ranked by the extent to which they manifest the time of modernity. Within this scheme, nations like Ghana enter time and history by becoming modern. However, their status as "new" to modernity means that their integration into this temporal scheme is only partial, and one thus finds different modes of time existing side by side in the same location. It is this juxtaposition of different kinds of temporality, in the case of India, that Dipesh Chakrabarty frames and interrogates as "the time of history and the times of gods." The time of history is structured by the rationality and order of modernity.

It is singular and universal, while the times of the gods are locally specific and marked by their presumed irrationality.[3]

The arguments of scholars like Chakrabarty offer a corrective to the standard view that the times of the gods—or the temporal modes of the non-modern elements in Third World societies—are not merely different but inferior. Yet that view remains extremely strong, and its shorthand includes words like *traditional, developing, underdeveloped, backward,* and even *primitive.* As Chakrabarty and other postcolonial scholars have argued, different ways of accounting for temporality are productive of social relations.[4] Therefore, the understanding of time within the framework of modernity establishes the basis for "strategies of power," including "the strategy of contrasting development with backwardness which organizes the planning of programmes of economic 'modernization' by the international monetary agencies and by Third World governments themselves."[5] It is these strategies of power, rather than any features inherent in temporal frameworks themselves, that privilege the time of history over the time of the gods—or, in this case, the time of the ancestors.

While modernization or "development" frameworks are common sites for the exercise of such strategies of power, the encounter between intellectual property law and indigenous and local culture reveals yet another site. The status of the law, as a key ruling mechanism in a modern nation-state, gives it preeminence over indigenous norms. It is only when such norms are accorded formal legal recognition that they approach the authoritative status of the law. The temporal and spatial modes of cultural production sanctioned by intellectual property law therefore operate as strategies of power first through this structural location and second through the failure to grant equivalent status to the ways that space and time are organized in local cultural production. The effect of the law's formal separation of creative work from its spatial and temporal contexts is to magnify those contexts in modes of cultural production that do not insist on this separation and to render them problematic.

With modernity as the privileged mode of organizing the spatial and temporal dimensions of cultural production, the dynamism of cloth producers' creative practices and their participation in modern circuits of globalization are permanently obscured and diminished. In this framework intellectual property laws are important strategies of power whose operation becomes evident when they treat traditional knowledge and folklore as anomalies. The complex question of how to understand and organize the regulation of cultural production in ways that account for different temporal and social systems is reduced to the simpler one of how to deal with the presumed lack of fit between the tradition of folklore and the modernity of intellectual property law.

In the Ghanaian case, the hegemonic operation of modern time also occurs in the classification of cultural products like adinkra and kente as "traditional." The concept of modernity operates to distinguish between past and present and, further, to divide the world accordingly. Modernity is the site of the present, and tradition, the site of the past.[6] The temporality and social organization of adinkra and kente production is therefore inferior not only because it does not distinguish between persons in the same ways that modernity does but because, in being traditional, it resides permanently in the past. This occurs both externally and internally in Western and Ghanaian characterizations of such cultural production.

When Ghana promotes its "rich cultural heritage" to prospective visitors, it is presenting them with an opportunity to connect with the past. Marketing that past in the context of a nation that is simultaneously able to offer modern amenities to those visitors suggests that this tradition exists in a capsule, apart from modern Ghana. At the same time, implicit in the claim that one can witness a rich cultural heritage in Ghana is the premise that even as it indexes the past, this is a heritage that continues into the present. (This premise—of a "living heritage"—is also asserted by government officials and some scholars as a justification for not treating Ghanaian folklore as part of the public domain.)[7] The living heritage premise means, in effect, that objects that reside in museums in the West—repositories of congealed time—come to life in places like Ghana.

The same distinction occurs in adinkra and kente producers' claims about the authenticity of their work—for example, when adinkra maker Kwame says, "But ours is the *cultural* one" in distinguishing between mass-produced imitations and hand-stenciled adinkra cloth. It is clear from his words that handmade cloth embodies cultural authenticity in ways that mass-produced cloth cannot. Handmade cloth, in effect, differs from mass-produced cloth in being a bearer of tradition—the source of its authenticity. However strategic Ghana's (and Ghanaians') deployment of tradition may be, it reifies the tradition–modernity divide in ways that ultimately confirm the superior status of the latter. It also reinforces the country's status as one that aspires to modernity without having fully arrived.

In using intellectual property law to protect folklore, Ghana further confirms the tradition–modernity divide in not considering the possibility of a legal regime that validates the authorizing practices of local cultural producers and their alternative modes of organizing their work socially and temporally. Given the strength of local discourses, institutions, and practices that make tradition an important element in both cultural nationalism and tourism policy, it is unlikely that this privileging of modernity will change even under an alternative set of arrangements such as a sui generis set of laws to regulate the appropriation of local cultural production. If anything, such a set of laws, in being set apart from mainstream intellectual property laws, would only reinforce the divide.

Capital, the State, and Cultural Production

Ghana's use of intellectual property law to convert culture into an economic resource is an interesting variation on the relationship between intellectual property law and capital. In one version of that relationship, the culture industries use intellectual property law to reinforce and extend the boundaries around cultural goods they produce and strictly police those boundaries, permitting access only on payment of licensing fees and royalties.[8] In another version, individuals and corporations, from artists to pharmaceutical companies, appropriate indigenous and local cultural production that they regard as belonging in the public domain, convert it into "their" artistic or scientific work, and buttress those ownership claims with intellectual property laws that grant them the exclusive right to profit from "their" creations and inventions.[9]

In the Ghanaian version, a Third World nation, seeking to maximize its revenues, converts indigenous cultural production into national culture and claims state ownership over that culture by means of intellectual property law and, in effect, state control of any revenue from royalty payments. As noted in previous chapters, while the language of the law may describe this set of arrangements as custodianship rather than ownership, the result, in practice, is ownership. An appropriating practice that would be contested if it were undertaken by groups and individuals from outside Ghana becomes defensible because it is undertaken by the Ghanaian state, ostensibly on behalf of its citizens.

The first two versions are often justified by appeal to romantic ideas of creativity and authorship as well as Lockean ideas of the conditions under which one can extract from a commons (in the second case, the commons of "virgin knowledge" discussed in chapter 2). The third version is justified on the grounds of national unity and cultural sovereignty. In all three versions, intellectual property laws are used to legitimize certain ownership claims over cultural products, thereby granting those owners the exclusive right to profit from any further appropriation of those products. In all three cases, the application of intellectual property law underscores the power of corporations and the state in making claims over culture.

These parallels raise the important question of why Ghana should be able to pursue claims over adinkra and kente internationally when it is the state rather than cultural producers who are likely to benefit if those claims can be successfully made. They also help to reveal the links between some of the many dimensions of the problems with intellectual property law. The question of whether and how to protect traditional knowledge must be raised and settled on multiple fronts, and highlighting the links between those fronts helps to reveal the inconsistencies in Ghana's position at home and abroad that must be addressed if the country is to argue persuasively for normative changes in the international framework.

The Ghanaian state's claims over indigenous culture are unremarkable when viewed in the light of nationalist projects. In claiming a national culture, Ghana is no different from all other nations that use indigenous culture for the symbolic work of building national identity. It is also not unique in using the specific elements of adinkra and kente, along with other kinds of indigenous culture, in this project. Prior to the establishment of the Ghanaian state, those same elements served in establishing Asante as a culturally distinctive nation. More recently, black nationalism in the United States has drawn upon adinkra, kente, and elements from other parts of Africa to assert a heritage and identity that is distinct from that of the U.S. mainstream.

Given these cycles of appropriation of adinkra and kente for different nationalist projects, why should Ghana's claims be superior to the others? Since Asante was there first, does it not have a prior claim to adinkra and kente as *its* national heritage? But that claim, too, can be contested, and not only because Asante has long ceased to be a major West African power and has also been subsumed into Ghana. The claim of Asante rights to adinkra and kente can also be challenged because these textiles were *made* Asante rather than being inherently Asante. This excavation of the true origins of adinkra, kente, and other elements of Ghanaian culture could go on indefinitely, and what it reveals is that the simple fact of current location in a specific territory is not always a strong basis for pursuing proprietary claims over culture. Yet outside settler democracies, this basis is largely uncontested, and such culture is generally accepted as part of the national heritage.

What gives Ghana's claims over indigenous and local cultural production their authority is the country's status as a certain kind of political entity—a modern nation-state—and, as such, one whose right to a national culture is taken as a given.[10] In this case, modernity translates into distinct advantages for the Ghanaian state. The Asante people may still refer to Asante not only as an ethnic group but as a nation *(Asanteman)*, but internationally, it is Ghana that has the standing necessary to make formal claims over culture. Although the Ghanaian state grants a certain degree of authority to indigenous ethnopolitical groups like the Asante, these tacitly accept that they are different from, and subordinate to, the Ghanaian state. This hierarchical system of national and indigenous authority makes it possible for both to make claims over culture without those claims conflicting with each other.

This set of arrangements makes indigenous rulers collaborators with the Ghanaian state in the work of building a national culture out of indigenous and local sources. While this is a sound strategy in forging both cultural nationalism and national unity, it does not justify state custodianship of adinkra and kente and other folklore. Indeed that custodianship contradicts the state–ethnic partnership principle in effectively writing folklore producers (who come from different ethnic groups) out of intellectual property law. Although the law has fundamental flaws, it does apportion benefits from the appropriation of local culture, yet none of those benefits go to the individuals, communities, and ethnic groups that produce that culture. Ostensibly, reposing the rights to folklore in the state averts the possibility of conflict from competing ethnic and individual claims and further fosters national unity. This argument derives its strength from a key underlying assumption, namely that the nation-state takes precedence over its constituent ethnic groups.

This is an argument that Ghana can make with few adverse political consequences, partly because of the history by which it came to nationhood and also because of its history since becoming a nation. Essentially, the ethnic groups that make up Ghana became a single nation-state by defining themselves in opposition to a common source of oppression—British colonial rule. In the half century since independence, the premise that those ethnic groups belong together as a single nation has remained largely unchallenged. While this sets Ghana apart as an example of stability in a region prone to ethnic fragmentation, it has also allowed the Ghanaian state considerable flexibility in managing ethnic diversity. That diversity is acknowledged where it serves the interests of the state and ignored where to acknowledge it would be inconvenient. An example of the former is the use of multiple languages in national broadcasting, while the state custodianship of folklore illustrates the latter.

The privileged status of the modern nation-state as a political entity, Ghana's location in a region where there is a premium on the stability of multiethnic nation states, and the country's record of relative stability within that region combine to give the Ghanaian state considerable latitude in the degree to which it engages with multiethnicity. Another factor is the racial homogeneity that masks ethnic difference in Ghana. In Western settler democracies, indigenous peoples' struggles against the appropriation of their culture within the nation-states where they are located are struggles along lines of both ethnicity and race, with the latter giving those struggles a degree of visibility and moral authority that is harder to achieve in locations like Ghana, whose successful struggles against Western dominance can also be read as successful struggles against racial dominance.

As a racially homogenous modern nation-state, Ghana can assert claims of cultural sovereignty against the West without raising questions about the bases of that culture. This stands in contrast to nations like Australia and Canada, whose histories of settler colonization mean that any national claims over indigenous culture can be strongly challenged in ways that do not occur in the case of nations like Ghana. Stated differently, Ghana stands in relation to the West in ways that parallel the situation of indigenous peoples in Western nations. This lets Ghana off the hook with regard to questions of national appropriation of local and indigenous culture.

Exemplary and Anomalous Subjects

A third instance of the way that modernity functions as a hegemonic force can be seen in the ways that different kinds of cultural producers fare as subjects of laws in a modern state. In claiming custodianship over folklore through copyright law, the Ghanaian state allows for authorship claims by folklore producers. However, this requires these producers to constitute themselves as legal subjects in ways that are at variance with their subjectivity as cultural producers in temporal and spatial networks that differ from those recognized in intellectual property law. This is most evident when one compares adinkra and kente makers with musicians in the recording industry as subjects of copyright law. Although the law recognizes the rights of both groups, the two groups conceive of themselves very differently in relation to the law.

Ghanaian musicians' thirty-year history of activism around copyright law has made them into the quintessential subjects of that law. This is attested to both in cloth producers' perception of copyright as a musicians' issue and in musicians' own characterization of themselves in relation to the law—for example, in their resistance to the participation of other groups of cultural producers in COSGA, the collection society set up under the 1985 copyright law. The activism that makes musicians into a nuisance in the eyes of certain government officials also makes them ideal subjects precisely because of their challenges to the state. They embody the liberal ideal of an active civil society that holds the state accountable to the interests of the people.

In being active subjects, however, musicians in the recording industry act within a mode established for them within the framework of modernization. First, their right to copyright protection is taken as given because of their operation within a sphere of cultural production that fits within the norms of intellectual property law. Their operation within that sphere also means that they confirm rather than challenge the premises of subjectivity within the law as well as the law's spatial and temporal organization of cultural production. Thus, even though they challenge the Ghanaian state's custodianship of folklore, that challenge does not extend to radically questioning the status of local and indigenous cultural production within intellectual property law. Ultimately, musicians are model subjects because they confirm the framework of modernization within which intellectual property law is embedded.

In contrast to musicians, adinkra and kente producers barely view themselves as subjects of intellectual property law, and if one takes the model of an active civil society as the basis of evaluation, cloth makers seem to fall short of that standard. The problem with this standard of comparison is that it fails to take into account cloth makers' subjectivity as cultural workers who follow production norms different from those legitimized by intellectual property law. Within those norms, they are quite active in pursuing their interests. In the same way that musicians' activism is a function of their location in a site of production that is linked to the state and to intellectual property law in advantageous ways, adinkra and kente producers' lack of activism is because of their location in an area of production that has no easy connection to the sphere of the law.

Viewed in this way, cloth producers and musicians are produced as subjects by the norms of cultural production within which they operate. If adinkra and kente makers are inactive in relation to intellectual property law, it is because before that law, they are anomalous subjects. The factors that set their cultural production apart from those routinely regulated by intellectual property law also help to determine their subjectivity in relation to the law. At the same time, women cloth traders show that the law can be turned to the advantage of groups that typically do not fare well as citizens and subjects within the space of the nation. Like adinkra and kente producers, women are a relatively marginalized group as legal subjects and as citizens.

Yet, in spite of cycles of official and popular hostility as well as economic policies that shrink their options, Ghanaian women in the commercial sector continue to create spaces in which they can operate successfully. In doing so, they provide a model for exploring spaces of legal empowerment for cloth producers. However, an important aspect of the legal subjectivity of women and musicians is that their cultural production and the law coincide in ways that have not yet occurred with the cultural production of adinkra and kente makers. It is therefore unlikely that these cloth makers (and other folklore producers) can use the law to their advantage without further legal reform.

In principle, musicians, market women, and cloth producers are all citizens of Ghana and therefore equal before the country's laws. This is the assumption underpinning the copyright law's provision for individual claims of authorship by folklore producers. This liberal democratic assumption of equality, however, ignores the ways that factors other than formal instruments like national constitutions and laws mediate in the experience of citizenship. It fails to take into account structural sources of inequality, including class differences and differences in the spheres within which cultural production takes place. It also fails to consider the different ways in which those spheres are connected to the state. Citizens operating in spheres like mechanized cloth production and the recording music industry can use the laws governing those spheres to their advantage in ways that citizens outside those spheres cannot. Those spheres that afford the greatest scope for the exercise of rights are those spheres that conform to the structures of the modern nation-state. The simple fact of being a citizen does not, by itself, guarantee access to all the rights and benefits of citizenship.

The power that the Ghanaian state exercises in using national laws to protect folklore is a result of its conformity to the forms of governance mandated by globalized modernization. But this translates into very little power in the global sphere of cultural flows and the international system that regulates those flows. Further, the extent to which Ghana can shape its laws to suit local ends is constrained by international norms and regulations. In the case of intellectual property law, the TRIPS regime provides little scope for nations to challenge the basic premises of the law. Nonetheless, this has not stopped Ghana from including provisions in its intellectual property laws that are neither required nor enforceable under TRIPS. This suggests that within the constraints of the international regulatory system, there is still considerable leeway for individual nations to act.

So far, Ghana has used that space in ways that are relatively conservative, and this is not only because of state priorities or the problems inherent in intellectual property law. Ghana's use of intellectual property law is almost predictable when viewed in a broader global and historical context. The nationalist capture of the colonial state often included the retention of the colonial distinction between tradition and modernity. Where that distinction operated under colonialism as a means of subjugation, in the nationalist context, tradition was initially a resource for distancing the independent nation from the colonial state. However, tradition in nationalist hands often became a basis for bourgeois rather than radical or revolutionary nationalism.[11] This is evident in Ghana's narrow approach to the conversion of local culture into national culture partly through the use of intellectual property law. That application of the law demonstrates that Ghana is a viable nation state and is modernizing in accordance with all major indicators, including modern legal systems. However, as the Ghanaian application of intellectual property law to traditional knowledge shows, the problem with those indicators is that they are often externally determined, one-size-fits-all templates and, as such, are also often at variance with local realities.

Practices of Resistance

Despite the extent of the power derived from modern laws, political forms and modes of legal subjectivity, that power is not absolute, and this is most obvious in the case of the women cloth traders outlined earlier. The limits of state power are also evident in Ghanaians' resistance to the official nationalist discourses that are used to justify state custodianship of adinkra and kente designs and other forms of folklore. Within cloth-producing communities, Ghanaians challenge the idea that the state is an appropriate or trustworthy custodian of the designs that originate from those communities. For cloth producers who view the Asantehene as the proper custodian of adinkra and kente, the power of the indigenous state becomes more relevant and worthy of recognition than that of the modern nation-state—at least in relation to indigenous cultural production. Outside cloth-producing communities, Ghanaians use the very basis of state custodianship, namely, the premise that there is such a thing as *national* culture, to claim access to that culture as a citizenship right that must not attract the penalty of royalty payments. In this they, too, withhold recognition from the state as a mediator in their use of cultural elements like adinkra and kente.

A further check on the state's assertion of ownership rights over those cultural elements comes from the changing tastes and values of consumers within and beyond Ghana. Ghanaians' increasing acceptance of imitation adinkra and kente cloth makes them an attractive market for local factories whose calculation appears to be that the profits to be made outweigh any sanctions from a state with limited ability to enforce the law that makes their appropriations illegal. The copyright protection of local cultural production is further undermined by African Americans who view *all* African culture as their birthright and constitute an important external market for imitation adinkra and kente. In its interactions with this community, the Ghanaian state must balance its desire to regulate and profit from the circulation of appropriations of adinkra and kente with its equally strong desire to attract African American investment in Ghana both in the short term through tourism and in the long term through settlement and, ultimately, citizenship.

In sum, certain kinds of folklore producers have been absent from the debates on intellectual property law in Ghana, and it is not only the literal voices of cultural workers like adinkra and kente makers that are obscured in those debates but also what their practices say about different modes of temporality and social organization in relation to cultural production. The result is that the discussion of options for addressing cultural appropriation assumes the temporal and social modes of intellectual property law, and while challenges have been made to the existing order *within* that framework, the framework itself remains intact. At the same time, despite the superior power and legitimacy that Ghana derives from its status as a modern nation-state with modern laws and its use of these to make claims over culture, the practices of cultural producers and consumers function to limit the actual effects of state control over local culture. Further, as noted in chapter 5, the power that the state exercises at home virtually evaporates in the context of international regulatory regimes.

In order to arrive at a more viable and just alternative to the current copyright protection of traditional knowledge, it is necessary, first of all, to reevaluate Ghana's intellectual property laws in ways that undermine the temporal divisions of modernity that in turn devalue the ancestral time of kente and adinkra production. Such a reevaluation must also take into account the limited legitimacy of a regulatory regime that makes the state, rather than folklore producers, the arbiter of what constitutes authorized and unauthorized uses of local cultural production. The commons of cloth production, adinkra and kente makers' management of the boundaries of that commons, and their authorization strategies suggest a number of options.

The Outside of Property?

The concept of the commons has attracted a lot of attention among scholars of intellectual property law in industrialized nations, especially since the emergence of networks of software developers in the "open source" model of collaborative cultural production.[12] This attention has also resulted in the recognition that the commons is not very well understood beyond being, simply, "property's outside."[13] Discussions of the commons in relation to software development and other kinds of creative collaboration—especially in relation to digital technology and the Internet—have tended to focus on its openness rather than its boundaries. Yet, as James Boyle has pointed out, with reference to open source software production under the General Public License (GPL), the very possibility of enclosure can be a basis for effectively managing the commons.[14] A related point that is obscured or minimized in the celebration of the commons as an alternative mode of managing cultural production is the way that the digital commons is enclosed by the economic, technical, and cultural capital required for participation within it.

As is evident in adinkra and kente makers' management of the boundaries of cloth production, the principle that some enclosure may be desirable holds true for forms of cultural production that take place in commons other than those of digital technology. The importance of boundaries becomes especially evident when one considers the fragility of a space like that of adinkra and kente production. Here, the challenge becomes one of ensuring cloth makers' continued ability to maintain boundaries that are robust enough to withstand destruction through rampant appropriation while retaining the permeability that ensures the continuing dynamism and viability of adinkra and kente production. The challenge is also one of resisting excessive forms of enclosure that seek to prevent the "tragedy of the commons" (that is, its overexploitation and eventual destruction) by walling it off altogether.

Ghana's approach in its application of intellectual property law to adinkra and kente and other forms of local culture is close to this latter alternative and does little to ensure the continued viability of the commons while displacing part of its management from cloth makers and other producers to the state. As a result, although one of the arguments made for the copyright protection of Ghanaian folklore is its dynamism, the current set of legal arrangements does not ensure that dynamism.[15] This is not only because the law fails to address the fact of the commons but also because its emphasis is on the products of the commons rather than *processes* by which those products come into being and the people who manage those processes. Simply acknowledging the possibility of individual claims over folklore fails to get at the heart of the issue—protective measures must extend to the spaces within which those individuals work and engage with folklore producers as guides and collaborators in the management of those spaces.

In the GPL case that Boyle discusses, the rights granted to software producers through copyright law enabled them to determine the terms on which others could access, modify, and distribute their code.[16] In this instance, a standard form of intellectual property protection became the basis for establishing a commons and determining the conditions of participation within it—that is, in managing its boundaries. Those boundaries admitted collaborative and nonproprietary software production while excluding software developers for whom proprietary models of production were more attractive. Judging from this example, commons-based creativity does not preclude the existence of boundaries, whether those boundaries are made explicit or not, and this becomes even clearer when one considers the commons of adinkra and kente production and its management by cloth producers.

While articulating the commons of adinkra and kente production to intellectual property law is a possible alternative to the current legal framework in Ghana, it leaves intact the inferior status of traditional knowledge within the law—especially since the law completely ignores the nature and significance of the commons and the key roles that cloth makers play in its management. In the GPL example, an important first step was the inclusion of software in protected works under U.S. intellectual property laws. That inclusion has become the international norm through TRIPS, but industrialized nations' continuing resistance to according traditional knowledge the same status points to a deeper problem that will not be resolved by simply linking different protection norms while their differing philosophical premises remain intact.

Nonetheless, while failing to resolve the problems with intellectual property law in relation to traditional knowledge, the GPL model offers an example of productive interaction between the law and the commons and could work within the space of Ghana if not internationally. Applying this model in Ghana would require state recognition of the commons-based production of adinkra and kente and other kinds of folklore as well as cultural producers' roles in managing their respective commons. It would also require active engagement with those producers as legal subjects. This could provide a basis for collaboration between the state and folklore producers in not only managing the commons to ensure its continued survival but also regulating the appropriation of its products. A more radical alternative would be a commons-based system that is not linked to intellectual property laws and does not depend on the latter for its legitimacy. Environmentalist metaphors have appeared in some scholarship on the subject, and these offer a useful starting point.

Ecosystems of Culture

The language of environmentalism has featured in a number of analyses of intellectual property law, most notably in the work of scholar and activist Vandana Shiva. In Shiva's analyses of the threats posed by monocultural agriculture and plant patents to indigenous and local agricultural practices that sustain biodiversity, the language of environmentalism is both literal and metaphorical—the latter in her warnings of the dangers of "monocultures of the mind."[17] David Bollier has also pointed out the importance of the concept of the commons in environmental scholarship and activism.[18] Increasingly, the language and strategies of environmental activism are becoming important metaphors and models for other spheres of cultural production that have no direct links to the environment—most strikingly, in the context of networked creativity in the digital age. Some scholars have called for an environmentalist approach in protecting commons-based cultural production.[19]

While this language has so far been applied in separate spheres of cultural production, using it to link those spheres together would make it possible to reconceptualize them in terms that allow for strategies of authorization that differ from those in conventional practices of authorship. The concept of ecosystems, for example, provides a common framework for understanding natural environments that may be quite different from each other yet raise similar concerns with regard to their development and management. In the same way, it is possible to conceive of ecosystems of cultural production each with quite distinct features and products—from seeds to software to adinkra and kente—that are nonetheless related in being spheres of commons-based cultural production with strategies of authorization that have little in common with those sanctioned by intellectual property law.

In their edited volume on the commons of knowledge, Charlotte Hess and

Elinor Ostrom nod toward this possibility when they define knowledge as "all types of understanding gained through experience or study, whether indigenous, scientific, scholarly, or otherwise nonacademic."[20] Yet the ensuing discussion focuses almost exclusively on "knowledge in digital form." They also refer to knowledge as an ecosystem, but in order to use the commons as a basis for analyzing and managing different kinds of knowledge, it might be more productive to think of *multiple* ecosystems. Again, Hess and Ostrom index the possibility of such an approach when they note the wide range of commons and commons management principles in existence.

Instead of operating solely at the level of description and abstract analysis, the conceptualization of creative spheres as ecosystems could be a basis for formulating coordinated yet flexible local, national, and transnational cultural production management systems that provide a far more robust and radical alternative to standard intellectual property regimes like copyright protection as a basis for managing commons-based cultural production. In linking different ecosystems of cultural production, this could also be a basis for linking struggles that have so far been perceived as unrelated. The discussion of the digital commons, for example, is highly Western in focus and remains so even in its internationalized versions, such as Yochai Benkler's vision of a networked global economy.[21] Similarly, discussions of measures to protect the cultural production of indigenous peoples and local communities in Third World nations typically occur in opposition to the industrialized nations especially when they are conducted in standard international intellectual property arenas like WIPO and the WTO.

A transnational network of commons-based cultural production management systems could provide the basis for an alternative framework that overcomes the limitations of intellectual property law as conceptualized in the current international regulatory system. For example, it would undermine the law's rigid separation of past and present and of individual and communal creativity. It would further support the interaction between these temporal and creative spheres that is common in so many spheres of cultural production. Ideally, such a network would be neutral regarding the different kinds of commons within it, simply linking them together in a coherent system. This could help to offset or even eliminate the hierarchical ranking of different kinds of cultural production.

In focusing on the system rather than the site and content of cultural production, such a network would also accommodate a wider range of management options than the territory-based geographical indications option. Further, it could transcend established and emerging polarities of North and South and global East in fostering multidirectional alliances. Most importantly, in offering a common basis for managing different kinds of cultural production and in linking a wide range of actors across the old divides, the network could be a basis for legitimacy that cannot be achieved through sui generis systems tailored to specific cases in isolation from each other.

Alternative Visions

Against this background, an alternative starting point to that of protecting "national culture" would be to assess Ghana's intellectual property laws according to the extent to which they are compatible with the ways that folklore is produced and the spheres of its production are managed. Assessing the law would also entail critically reviewing what kinds of citizenship are possible within it and what alternative ways of conceptualizing authorship, authorization, and alienability give all cultural producers a stake in the project of managing cultural production so that it remains a viable resource for those producers and not only for the state. The networked ecosystems of commons-based cultural production and management constitute one set of alternatives that would provide more scope for cultural producers to shape the kinds of regulatory systems within which they work.

In being *trans*national rather than *inter*national, such a network would give nonstate actors greater power than they have in international regulatory systems in which states are the primary actors. They could also exert pressure on nations to be accountable to local and indigenous cultural producers. Adinkra and kente producers' presence in global circuits, however minimal, shows that the possibility exists for cloth makers to also participate in global networks of different kinds of commons. Rather than being bound by the limitations of national copyright law for both their work and subjectivity, Ghanaian adinkra and kente producers could become part of a transnational network of commons-based cultural production that, unlike intellectual property law, recognizes and supports the complex structures of authorship, authorization, and alienability within which they work.

Acknowledgments

I am grateful, first, to the cloth producers who shared their life histories with me and to all the other artists, activists, scholars, policy advisers, and government officials who granted me the interviews that made this book possible. I thank Mrs. Sabina Ofori-Boateng for facilitating my research.

The University of California, San Diego gave me a Faculty Career Development Grant and an Academic Senate Research Grant that enabled me to undertake additional research in 2004, and the University of California Humanities Research Institute provided a fellowship that allowed me to begin the gender analysis in my second chapter. Special thanks to Peter Jaszi and Ann Shalleck of the Washington College of Law at American University for inviting me to be a part of their Intellectual Property and Gender network of scholars; the group was a supportive community for my work on gender. Thanks also to Jean Allman, Paula Chakravartty, and Yuezhi Zhao, who helped me to further clarify my thinking on gender, diaspora, and globalization.

My colleagues in the Department of Communication at the University of California, San Diego, have been a tremendous source of support throughout this project. I am particularly indebted to those who read and commented on all or part of the manuscript: Lisa Cartwright, Zeinabu Davis, Kelly Gates, Brian Goldfarb, Nitin Govil, Dan Hallin, Val Hartouni, Robert Horwitz, Chandra Mukerji, and Elana Zilberg. I also thank those who added friendship to collegiality and shared their homes and families with me: Lisa Cartwright, Giovanna Chesler, Zeinabu Davis, Brian Goldfarb, and Olga Vasquez.

Thanks to Carol Padden for her mentoring, to David Serlin for his encouragement, and to Peter Bloom and Jonathan Zilberg for their comments. Special thanks to Chandra Mukerji for her clear-sighted wisdom and the gift of "flow." Susan Leigh Star and Soek Fang Sim were sources of strength at difficult points in my work; I am sorry they did not live to see the results of their encouragement, and I will always remember them with deep gratitude.

Denise Ferreira da Silva's insights were very helpful to me in conceptualizing the overall project, and John Nerone's generosity and encouragement were invaluable as I struggled to complete the first draft of the manuscript. Katie Pearson has been a source of wise counsel in difficult times, while Jean Allman and Edward Reynolds were generous and steadfast in their encouragement and mentoring. I am also grateful to my good friends Patience Sowa, Nii Sai Doku, Alice Impraim, Carol Rogers, and Judy Husband for their constant support. Special thanks to Judy for the "book quilt" that helped me to finish this work.

I could not have asked for a better editor than Richard Morrison, who guided me through the publication process with grace and tremendous generosity. Adam Brunner and Erin Warholm-Wohlenhaus took care of the manuscript preparation. Two anonymous reviewers offered very helpful comments and suggestions, and I also thank Brian Goldfarb and Claudia da Metz for their help with photographs and Tracey Hughes for her work on the map of Ghana. I am also grateful to Carol Lallier for her careful copyediting and to Rachel Moeller for her work on the book.

And then there are my sisters—in spirit and birth. I am grateful to Judith Atala, who constantly inspires me with her example of tenacity and courage, and to Denise Ferreira da Silva, my sister in exile, for all those times she provided me with a space where explanations were unnecessary. Special thanks to Oduraa Boateng, who went out of her way to support me in this project as she generously added unpaid research assistance to her busy schedule as a lawyer and mother. Thanks also to Amanobea Adjepong-Boateng and Akua Ofori-Ampofo, who continually encourage and challenge me to strive and succeed.

Finally, I owe a deep debt of gratitude to my parents: my late father, Ernest Amano Boateng, my first role model in academia, and my mother, Evelyn Kensema Boateng, who is a steadfast source of love and encouragement. I thank them for sharing their intellectual gifts with their daughters and insisting that we use them well. I hope the better parts of this book reflect those gifts.

Notes

Introduction

1. "Intellectual Property in Ghana."

2. Government of Ghana, *Geographical Indications Act.*

3. Rattray, *Religion and Art in Ashanti*; Mould-Iddrisu, "Protection of Folklore in Ghana"; Kuruk, "Protecting Folklore."

4. Personal Narratives Group, *Interpreting Women's Lives*; Reinharz, *Feminist Methods in Social Research* (see, especially, chapter 7, "Feminist Oral History").

5. Wilks, *Asante in the 19th Century.*

6. Korang, *Writing Ghana.*

7. The term *ethnicity* denotes several different kinds of identification that may be based on language, race, or, in the case of immigrant communities, national origin. As used in this book, it refers to groups that can be distinguished from each other primarily on the basis of language. Those groups may also vary from one another in social and political structure.

8. Korang, *Writing Ghana*, 166.

9. Shillington, *History of Africa.*

10. Mamdani, *Citizen and Subject*, 17.

11. See, for example, Alexandra Wilson's account of the nineteenth-century shift in the significance of the office of the *Konor*, or war chief, among the Krobo people, from an intermediary between the priests and priestesses and the Europeans to a paramount ruler similar to an Akan chief in *The Bead Is Constant*, 6–7.

12. Rathbone, *Nkrumah and the Chiefs.*

13. National Commission on Culture, *The Cultural Policy of Ghana*, 8.

14. Posey and Dutfield, *Beyond Intellectual Property*; McLeod, *Owning Culture.*

15. For example, in *Owning Culture*, McLeod discusses the protection of Ed McMahon's distinctive call, "Here's Johnny."

16. *Oxford English Dictionary.*

17. Posey and Dutfield, *Beyond Intellectual Property*, 230.

18. Drahos, *A Philosophy of Intellectual Property*, 5.

19. Posey and Dutfield, *Beyond Intellectual Property.*

185

20. Ibid.

21. Halbert, "Feminist Interpretations of Intellectual Property Law." As Halbert notes, women have begun to protect their rights over knitting patterns under copyright law. A similar trend is occurring with quilting designs. In the latter case, the extent of copyright protection can vary, from books whose authors permit reproduction of their designs for personal, noncommercial use (e.g., Mary Hickey, in her book *Sweet and Simple Baby Quilts*) to those who only permit photocopying of specific designs within a book (for example, M'Liss Rae Hawley's *Phenomenal Fat Quarter Quilts*, in which all designs in the book are protected from reproduction with one exception that reads, "Attention Copy Shops: Please note the following exception—Publisher and author give permission to photocopy page 53 for personal use only").

22. Posey and Dutfield, *Beyond Intellectual Property*, 95.

23. Sell and May, "Moments in Law."

24. McLeod, *Owning Culture* and *Freedom of Expression®*; Boyle, *The Public Domain*; and Thomas and Servaes, "Introduction."

25. In the United States, Lawrence Lessig is one of the strongest voices expressing this concern. Others are Kembrew McLeod and James Boyle.

26. Rose, *Authors and Owners*.

27. Posey and Dutfield, *Beyond Intellectual Property*, 76.

28. A point made by several commentators, including Bettig in *Copyrighting Culture*; Posey and Dutfield, in *Beyond Intellectual Property*; McLeod, in *Owning Culture* and *Freedom of Expression*; and Yudice, in *The Expediency of Culture*.

29. Boyle, *The Public Domain*.

30. Amegatcher, *Ghanaian Law of Copyright*.

31. Interview with former official in Copyright Administration, September 24, 1999.

32. UNESCO is the institutional home of another international copyright agreement (the Universal Copyright Convention, or UCC) and is also responsible for overseeing the protection of cultural heritage. The model provisions were eventually published in 1985.

33. Tsikata and Anyidoho, "Copyright and Oral Culture"; Collins, "The 'Folkloric Copyright Tax' Problem in Ghana."

34. Government of Ghana, *Copyright Act*.

35. Kuruk, "Protecting Folklore."

36. Hountodji, "Introduction: Recentering Africa," 18.

37. Posey and Dutfield, *Beyond Intellectual Property*.

38. Harding, *Whose Science?* and Hill Collins, *Black Feminist Thought* (see, especially, Hill Collins's discussion in chapter 11, "Black Feminist Epistemology").

39. For example, Posey and Dutfield (in *Beyond Intellectual Property*, 92) question the usefulness of intellectual property rights for protecting indigenous knowledge given the unequal power relations between indigenous peoples and corporations (an inequality that also applies to Third World nations and the industrialized nations that define

those rights). I have also encountered such arguments when presenting this work at scholarly meetings.

40. Yudice, *The Expediency of Culture*, 9.

41. Canclini, *Transforming Modernity*, 10.

42. Wallerstein, "Culture as the Ideological Battleground of the Modern World-System."

43. Lowe and Lloyd, "Introduction," 2.

44. Ibid., 2.

45. Mama, "Shedding the Masks and Tearing the Veils"; Oyêwùmí, *The Invention of Women*.

46. Foucault, "What Is an Author?"

47. Gramsci, *Selections from the Prison Notebooks*.

48. Felski, *The Gender of Modernity*, 13.

49. Frow, *Time and Commodity Culture*.

50. Held and McGrew, "The Great Globalization Debate."

51. Wallerstein, *The Capitalist World Economy*.

52. For example, the manager of the Printex factory mentioned competition from textiles imported from China as one of the challenges facing his factory (interview, February 23, 2000).

53. Personal observation in fabric stores in the United States and cloth markets in Ghana.

54. See, for example, Ake, *The New World Order*.

55. Mohanty, "Introduction: Cartographies of Struggle."

56. Mohanty, "'Under Western Eyes' Revisited."

57. Shohat and Stam, *Unthinking Eurocentrism*.

58. Mohanty, "Introduction: Cartographies of Struggle."

59. Posey and Dutfield, *Beyond Intellectual Property*, 230.

60. Shohat and Stam, *Unthinking Eurocentrism*, 32. Other scholars, like Chandra Mohanty (in "'Under Western Eyes' Revisited"), also use the term *Fourth World* to refer to indigenous people.

61. Examples of this focus on indigenous peoples include the essays in Greaves, *Intellectual Property Rights for Indigenous Peoples*; Brown, *Who Owns Native Culture?*; and Coombe, *The Cultural Life of Intellectual Properties*.

62. Life history narration, Asokwa, November 9, 1999.

63. Arthur, *Cloth as Metaphor*.

64. Ibid.

65. Ibid.

66. Ibid., 25.

67. Obawale, "Choice of Color of Textile Fabrics among the Peoples of Ghana." See also Ross, *Wrapped in Pride*.

68. Ross, *Wrapped in Pride*.

69. Rattray, *Religion and Art in Ashanti*.

70. Obawale, "Choice of Color of Textile Fabrics among the Peoples of Ghana."

71. Life history narration, Adanwomase, November 27, 1999.

72. The distinction between the two kinds of communities is not watertight—both kinds of cloth production are found in several communities, but usually one is predominant. Thus, there are kente weavers at Ntonso and adinkra makers at Bonwire.

73. Nana Berhene, life history narration, Kumasi, November 25, 1999.

74. See Arthur, *Cloth as Metaphor,* for a detailed discussion of the meanings of color and cloth among the Akan.

75. Life history narration, Asokwa, 1999.

76. Yankah, *Speaking for the Chief,* 81–82.

77. Interview with GTP manager, Tema, December 10, 1999.

78. Ross, *Wrapped in Pride,* 91.

79. Interview with marketing manager of Printex (formerly Spintex factory), February 23, 2000.

1. The Tongue Does Not Rot

1. Life history narration, Ntonso, November 22, 1999.

2. Life history narration, Asokwa, December 1, 1999.

3. Agbo, *Values of Adinkra Symbols.*

4. Ross, *Wrapped in Pride,* 101.

5. Life history narration, Asokwa, December 1, 1999.

6. Ross, *Wrapped in Pride,* note 4.

7. He had waived the fees in my case.

8. Life history narration, Ntonso, November 22, 1999.

9. This is not limited to Akan society; Elisha Renne notes a similar relationship between the living and the dead among the Bunu people in Nigeria in *Cloth That Does Not Die.*

10. Kopytoff, "Ancestors as Elders in Africa."

11. This is done through the pouring of libation, during which each ancestor is summoned by name to bear witness to the occasion and is also offered a drink.

12. He relented in the course of his narration and provided a particularly rich historical account of the craft.

13. Currently, in both Ghanaian and U.S. copyright law, that expiration occurs seventy years after the death of an author.

14. Tsikata and Anyidoho, "Copyright and Oral Literature"; WIPO, *Revised Draft Provisions for the Protection of Traditional Cultural Expressions/Expressions of Folklore.*

15. See, for example, McLeod, *Owning Culture.*

16. Several scholars have commented on the enlightenment and Romantic roots of authorship under intellectual property law. See, for example, Coombe, *The Cultural Life of Properties* (especially her discussion in the chapter "The Properties of Culture and the Politics of Possessing Identity"); McLeod, *Owning Culture;* and Rose, *Authors and Owners.*

17. Anderson, *Imagined Communities.*

18. Frow, *Time and Commodity Culture;* McClintock, "Family Feuds"; Chakrabarty, *Provincializing Europe.*

19. Postcolonial scholars (for example, those listed in note 18) tackle the issue of different modes of time existing contemporaneously with each other. However, with a few exceptions (such as Frow, in *Time and Commodity Culture,* and Strathern, in "Imagined Collectivities and Multiple Authorship"), the discussion of different temporal modes is seldom linked with analyses of intellectual property law.

20. Frow, *Time and Commodity Culture,* 2.

21. McLeod, *Owning Culture;* Bettig, *Copyrighting Culture.*

22. Tsikata and Anyidoho, "Copyright and Oral Literature."

23. Foucault, "What Is an Author?"

24. Life history narration, Bonwire, November 26, 1999.

25. Government of Ghana, *Constitution of the Republic of Ghana.*

26. Life history narration, Accra, March 2, 2000.

27. One of Baffour Gyimah's designs features two figures seated at a table. One person is eating while the other watches. Baffour Gyimah's name for this design is, "It is the one who has food who eats, and not the one who is hungry."

28. The decree has been replaced by an industrial designs law and is discussed in greater detail in chapter 2.

29. Cochrane, "Senegalese Weavers' Ethnic Identities, in Discourse and in Craft."

30. Life history narration, Accra, March 2, 2000.

31. Life history narration, Asokwa, November 9, 1999.

32. Life history narration, Ntonso, November 22, 1999.

33. Ibid.

34. Ibid.

35. Life history narration, Accra, March 2, 2000.

36. Locke, "Two Treatises of Government."

37. According to Hess and Ostrom ("Introduction: An Overview of the Knowledge Commons," 3–4), interest in the commons as an analytical framework for knowledge and information began in the mid-1990s.

38. Boyle, *The Public Domain.*

39. Rose, "The Comedy of the Commons."

40. Boyle, *The Public Domain.*

41. Bollier, "Why We Must Talk about the Information Commons," 272.

42. Benkler, *The Wealth of Networks,* 60.

43. Ibid., 61.

44. See Lessig (*The Future of Ideas,* 23) on the Internet commons and Leach ("Modes of Creativity and the Register of Ownership") on the tribal commons.

45. Benkler, *The Wealth of Networks,* 61.

46. Appadurai, "Introduction: Commodities and the Politics of Value."

47. Government of Ghana, *Textile Designs (Registrations) Decree.*

48. Mould-Iddrisu, "Industrial Designs—the Ghanaian Experience."

49. See, for example, McLeod, *Owning Culture.*
50. Collins, "The 'Folkloric Copyright Tax' Problem in Ghana."

2. The Women Don't Know Anything!

1. Butler, *Gender Trouble.*
2. Amadiume, *Male Daughters, Female Husbands.*
3. Oyêwùmí. *The Invention of Women,* 42.
4. Ibid., 78.
5. Harding, *Whose Science?* and Hill Collins, *Black Feminist Thought.*
6. See, for example, Shiva, *Biopiracy.*
7. See, for example, Oakes, "Bathing in the Far Village."
8. Halbert, *Intellectual Property in the Information Age* and "Feminist Interpretations of Intellectual Property Law."
9. Shiva, *Biopiracy.*
10. Polakoff, *Into Indigo.*
11. Renne, "Traditional Modernity."
12. Several respondents referred to this as Oyokomanhene, king of the Oyoko *state,* but the holder of the title insisted that the proper designation was Oyokomaahene, king of the Oyoko *women,* based on his version of the origin of the cloth.
13. Nana Berhene, Oyokomaahene, life history narration, Kumasi, November 25, 1999.
14. Life history narration, Asokwa, November 10, 1999.
15. Rattray, *Religion and Art in Ashanti.*
16. Nana Antwi Boasiako, former linguist of the Asantehene, interview, February 16, 1999.
17. I am grateful to Lisa Cartwright for suggesting this interpretation.
18. Life history narration, Kumasi, October 13, 1999.
19. Life history narration, Bonwire, November 26, 1999.
20. Interview with Assistant Program Officer, Center for the Development of People (CEDEP), Kumasi, October 11, 1999.
21. Life history narration, Asokwa, November 9, 1999.
22. Etienne, "Women and Men, Cloth and Colonization."
23. Rattray, *Religion and Art in Ashanti.*
24. Nana Antwi Boasiako, Kumasi, February 16, 1999.
25. Mama, "Shedding the Masks and Tearing the Veils"; Adomako Ampofo, "'My Cocoa Is between My Legs.'"
26. A photograph of machine-printed adinkra is shown in Claire Polakoff's book *Into Indigo,* published in 1980, while Doran Ross reports in *Wrapped in Pride* (283) that adinkra cloth was mass-produced by the British for sale in Ghana as far back as the late nineteenth century.
27. Observation in cloth markets in Ghana in 2004, confirmed by the executive secretary of the National Folklore Board in an interview on December 15, 2004.

28. Life history narration, Asokwa, November 9, 1999.

29. See, for example, Domowitz, "Wearing Proverbs."

30. Darkwah, "Trading Goes Global."

31. Interview, Accra, February 23, 2000.

32. Yankah, *Speaking for the Chief* (68), notes that men dominate public speaking in Africa.

33. Domowitz, "Wearing Proverbs."

34. Government of Ghana, *Textile Designs (Registration) Decree.*

35. Felski, *The Gender of Modernity;* Lloyd, "The Man of Reason."

36. Kesson-Smith and Tettey, "Citizenship, Customary Law and Gendered Jurisprudence."

37. Coalition on the Women's Manifesto for Ghana, *The Women's Manifesto for Ghana.*

38. For example, in the area of domestic violence, with the passage of the Domestic Violence Act in 2007.

39. This is also the view adopted by scholars and activists in the Ghanaian music industry.

40. Conseil National du Ghana pour les Femmes et le Développement, "Groupements a but économique de femmes solidaires."

41. Arthur, *Cloth as Metaphor.*

42. One respondent reported working on a commission to produce such stoles. This and other diasporic uses of kente cloth are reported by Ross in *Wrapped in Pride.*

43. Boateng, "Equality, Development, Peace and Inverted Pyramids"; Tsikata, "Gender Equality and the State in Ghana"; Darkwah, "Trading Goes Global."

44. Adomako Ampofo, "My Cocoa Is between My Legs."

45. The Coalition on the Women's Manifesto for Ghana, *The Women's Manifesto for Ghana.*

46. Darkwah, "Trading Goes Global."

47. McClintock, "Family Feuds"; Mohanty, "Cartographies of Struggle."

48. Rattray, *Religion and Art in Ashanti;* Stoller, *Money Has No Smell.*

49. Halbert, *Intellectual Property in the Information Age* and "Feminist Interpretations of Intellectual Property Law."

50. Shohat and Stam, *Unthinking Eurocentrism.*

51. This often happens when a sphere of female knowledge becomes profitable beyond local communities and markets or when modern technology is applied to it. In Ghana, it has often been the case that the application of technology to female activities like vegetable oil extraction has led to male control of those activities.

3. Your Face Doesn't Go Anywhere

1. *Lobby* is used here in the sense of an interest group rather than specialists who are paid by such groups to influence legislators.

2. Collins, "The Early History of West African Highlife Music," 221.

3. Collins, "The 'Folkloric Copyright Tax' Problem in Ghana."

4. Collins, "The Early History of West African Highlife Music."

5. Ibid.

6. The 1990 edition of *Ghana Copyright News* gives the date as 1922, while Collins, in "The 'Folkloric Copyright Tax' Problem in Ghana," gives 1928 as the date of that first recording.

7. Carey, "Historical Pragmatism and the Internet," 451.

8. Toynbee, "Musicians," 127.

9. Ibid.

10. John Collins, interview, November 30, 2004.

11. van Dantzig, *Forts and Castles of Ghana*.

12. Castles served a number of purposes, from provisioning ships to—more notoriously—holding slaves before they were transported across the Atlantic. Several of these forts have become museums, tourist attractions, and sites of pilgrimage for Africans in the diaspora. Others, like Christiansborg, have been incorporated into the network of administrative buildings.

13. See, for example, Halbert, *Intellectual Property in the Information Age*; Boyle, *Shamans, Software, and Spleens*.

14. John Collins, interview, November 30, 2004.

15. Ibid.

16. Interview, September 16, 1999. This point is also made by several scholars of intellectual property law. For example, Sell and May argue in "Moments in Law" that technological innovations constitute one of three key factors that come together at various points in time to create significant shifts in intellectual property regulation (the other two factors are ideas and institutions).

17. The law was also significant in its responsiveness to that part of the international intellectual property law agenda that was concerned with regulating the appropriation of local and indigenous cultural production (or folklore). As a result, the law included measures to protect folklore based on the model provisions of UNESCO and WIPO.

18. John Collins, interview, November 30, 2004.

19. Ghana Copyright Administration, "Copyright Changes Hats," 3.

20. Ghana Copyright Administration, "The Banderole System," 4–5.

21. Ghana Copyright Administration, "1991 Distribution Figures," 5.

22. Collins, "The 'Folkloric Copyright Tax' Problem in Ghana."

23. Ibid.

24. Simon, *Rhythm of the Saints*.

25. Collins, note 22.

26. Ghana Copyright Administration, "Musicians Meet Secretary for Information," 1. The meeting may have been held in early 1990, since the report did not give an exact date but said that it was a follow-up to a meeting between musicians and the Head of State in August 1989.

27. Copyright Administrator, interview, September 16, 1999.

28. Interview, December 29, 2000. "Book-long" is a Ghanaian-English term that roughly translates as bookish or nerdy.

29. Interview, December 8, 2004.

30. See Ryan, *Knowledge Diplomacy.*

31. Carlos Sakyi, interview, December 8, 2004.

32. Ibid.

33. WIPO, *Agreement between the World Intellectual Property Organization and the World Trade Organization (1995); Agreement on Trade-Related Aspects of Intellectual Property Rights (TRIPS Agreement) (1994); Provisions mentioned in the TRIPS Agreement of the Paris Convention etc.,* 54–55.

34. Other laws included in this reform were the *Industrial Designs Act,* which replaced the 1973 *Textile Designs (Registration) Decree; Trade Marks Act; Geographical Indications Act;* and *Layout Designs (Topographies) of Integrated Circuits Act.*

35. John Collins, interview, November 30, 2004; Carlos Sakyi, interview, December 8, 2004.

36. I am grateful to Mr. Apodollah, Parliament House, Ghana, for pointing this out in a discussion on November 29, 2004.

37. Personal observation of forum and of parliamentary session where bill was passed.

38. Interview, December 29, 1999.

39. Interview, September 24, 1999.

40. Interview, December 8, 2004.

41. Life history narration, Asokwa, November 9, 1999.

42. Most cloth producers had some formal education, but only one had completed high school. Obviously, as skilled weavers and adinkra makers, they were very highly educated in their respective areas, but this was outside the sphere of officially recognized formal education.

43. Life history narration, March 2, 2000.

44. This may be a generational problem—particularly in the case of kente, as there was an organized group of young weavers at Bonwire at the time that these life histories were conducted. However, the main objective of such groups appears to be to pool resources for kente production, and no such group appears to have taken up the issue of the protection of kente designs at the national level.

45. See Giroux, "The Terror of Neoliberalism"; Mkandawire, "The Global Economic Context"; and Ferguson, *Global Shadows.*

46. Giroux, "The Terror of Neoliberalism," 4.

47. Hearn, "The 'Uses and Abuses' of Civil Society in Africa."

48. As noted in the Introduction, the national constitution formally recognizes the rulers of indigenous states within Ghana, although their authority in their respective territories is no longer absolute.

49. Life history narration, Tewobaabi, November 27, 1999.

50. A number of scholars, including Chander and Sunder (in "The Romance of the Public Domain") and Jaszi and Woodmansee (in "Beyond Authorship") point to this element of ignorance as one of the challenges in gaining protection for indigenous and local cultural production under intellectual property laws.

51. Sell and May, "Moments in Law."

52. Foucault "What Is an Author?"

53. Ibid., 118.

54. See Rose, *Authors and Owners;* Jaszi and Woodmansee, "Beyond Authorship"; Coombe, *The Cultural Life of Properties;* and McLeod, *Owning Culture.*

55. Government of Ghana, *Copyright Act,* Section 76.

56. Collins makes a similar observation in "The 'Folkloric Copyright Tax' Problem in Ghana."

57. Life histories, Bonwire, November 26, 1999; Adanwomase, November 27, 1999.

58. See Mamdani, *Citizen and Subject,* for this analysis of the urban–rural divide.

59. The portion of Asokwa where the adinkra-making community is located is an example of a community that is urban yet marginal.

60. See Mkandawire, "The Global Economic Context"; Ferguson, *Global Shadows.*

61. George F. Kojo Arthur, personal communication, January 28, 2008.

62. Centre for Indigenous Knowledge Systems. Homepage. http://www.cefiks.org (accessed December 13, 2009).

4. We Run a Single Country

1. Life history narration, Accra, December 8, 1999.

2. Ibid.

3. Agbenaza, *The Ewe 'Adanudo.'*

4. Ziff and Rao, *Borrowed Power,* 1.

5. Ibid.

6. According to Rosemary Coombe (in *The Cultural Life of Properties*), this view represents a shift in the understanding of cultural appropriation from an act of subversion and resistance by the marginalized to an act of domination by the powerful.

7. An exception to this is Coombe's discussion of subversive appropriation by marginalized groups.

8. Appadurai, *Modernity at Large* (see, especially, chapter 2, "Disjuncture and Difference in the Global Cultural Economy").

9. Additional factors are global art and tourist markets.

10. Wilks, *Asante in the 19th Century.*

11. Following the defeat of Germany in the First World War, the German territory of Togoland, to the east of the Gold Coast, was divided up between Britain and France.

12. Anderson, *Imagined Communities.*

13. Fanon, *The Wretched of the Earth.*

14. Askew, *Performing the Nation.*

15. Korang, *Writing Ghana.*

16. Ansah, *Golden Jubilee Lectures.*

17. Chazan et al., *Politics and Society in Contemporary Africa.*

18. Allman, *Quills of the Porcupine.*

19. This was standard colonial practice, as discussed by Mamdani in *Citizen and Subject.*

20. Korang, *Writing Ghana.* Korang notes that these claims were supported by the work of anthropologist Eva Meyerowitz, but the latter's findings have been disputed.

21. See Molefi Asante, "The Principal Issues of Afrocentric Identity," for a discussion of Afrocentric thought.

22. Arthur, *Cloth as Metaphor.*

23. Personal observation in Ghana on several occasions.

24. The Big Six were the leaders of Nkrumah's Convention People's Party, which came to the forefront of the nationalist movement through its effective mass mobilization strategies.

25. Ross, *Wrapped in Pride.*

26. Personal observation, confirmed as deliberate state policy by the manager of the Ghana Tourist Board (Kumasi office) in an interview on February 4, 2000.

27. Ross, *Wrapped in Pride,* note 27.

28. Personal observation, December 1999.

29. Yankah, *Speaking for the Chief.*

30. Life history narration, Bonwire, November 26, 1999.

31. Ibid.

32. Ibid.

33. Life history narration, Kumasi, October 13, 1999.

34. Ross, *Wrapped in Pride.*

35. Life history narration, Accra, March 2, 2000.

36. Interview, December 15, 2004.

37. Collins, "The 'Folkloric Copyright Tax' Problem in Ghana"; COCCA, *Copyright Bill Is Inadequate.*

38. Life history narration, Adanwomase, November 27, 1999.

39. The official view as reported by Nana Antwi Boasiako, former linguist of the Asantehene, Kumasi, October 13, 1999.

40. Life history narration, November 25, 1999.

41. Life history narration, Accra, February 29, 2000.

42. Ibid.

43. Ibid.

44. This position is also held by several folklore specialists and by activists in the musicians' lobby. See, for example, Collins, "The 'Folkloric Copyright Tax' Problem in Ghana"; and COCCA, *Copyright Bill Is Inadequate.*

45. Gyaman, the origin of adinkra, is located near the Ghana–Ivory Coast border. However, the craft appears not to have survived in the Ivory Coast, which is best known

for Korhogo cloth. This bears some resemblance to adinkra in its application of designs in black to a plain cotton background. However, the production techniques of this cloth are closer to those of Malian bogolanfini than to adinkra, and its symbolic system is entirely different from that of adinkra cloth. See Polakoff, *Into Indigo.*

46. It is important to note that Mansah's and Akosua's views are reported here not because they are necessarily representative but because they are helpful for understanding the ways in which some Ghanaian artists view the issue of rights to cultural production. Another artist, interviewed in 2004, expressed a contrary view and thought the payment of royalties for folklore was a reasonable requirement.

47. Chazan and others, *Politics and Society in Contemporary Africa.*

48. Akyeampong, "Africans in the Diaspora."

49. Ibid.

50. Ibid.

51. Boateng, "African Textile and the Politics of Diasporic Identity-Making."

52. White and White, *Stylin'.*

53. Ibid.

54. Ibid., 23.

55. Brown, *Fighting for US.*

56. Martin, "Karenga, Maulana (Everett, Ronald McKinley)," 1526.

57. Although it is widely spoken in East Africa, Swahili is not an indigenous African language but an amalgam of Arabic and indigenous languages. In this respect, it is something of a pan-African language that would have been particularly appealing in the 1960s when the pan-African movement linking people of African descent was still active.

58. For detailed discussions of the pan-African movement, see P. Olisanwuche Esedebe, *Pan-Africanism;* W. Ofuatey-Kodjoe, *Pan Africanism;* Immanuel Geiss, *The Pan-African Movement.* Some commentators see the pan-African movement as a thing of the past, while others, like Ofuatey-Kodjoe and Esedebe, see it more as a continuing and mutating phenomenon.

59. This point is also noted by Doran Ross in *Wrapped in Pride,* 171.

60. De Veaux, *Warrior Poet,* 144–45.

61. Ibid.

62. The use of kente in such celebrations is exhaustively discussed in Doran Ross's *Wrapped in Pride.*

63. Personal observation in fabric stores in Illinois and California from 2001 to the present.

64. Hicks, *Black Threads.*

65. Ibid.

66. See Coombe, *The Cultural Life of Properties.*

67. In the work of recording and visual artists like Cassandra Wilson and Varnette Honeywood, for example, and also in Sankofa societies.

68. Interview, Champaign, Illinois, October 2001.

69. Boateng, "African Textiles and the Politics of Diasporic Identity-Making."

70. Stoller, *Money Has No Smell.*

71. Ross, *Wrapped in Pride.*

72. Bourdieu, *Distinction.*

73. Life history narration, Bonwire, November 26, 1999.

74. See also Coombe's discussion of Western criteria for judging non-Western art in "The Properties of Culture and the Politics of Possessing Identity" in *The Cultural Life of Properties.*

75. Frow, *Time and Commodity Culture;* Mauss, *The Gift.*

76. Frow, *Time and Commodity Culture,* 114.

77. Ibid.,124.

78. One weaver reported that he had worked on such commissions. Life history narration, Accra, December 8, 1999.

79. Ross, *Wrapped in Pride;* Boateng, "African Textiles and the Politics of Diasporic Identity-Making."

80. Interview, Champaign, Illinois, October 2001.

81. Boateng, "African Textiles and the Politics of Diasporic Identity-Making."

82. Askew, *Performing the Nation,* 273.

83. In a 2004 interview, the executive secretary of the National Folklore Board indicated that the law was likely to be applied most vigorously to those whose appropriation of folklore occurs on a large scale (such as textile companies).

84. Jennifer Hasty, "Rites of Passage, Routes of Redemption."

5. This Work Cannot Be Rushed

1. Life history narration, 1999.

2. Feld, "A Sweet Lullaby for World Music."

3. Naples and Desai, "Changing the Terms."

4. See Feld, "A Sweet Lullaby for World Music," and Seeger, "Who Got Left Out of the Property Grab Again," for musical examples. For scholarship on the appropriation of other forms of indigenous culture, see Ziff and Rao, "Introduction to Cultural Appropriation"; Coombe, *The Cultural Life of Properties;* Jaszi and Woodmansee "Beyond Authorship."

5. Carmody and Owusu, "Competing Hegemons?"

6. Held and McGrew, "The Great Globalization Debate."

7. Appadurai, *Modernity at Large,* chapter 2, "Disjuncture and Difference."

8. Morris and Waisbord, "Introduction: Rethinking Media Globalization and State Power" in *Media and Globalization.*

9. Held and McGrew, "The Great Globalization Debate."

10. Appadurai, "Disjuncture and Difference."

11. Ibid.; Arnason, "Nationalism, Globalization and Modernity"; Bergesen, "Turning World-System Theory on Its Head."

12. Robertson, "Mapping the Global Condition."

13. Held and McGrew, in their overview of the literature on globalization (see note 10), outline scholarship that identifies colonial and imperialist projects, old and new, as factors that have introduced deep structural inequalities into the global economy.

14. Mkandawire, "The Global Economic Context," 172.

15. Ibid.

16. Self-serving when it comes from industrialized nations or, in the past, from racist settler regimes on the continent. This view is very common in popular discourse as evidenced, for example, in references to "the African problem," Africa as a "basket case," and so forth.

17. Appadurai, "Introduction: Commodities and the Politics of Value."

18. Collins, "The 'Folkloric Copyright Tax' Problem in Ghana."

19. See Mkandawire, "The Global Economic Context"; Ferguson, *Global Shadows*; and Jensen and Gibbon, "Africa and the Doha Round," for examples of scholarship on the adverse consequences of World Bank/IMF–led policies and equally adverse implications of the WTO and its agreements for African countries.

20. This series of events has been discussed by several commentators, including Ryan, *Knowledge Diplomacy*; Sell, *Power and Ideas*; Sell and May, "Moments in Law"; and Drahos and Braithwaite, *Information Feudalism*.

21. World Intellectual Property Organization, http://www.wipo.int/treaties/general (accessed August 20, 2008). An exception to the agreements administered by WIPO was UNESCO's Universal Copyright Convention.

22. An obvious exception to this principle of equality is the U.N. Security Council of which five nations are permanent members and hold veto rights that are not shared by the other members who participate in the council on a rotating basis.

23. Jaszi and Woodmansee, "Introduction," 12.

24. For example, the patenting of plant material became an accepted premise in intellectual property law as early as 1980. See McLeod, *Owning Culture*.

25. Ryan, *Knowledge Diplomacy*.

26. "US Vows to 'Fight' the Push for WIPO Reform." *Intellectual Property Watch* 1, no. 2 (November 4, 2004).

27. Mara, "'Turning Point' at WIPO."

28. Jensen and Gibbon, "Africa and the Doha Round."

29. McLeod, *Freedom of Expression*.

30. Teitel and Shand, *The Ownership of Life*.

31. Nnaemeka, "Nego-Feminism"; Hountondji, "Introduction: Recentring Africa."

32. Boyle, *Shamans, Software, and Spleens*, 141.

33. In *Money Has No Smell*, Paul Stoller gives China as the source of the imitations sold by West African vendors in New York. Based on my personal observation in U.S. fabric stores, imitations are also produced in India.

34. See Horyn, "A Few Jewels Left in Milan's Crown"; Barboza, "People's Republic of Exports."

35. Carmody and Owusu, "Competing Hegemons?"

36. Ibid.

37. Taylor, "China's Foreign Policy."

38. Ibid.

39. Carmody and Owusu, "Competing Hegemons."

40. Taylor, "China's Foreign Policy," 458.

41. Sautman and Hairong, "Friends and Interests," 86.

42. Ibid.

43. Carmody and Owusu, "Competing Hegemons," 507.

44. Ibid.

45. See Jaszi and Woodmansee, "Beyond Authorship," for examples of this.

46. McLeod, *Owning Culture*; Drahos and Braithwaite, *Information Feudalism.*

47. Mulama, "East Africans May Be Stripped of the Kikoi."

48. Hearn, "The 'Uses and Abuses' of Civil Society in Africa.

Conclusion

1. Mkandawire, "The Global Economic Context."

2. Ferguson, *Global Shadows*, 10.

3. Chakrabarty, *Provincializing Europe* (see, especially, chapter 3, "Translating Life-Worlds into Labor and History"). An earlier version of the chapter was published as "The Time of History and the Times of Gods" in Lowe and Lloyd, *The Politics of Culture.*

4. Chakrabarty, *Provincializing Europe*; McClintock, "Family Feuds"; Lowe and Lloyd, *The Politics of Culture in the Shadow of Capital*; Frow, *Time and Commodity Culture*; Ferguson, *Global Shadows.*

5. Frow, *Time and Commodity Culture*, 2.

6. McClintock, "Family Feuds"; Chakrabarty, *Provincializing Europe*; and Frow, *Time and Commodity Culture.*

7. Collins, "The Problem of Oral Copyright."

8. See Bettig, *Copyrighting Culture*; McLeod, *Owning Culture*; and McLeod, *Freedom of Expression*, for examples of this version.

9. See Coombe, *The Cultural Life of Properties*; McLeod, *Owning Culture*; McLeod, *Freedom of Expression*; and Jaszi and Woodmansee, "Beyond Authorship," for examples of this version.

10. Hobsbawm, *Nations and Nationalism.*

11. Lowe and Lloyd make this argument in their introduction to the anthology *The Politics of Culture in the Shadow of Capital*. See also, Fanon, *The Wretched of the Earth.*

12. Lessig, *The Future of Ideas*; Boyle, *The Public Domain*; Benkler, *The Wealth of Networks.*

13. See Benkler, *The Wealth of Networks*; Boyle, *The Public Domain.*

14. Boyle, *The Public Domain*, 167.

15. This point is also made by Tsikata and Anyidoho, "Copyright and Oral Literature"; and Collins, "The Problem of Oral Copyright."

16. Ibid.

17. Shiva, *Monocultures of the Mind.*

18. Bollier, "The Growth of the Commons Paradigm."

19. Bollier, "Why We Must Talk about the Information Commons"; Boyle, *The Public Domain.*

20. Hess and Ostrom, *Understanding Knowledge as a Commons,* 8.

21. Benkler, *The Wealth of Networks.*

Bibliography

Adomako Ampofo, Akosua. "'My Cocoa Is between My Legs': Sex as Work among Ghanaian Women." In *Women's Labor in the Global Economy*, edited by Sharon Harley, 182–205. New Brunswick, N.J.: Rutgers University Press, 2007.

Agbenaza, Edith Happy. "The Ewe 'Adanudo' (A Piece of Creative Cloth Woven Locally by Ewes)." Unpublished B.A. thesis, University of Science and Technology, Kumasi, Ghana, n.d.

Agbo, Adolph. *Values of Adinkra Symbols.* Kumasi, Ghana: Ebony Designs and Publications, 1999.

Ake, Claude. *The New World Order: A View from the South.* Lagos, Nigeria: Malthouse Press, 1992.

Akyeampong, Emmanuel. "Africans in the Diaspora: The Diaspora and Africa." *African Affairs* 99 (2000): 183–215.

Allman, Jean. *The Quills of the Porcupine: Asante Nationalism in an Emergent Ghana.* Madison: University of Wisconsin Press, 1993.

Amadiume, Ifi. *Male Daughters, Female Husbands: Gender and Sex in an African Society.* Atlantic Highlands, N.J.: Zed Books, 1987.

Amegatcher, Andrew O. *Ghanaian Law of Copyright.* Accra, Ghana: Omega Law Publishers, 1993.

Anderson, Benedict. *Imagined Communities: Reflections on the Origin and Spread of Nationalism,* rev. ed. London: Verso, 1991.

Ansah, Paul A.V. *Golden Jubilee Lectures: Broadcasting and National Development.* Accra, Ghana: Ghana Broadcasting Corporation, 1985.

Appadurai, Arjun. "Introduction: Commodities and the Politics of Value." In *The Social Life of Things: Commodities in Cultural Perspective,* edited by Arjun Appadurai, 3–63. Cambridge: Cambridge University Press, 1986.

———. *Modernity at Large: Cultural Dimensions of Globalization.* Minneapolis: University of Minnesota Press, 1996.

Arnason, Johann P. "Nationalism, Globalization, and Modernity." In Featherstone, *Global Culture,* 207–36.

Arthur, G. F. Kojo. *Cloth as Metaphor: (Re)-reading the Adinkra Cloth Symbols of the*

Akan of Ghana. Legon, Ghana: Centre for Indigenous Knowledge Systems (CEFIKS), 1999/2001.

Asante, Molefi Kete. "The Principal Issues in Afrocentric Identity." In *African Intellectual Heritage: A Book of Sources,* edited by Molefi Kete Asante and Abu S. Abarry. Philadelphia: Temple University Press, 1996.

Askew, Kelly M. *Performing the Nation: Swahili Music and Cultural Politics in Tanzania.* Chicago: University of Chicago Press, 2002.

Barboza, David. "People's Republic of Exports." *New York Times,* October 14, 2009.

Benkler, Yochai. *The Wealth of Networks: How Social Production Transforms Markets and Freedom.* New Haven, Conn.: Yale University Press, 2006.

Bergesen, Albert. "Turning World-System Theory on Its Head." In Featherstone, *Global Culture,* 67–81.

Bettig, Ron. *Copyrighting Culture: The Political Economy of Intellectual Property.* Boulder, Colo.: Westview Press, 1996.

Boateng, Boatema. "African Textiles and the Politics of Diasporic Identity-Making." In *Fashioning Africa: Power and the Politics of Dress,* edited by Jean Allman, 212–26. Bloomington: Indiana University Press, 2004.

———. "Equality, Development, Peace, and Inverted Pyramids: A Study of West Africa Magazine and the United Nations Women's Decade." Master's thesis, University of Leicester, England, 1989.

———. "Walking the Tradition–Modernity Tightrope: Gender Contradictions in Textile Production and Ghanaian Intellectual Property Law." *American University Journal of Gender, Social Policy and the Law* 15, no. 2 (2007): 341–57.

Bollier, David. "The Growth of the Commons Paradigm." In Hess and Ostrom, *Understanding Knowledge as a Commons,* 27–40.

———. "Why We Must Talk about the Information Commons." *Law Library Journal* 96, no. 2 (2004): 267–82.

Bourdieu, Pierre. *Distinction: A Social Critique of the Judgment of Taste.* Cambridge, Mass.: Harvard University Press, 1984.

Boyle, James. *Shamans, Software, and Spleens: Law and the Construction of the Information Society.* Cambridge, Mass.: Harvard University Press, 1996.

———. *The Public Domain: Enclosing the Commons of the Mind.* New Haven, Conn.: Yale University Press, 2008.

Boyle, James, and Lawrence Lessig, eds. "Cultural Environmentalism @10." Special Issue, *Law and Contemporary Problems* 70, no. 2 (2007).

Brown, Michael. *Who Owns Native Culture?* Cambridge, Mass.: Harvard University Press, 2003.

Brown, Scot. *Fighting for US: Maulana Karenga, the US Organization, and Black Cultural Nationalism.* New York: New York University Press, 2003.

Butler, Judith. *Gender Trouble: Feminism and the Subversion of Identity.* New York: Routledge, 1990.

Canclini, Néstor García. *Transforming Modernity: Popular Culture in Mexico.* Translated by Lidia Lozano. Austin: University of Texas Press, 1993.

Carey, James. "Historical Pragmatism and the Internet." *New Media and Society* 7, no. 4 (2005): 443–55.

Carmody, Padraig R., and Francis Y. Owusu. "Competing Hegemons? Chinese versus American Geo-economic Strategies in Africa." *Political Geography* 26 (2007): 504–24.

Chakrabarty, Dipesh. *Provincializing Europe: Postcolonial Thought and Historical Difference.* Princeton, N.J.: Princeton University Press, 2000.

Chakravartty, Paula, and Yuezhi Zhao, eds. *Global Communications: Toward a Transcultural Political Economy.* Lanham, Md.: Rowman & Littlefield, 2008.

Chander, Anupam, and Madhavi Sunder. "The Romance of the Public Domain." *California Law Review* 92, no. 5 (October 2004): 1331–73.

Chazan, Naomi, Peter Lewis, Robert Mortimer, Donald Rothchild, and Stephen John Stedman. *Politics and Society in Contemporary Africa,* 3rd ed. Boulder, Colo.: Lynne Rienner Publishers, 1999.

Coalition of Concerned Copyright Advocates (COCCA). *Copyright Bill Is Inadequate.* Accra, Ghana, 2004.

Coalition on the Women's Manifesto for Ghana. *The Women's Manifesto for Ghana.* Accra, Ghana, 2004.

Cochrane, Laura L. "Senegalese Weavers' Ethnic Identities, in Discourse and in Craft." *African Identities* 7, no. 1 (February 2009): 3–15.

Collins, John. "The Early History of West African Highlife Music." *Popular Music* 8, no. 3 (1989): 221–30.

———. "The 'Folkloric Copyright Tax' Problem in Ghana." *Media Development* 50, no. 1, (2003): 10–14.

———. "The Problem of Oral Copyright: The Case of Ghana." In *Music and Copyright,* edited by Simon Frith, 146–58. Edinburgh: Edinburgh University Press, 1993.

———. *Transnational Culture and Ghanaian Music: Copyright Conundrums in a Developing Nation.* Presented at the Center for African Studies Fall Colloquium on Transnational Culture Industries in Africa and Local Sites of Production. University of Illinois at Urbana–Champaign, 2000.

Conseil National du Ghana pour les Femmes et le Développement [Ghana National Council on Women and Development]. "Groupements a but économique de femmes solidaires: L'expérience du ghana" [Women's economic mutual help groups]. *Revue Tiers Monde* 26, no. 102, (April–June 1985): 451–56.

Coombe, Rosemary. *The Cultural Life of Properties: Authorship, Appropriation and the Law.* Durham, N.C.: Duke University Press, 1998.

Darkwah, Akosua K. "Trading Goes Global: Market Women in an Era of Globalization." *Asian Women* 15 (2002): 31–49.

De Veaux, Alexis. *Warrior Poet: A Biography of Audre Lorde.* New York: W. W. Norton, 2004.

Domowitz, Susan. "Wearing Proverbs: *Anyi* Names for Printed Factory Cloth." *African Arts* 25, no. 2 (1992): 82–87.

Drahos, Peter. *A Philosophy of Intellectual Property.* Aldershot, England: Ashgate Publishing, 1996.

Drahos, Peter, and John Braithwaite. *Information Feudalism: Who Owns the Knowledge Economy?* New York: New Press, 2002.

Esedebe, P. Olisanwuche. *Pan-Africanism: The Idea and Movement, 1776–1991,* 2nd ed. Washington, D.C.: Howard University Press, 1994.

Etienne, Mona. "Women and Men, Cloth and Colonization: The Transformation of Production–Distribution Relations among the Baule." In Grinker and Steiner, *Perspectives on Africa,* 518–35.

Fanon, Frantz. *The Wretched of the Earth.* New York: Grove Press, 1963.

Featherstone, Mike, ed. *Global Culture: Nationalism and Modernity.* London: Sage, 1990.

Feld, Steven. "A Sweet Lullaby for World Music." *Public Culture* 12, no. 1 (2000): 145–71.

Felski, Rita. *The Gender of Modernity.* Cambridge, Mass.: Harvard University Press, 1995.

Ferguson, James. *Global Shadows: Africa in the Neoliberal World Order.* Durham, N.C.: Duke University Press, 2006.

Foucault, Michel. "What Is an Author?" In *The Foucault Reader,* edited by Paul Rabinow, 101–20. New York: Pantheon Books, 1984.

Frow, John. *Time and Commodity Culture: Essays in Cultural Theory and Postmodernity.* Oxford: Clarendon Press, 1997.

Geiss, Immanuel. *The Pan-African Movement: A History of Pan-Africanism in America, Europe and Africa.* New York: Africana Publishing Co., 1974.

Ghana Copyright Administration. "The Banderole System." *Ghana Copyright News: The Organ of the Copyright Office and the Copyright Society of Ghana* 3, January 1991–December 1992.

———. "Copyright Changes Hats." *Ghana Copyright News* 2, December 1990.

———. "Musicians Meet Secretary for Information." *Ghana Copyright News* 1, March 1990.

———. "1991 Distribution Figures." *Ghana Copyright News* 3, January 1991–December 1992, 5.

Ghosh, Rishab Ayer, ed. *CODE: Collaborative Ownership and the Digital Economy.* Cambridge, Mass.: MIT Press, 2005.

Giroux, Henry A. "The Terror of Neoliberalism: Rethinking the Significance of Cultural Politics." *College Literature* 32, no. 1 (Winter 2005): 1–19.

Government of Ghana. *Constitution of the Republic of Ghana,* Accra, Ghana: Government Printer, Assembly Press, 1998.

———. *Copyright Act (Act 690),* 2005.

———. *Copyright Law,* 1985 (P.N.D.C.L. 110).

———. *Domestic Violence Act,* 2007.

———. *Geographical Indications Act,* 2003.

———. *Industrial Designs Act,* 2003.

———. *Layout Designs (Topographies) of Integrated Circuits Act,* 2004.

———. *Textile Designs (Registration) Decree,* 1973.

———. *Trade Marks Act,* 2004.

Gramsci, Antonio. *Selections from the Prison Notebooks of Antonio Gramsci,* edited by Quintin Hoare and Geoffrey Nowell Smith. New York: International Publishers, 1971.

Greaves, Tom, ed. *Intellectual Property Rights for Indigenous Peoples: A Source Book.* Oklahoma City: Society for Applied Anthropology, 1994.

Grinker, Roy Richard, and Christopher B. Steiner, eds. *Perspectives on Africa: A Reader in Culture, History, and Representation.* Malden, Mass.: Blackwell, 1997.

Halbert, Debora J. "Feminist Interpretations of Intellectual Property Law." *American University Journal of Gender, Social Policy and the Law* 14, no. 3 (2006): 431–60.

———. *Intellectual Property in the Information Age: The Politics of Expanding Ownership Rights.* Westport, Conn.: Quorum Books, 1999.

Harding, Sandra. *Whose Science? Whose Knowledge? Thinking from Women's Lives.* Ithaca, N.Y.: Cornell University Press, 1991.

Hasty, Jennifer. "Rites of Passage, Routes of Redemption: Emancipation Tourism and the Wealth of Culture." *Africa Today* 49, no. 3 (2002): 47–76.

Hawley, M'Liss Rae. *Phenomenal Fat Quarter Quilts.* Lafayette, Calif.: C&T Publishing, 2004.

Hearn, Julie. "The 'Uses and Abuses' of Civil Society in Africa." *Review of African Political Economy* 88 (2001): 45–53.

Held, David, and Anthony McGrew. "The Great Globalization Debate: An Introduction." In *The Global Transformations Reader: An Introduction to the Globalization Debate,* edited by David Held and Anthony McGrew, 1–45. Malden, Mass.: Polity Press, 2000.

Hess, Charlotte, and Elinor Ostrom, eds. *Understanding Knowledge as a Commons: From Theory to Practice.* Cambridge, Mass.: MIT Press, 2007.

———. "Introduction: An Overview of the Knowledge Commons." In Hess and Ostrom, *Understanding Knowledge as a Commons,* 3–26.

Hickey, Mary. *Sweet and Simple Baby Quilts.* Woodinville, Wash.: Martingale & Company, 2003.

Hicks, Kyra. *Black Threads: An African American Quilting Sourcebook.* Jefferson, N.C.: McFarland, 2003.

Hill Collins, Patricia. *Black Feminist Thought: Knowledge, Consciousness, and the Politics of Empowerment,* 2nd ed. New York: Routledge, 2000.

Hobsbawm, E. J. *Nations and Nationalism since 1870: Programme, Myth, Reality.* Cambridge: Cambridge University Press, 1992.

Horyn, Cathy. "A Few Jewels Left in Milan's Crown." *New York Times,* September 29, 2009.

Hountondji, Paulin J. "Introduction: Recentring Africa." In *Endogenous Knowledge: Research Trails,* edited by Paulin J. Hountodji, 1–39. Dakar, Senegal: CODESRIA, 1997.

Imam, Ayesha, Amina Mama, and Fatou Sow, eds. *Engendering African Social Sciences.* Dakar, Senegal: CODESRIA, 1997.

"Intellectual Property in Ghana: Kente, Folklore Need Protection." *Public Agenda* (Accra, Ghana), November 4–10, 1996.

Jaszi, Peter, and Martha Woodmansee. "Beyond Authorship: Refiguring Rights in Traditional Culture and Bioknowledge." In *Scientific Authorship: Credit and Intellectual Property in Science,* edited by Mario Biagioli and Peter Galison, 195–223. New York: Routledge, 2003.

———. "Introduction." In *The Construction of Authorship: Textual Appropriation in Law and Literature,* edited by Martha Woodmansee and Peter Jaszi, 1–13. Durham, N.C.: Duke University Press, 1994.

Jensen, Michael Friis, and Peter Gibbon. "Africa and the Doha Round: An Overview." *Development Policy Review* 25, no. 1 (2007): 5–24.

Kesson-Smith, Charlotte, and Wisdom J. Tettey. "Citizenship, Customary Law and Gendered Jurisprudence: A Socio-Legal Perspective." In *Critical Perspectives on Politics and Socio-Economic Development in Ghana,* edited by Wisdom J. Tettey, Korbla B. Puplampu, and Bruce J. Berman, 305–32. Leiden, The Netherlands: Koninlijke Brill, 2003.

Kopytoff, Igor. "Ancestors as Elders in Africa." In Grinker and Steiner, *Perspectives on Africa: A Reader in Culture, History and Representation,* 412–21.

Korang, Kwaku. *Writing Ghana, Imagining Africa: Nation and African Modernity.* Rochester, N.Y.: University of Rochester Press, 2003.

Kuruk, Paul. "Protecting Folklore under Modern Intellectual Property Regimes: A Reappraisal of the Tensions between Individual and Communal Rights in Africa and the United States." *American University Law Review* 48, no. 4 (April 1999): 769–849.

Leach, James. "Modes of Creativity and the Register of Ownership." In Ghosh, *CODE: Collaborative Ownership and the Digital Economy,* 29–44.

Lessig, Lawrence. *The Future of Ideas: The Fate of the Commons in a Connected World.* New York: Vintage Books, 2001/2002.

Lloyd, Genevieve. "The Man of Reason." In *Feminist Theory: A Philosophical Anthology,* edited by Ann E. Cudd and Robin O. Andreasen, 177–87. Malden, Mass.: Blackwell, 2005.

Locke, John. "Two Treatises of Government." In *The Works of John Locke (Vol. V),* edited by T. Tegg et al. London: Thomas Davison, 1823.

Lowe, Lisa, and David Lloyd, eds. *The Politics of Culture in the Shadow of Capital.* Durham, N.C.: Duke University Press, 1997.

Mama, Amina. "Shedding the Masks and Tearing the Veils: Cultural Studies for a Post-Colonial Africa." In Imam, Mama, and Sow, *Engendering African Social Sciences,* 61–80.

Mamdani, Mahmood. *Citizen and Subject: Contemporary Africa and the Legacy of Late Colonialism.* Princeton, N.J.: Princeton University Press, 1996.

Mara, K. (2009) "'Turning Point' at WIPO Pulls Traditional Knowledge Debate Out at Eleventh Hour." *Intellectual Property Watch.* http://www.ip-watch.org/weblog/2009/10/03/"turning-point"-at-wipo-pulls-traditional-knowledge-debate-out-at-eleventh-hour (accessed November 29, 2009).

Martin, Waldo E. "Karenga, Maulana (Everett, Ronald McKinley)." In *Encyclopedia of African-American Culture and History,* edited by Jack Salzman, David L. Smith, and Cornel West. New York: Macmillan Reference, 1996.

Mauss, Marcel. *The Gift: Forms and Functions of Exchange in Archaic Societies.* Translated by Ian Cunnison. New York: Norton, 1967.

McClintock, Anne. "Family Feuds: Gender, Nationalism and the Family." *Feminist Review* 44, no. 2 (1993): 61–80.

McLeod, Kembrew. *Freedom of Expression®: Resistance and Repression in the Age of Intellectual Property.* Minneapolis: University of Minnesota Press, 2007.

———. *Owning Culture: Authorship, Ownership and Intellectual Property Law.* New York: Peter Lang, 2001.

Mkandawire, Thandika. "The Global Economic Context." In *Towards a New Map of Africa,* edited by Ben Wisner, Camilla Toulmin, and Rutendo Chitiga, 155–82. London: Earthscan, 2005.

Mohanty, Chandra T. "Introduction: Cartographies of Struggle: Third World Women and the Politics of Feminism." In *Third World Women and the Politics of Feminism,* edited by Chandra Talpade Mohanty, Anne Russo, and Lourdes Torres, 1–47. Bloomington: Indiana University Press, 1991.

———. "'Under Western Eyes' Revisited: Feminist Solidarity through Anticapitalist Struggles." In *Feminism without Borders: Decolonizing Theory, Practicing Solidarity.* Durham, N.C.: Duke University Press, 2003.

Morris, Nancy, and Silvio Waisbord, eds. *Media and Globalization: Why the State Matters.* Lanham, Md.: Rowman & Littlefield, 2001.

Mould-Iddrisu, Betty N. "Industrial Designs—the Ghanaian Experience." *Managing Intellectual Property,* no. 7/8 April May, 1991.

———. "Protection of Folklore in Ghana." Prepared for the Second National Seminar on Folklore. Tamale, Ghana, 1994.

Mulama, Joyce. "East Africans May Be Stripped of the Kikoi." *International Press Services,* Nairobi, May 2006.

Naples, Nancy A., and Manisha Desai. "Changing the Terms: Community Activism, Globalization and the Dilemma of Transnational Feminist Praxis." In *Women's Activism and Globalization: Linking Local Struggles and Transnational Politics,* edited by Nancy Naples and Manisha Desai, 3–14. New York: Routledge, 2002.

National Commission on Culture. *The Cultural Policy of Ghana.* Accra, Ghana: National Commission on Culture, 2004.

Nnaemeka, Obioma. "Nego-Feminism: Theorizing, Practicing, and Pruning Africa's Way." *Signs: Journal of Women in Culture and Society* 29, no. 2 (2003): 357–85.

Oakes, Tim. "Bathing in the Far Village: Globalization, Transnational Capital, and the

Cultural Politics of Modernity in China." *Positions: East Asia Cultures Critique* 7, no. 2 (1999): 307–42.

Obawale, Gidoen Yekini. "Choice of Colour of Textile Fabrics among the Peoples of Ghana." Bachelor's thesis, University of Science and Technology, Kumasi, Ghana, n.d.

Ofuatey-Kodjoe, W. *Pan Africanism: New Directions in Strategy.* Lanham, Md.: University Press of America, 1986.

Oxford University Press. *Oxford English Dictionary.* http://dictionary.oed.com.

Oyêwùmí, Oyèrónkẹ́. *The Invention of Women: Making an African Sense of Western Gender Discourses.* Minneapolis: University of Minnesota Press, 1997.

Personal Narratives Group. *Interpreting Women's Lives: Feminist Theory and Personal Narratives.* Bloomington: Indiana University Press, 1989.

Polakoff, Claire. *Into Indigo: African Textiles and Dyeing Techniques.* Garden City, N.Y.: Anchor Books, 1980.

Posey, Darrell, and Graham Dutfield. *Beyond Intellectual Property: Toward Traditional Resource Rights for Indigenous Peoples and Local Communities.* Ottawa: IDRC, 1996.

Ranger, Terence. "The Invention of Tradition in Colonial Africa." In *The Invention of Tradition,* edited by Eric Hobsbawm and Terence Ranger, 211–62. Cambridge: Cambridge University Press, 1992.

Rathbone, Richard. *Nkrumah and the Chiefs: The Politics of Chieftaincy in Ghana 1951–60.* Accra, Ghana: F. Reimmer Book Services; Athens: Ohio University Press/Oxford: James Currey, 2000.

Rattray, Robert S. *Religion and Art in Ashanti.* Accra, Ghana: Presbyterian Book Depot; London: Oxford University Press, 1927.

Reinharz, Shulamit. *Feminist Methods in Social Research.* New York: Oxford University Press, 1992.

Renne, Elisha P. *Cloth That Does Not Die: The Meaning of Cloth in Bunu Social Life.* Seattle: University of Washington Press, 1995.

———. "Traditional Modernity and the Economics of Handwoven Cloth Production in Southwestern Nigeria." *Economic Development and Cultural Change* 45 (July 1997): 773–92.

Robertson, Roland. "Mapping the Global Condition: Globalization as the Central Concept." In Featherstone, *Global Culture,* 15–30.

Rose, Carol M. "The Comedy of the Commons: Custom, Commerce, and Inherently Public Property." In Rose, *Property and Persuasion: Essays on the History, Theory, and Rhetoric of Ownership,* 105–62. Boulder, Colo.: Westview Press, 1994.

Rose, Mark. *Authors and Owners: The Invention of Copyright.* Cambridge, Mass.: Harvard University Press, 1993.

Ross, Doran. *Wrapped in Pride: Ghanaian Kente and African-American Identity.* Los Angeles: UCLA Fowler Museum of Cultural History, 1998.

Ryan, Michael P. *Knowledge Diplomacy: Global Competition and the Politics of Intellectual Property.* Washington, D.C.: Brookings Institution Press, 1996.

Sautman, Barry, and Yan Hairong. "Friends and Interests: China's Distinctive Links with Africa." *African Studies Review* 50, no. 3 (December 2007): 75–114.

Seeger, Anthony. "Who Got Left Out of the Property Grab Again: Oral Traditions, Indigenous Rights, and Valuable Old Knowledge." In Ghosh, *CODE: Collaborative Ownership and the Digital Economy,* 75–84.

Sell, Susan. *Power and Ideas: North–South Politics of Intellectual Property and Antitrust.* Albany: State University of New York Press, 1998.

Sell, Susan, and Christopher May. "Moments in Law: Contestation and Settlement in the History of Intellectual Property Law." *Review of International Political Economy* 8, no. 3 (2001): 467–500.

Shillington, Kevin. *History of Africa.* New York: St. Martin's Press, 1995.

Shiva, Vandana. *Biopiracy: The Plunder of Nature and Knowledge.* Boston: South End Press, 1997.

———. *Monocultures of the Mind: Biodiversity, Biotechnology and the Third World.* Penang, Malaysia: Third World Network, 1993.

Shohat, Ella, and Robert Stam. *Unthinking Eurocentrism: Multiculturalism and the Media.* New York: Routledge, 1994.

Simon, Paul. *Rhythm of the Saints.* Music CD. Burbank, Calif.: Warner Brothers, 1990.

Stoller, Paul. *Money Has No Smell: The Africanization of New York City.* Chicago: Chicago University Press, 2002.

Strathern, Marilyn. "Imagined Collectivities and Multiple Authorship." In Ghosh, *CODE: Collaborative Ownership and the Digital Economy,* 13–28.

Taylor, Ian. "China's Foreign Policy towards Africa in the 1990s." *Journal of Modern African Studies* 36, no. 3 (1998): 443–60.

Teitel, Martin, and Hope Shand. *The Ownership of Life: When Patents and Values Clash.* Freeston, Calif.: CS Fund; New York: The HKH Foundation, 1997.

Thomas, Pradip Ninan, and Jan Servaes. "Introduction." In *Intellectual Property Rights and Communications in Asia: Conflicting Traditions,* edited by Pradip Ninan Thomas and Jan Servaes. New Delhi: Sage, 2006.

Toynbee, Jason. "Musicians." In *Music and Copyright,* edited by Simon Frith and Lee Marshall, 123–38. New York: Routledge, 2004.

Tsikata, Dzodzi. "Gender Equality and the State in Ghana: Some Issues of Policy and Practice." In Imam, Mama, and Sow, *Engendering African Social Sciences,* 381–412.

Tsikata, Fui S., and Anyidoho, Kofi. "Copyright and Oral Literature." In *Power of Their Word: Selected Papers from Proceedings of the 1st National Conference on Oral Literature in Ghana.* Legon, Ghana, 1988.

UNESCO; World Intellectual Property Organization. *Model Provisions for National Laws on Protection of Expressions of Folklore against Illicit Exploitation and Other Prejudicial Actions.* Geneva: UNESCO, 1985.

van Dantzig, Albert. *Forts and Castles of Ghana.* Accra, Ghana: Sedco Publishing, 1980.

Wallerstein, Immanuel. *The Capitalist World Economy.* Cambridge: Cambridge University Press, 1979.

———. "Culture as the Ideological Battleground of the Modern World-System." In Featherstone, *Global Culture: Nationalism and Modernity*, 31–55.

White, Shane, and Graham White. *Stylin': African-American Expressive Culture from Its Beginnings to the Zoot Suit*. Ithaca, N.Y.: Cornell University Press, 1998.

Wilks, Ivor. *Asante in the 19th Century: The Structure and Evolution of a Political Order*. Cambridge: Cambridge University Press, 1975.

Wilson, Alexandra. *The Bead Is Constant*. Legon: Ghana Universities Press, 2003.

Woodmansee, Martha, and Peter Jaszi, eds. *The Construction of Authorship: Textual Appropriation in Law and Literature*. Durham, N.C.: Duke University Press, 1994.

World Intellectual Property Organization (WIPO). *Agreement between the World Intellectual Property Organization and the World Trade Organization (1995)*. Geneva: WIPO, 1995.

———. *Agreement on Trade-Related Aspects of Intellectual Property Rights (TRIPS Agreement) (1994)*. Geneva: WIPO, 1994.

———. *Provisions Mentioned in the TRIPS Agreement of the Paris Convention etc.* Geneva: WIPO, 1996.

———. *Revised Draft Provisions for the Protection of Traditional Cultural Expressions/Expressions of Folklore: Policy Objectives and Core Principles*. Geneva: WIPO, 2010.

Yankah, Kwesi. *Speaking for the Chief: Okyeame and the Politics of Akan Royal Oratory*. Bloomington: Indiana University Press, 1995.

Yudice, George. *The Expediency of Culture: The Uses of Culture in the Global Era*. Durham, N.C.: Duke University Press, 2003.

Ziff, Bruce, and Pratima Rao. "Introduction to Cultural Appropriation: A Framework for Analysis." In *Borrowed Power: Essays on Cultural Appropriation*, edited by Bruce Ziff and Pratima Rao, 1–27. New Brunswick, N.J.: Rutgers University Press, 1997.

Index

Abdallah, Mohammed Ben, 96
adanudo, 23, 117. *See also* Ewe kente
Adanwomase, 24, 26, 37, 130
adinkra cloth: cultural significance of, 22–23, 26; and imitations in non-textile form, 28; symbols of, 22, 29, 38–39, 134–35. *See also* cloth
African Americans, 4, 28, 86, 133–41, 177
African diaspora, 18, 20, 32, 132–33
African feminism, 16–17, 68
Afrocentrism, 124
Agbozume, 117
Akan culture, 5, 123–25
Akan states, 22, 23
alienability, 8, 30, 155. *See also* ownership
Amadiume, Ifi, 68
American Society of Composers, Authors and Publishers (ASCAP), 98
Amu, Ephraim, 24, 128
Anderson, Benedict, 122
Appadurai, Arjun: and consumption and production knowledge, 62, 152; and global cultural landscapes, 119, 149
Asante chief or king. *See* Asantehene
Asantehene, 18, 50, 71–72, 102, 104–5, 106; as mediator between cloth

producers and state, 18, 102, 105, 114; and ownership of adinkra and kente, 3, 37, 130; and prestige of adinkra and kente 7, 53; production of cloth for, 37; as spiritual ruler, 71
Asante state, 3, 5, 172; cloth producers and, 21, 48, 50
Asokwa, 22, 24–26, 37, 113
authenticity, 138–39, 169; and adinkra designs; 37, 51–53; and consumption, 62
author function, 48, 49, 109
authorship, 30, 48; and author–owner distinction, 8–9, 11; and naming of cloth designs, 38–39, 43, 81–82, 109; and social context, 47–48, 54; temporal dimensions of, 36. *See also* creativity

Balfour Gyimah, Nana, **51–55**, 61, 90, 105–6, 113–14
banderole, 96, 98
batik: Ghanaian, 28, 53; Indonesian, 27, 82, 85
Benkler, Yochai, 59, 181
Berne Convention for the Protection of Artistic and Literary Works, 9, 10, 154
black nationalism. *See* nationalism: African American

211

Boatema Boateng is associate professor of communication at the University of California, San Diego.